END

Ground-breaking revelation on how to dismantle a lifetime of toxic thinking that interferes with your peace and destiny in God!

SID ROTH

Host, *It's Supernatural!*

Charlotte, North Carolina

Ken and Jeanne Harrington live what they write and preach. They have tested the revelations that God has given to them through both life's valleys and mountain tops. They also actively engage in the life of their local church body as examples of servant leaders. What you hold in your hand is a book that brilliantly connects science and the things of the Spirit that, in their words, will help discern between fact and truth. Ken and Jeanne have given another gift to the body of Christ through their hard work. This is a gift that will bring people freedom from their past, hope for their future, and a revelation of God's love for their present.

REV. LANDEN DORSCH

Lead Pastor, Gateway Family Church

Leduc, Alberta, Canada

This is a book that will help bring deliverance from those bad choices and memories of the past and release you, by His grace, to be the person God created you to be. This book exposes the world we live in but exalts the Word we must live by to experience true deliverance.

JOHN M. DOYLE

Executive Director, Cape Missions International

Cape Town, South Africa

I am pleased to recommend this volume to the restless heart. It is unusual to come across a thesis that harmonizes the best of medical science with the less empirically definable spiritual capacity in all of us. With an emphasis on memory, Ken and Jeanne's detailed research of the biochemical and physical makeup of the brain leads the reader to contemplate how and why we react as we do, even after spiritual regeneration. They detail the often unrecognized influences we experience through our physical senses, stored memories, the people around us, and our own corrupt thinking. The theoretical turns practical as the authors offer generous insight into how to manage stress and disappointment through the "renewing of our mind." Sounds simple, but get ready for some vigorous emotional and mental calisthenics as these two veterans gently lead you on a journey they have well charted.

MOHAN MAHARAJ
Missions Pastor, Gateway Family Church
Leduc, Alberta, Canada
President, Global Ministries
President, Aspire Group Realty Inc.
Edmonton Alberta, Canada

I have known Jeanne and Ken for seven years and the Lord gave me the privilege to share in their lives. They have the Love of God and are hungry to serve people more. I believe the Lord gave them the honor to write this book in this context.

As a Christian, I think we need to know the Love of God for this world and desire that that knowledge be increased. I believe the Father wishes that all people will live healthy and happy regardless of their faith.

There are number of good books in the world and among them are Christian books. I think this book is not only for Christians but for everyone. This book deals with the roots so that we can abundantly reap good fruits. Not only will many people receive healing and gain happiness but will come to know the Love of Father. If people recover, nations and the world will be recovered. I strongly believe that the Father's will in this area will be done by applying the principles in this book.

CHANG SU YOO
Managing Director
AIP Securities Co., Ltd.
Hong Kong, China; Seoul, Korea

Once again, Ken and Jeanne have brought us a book that empowers believers. The first part of the book explains the physiology of the brain, the wonder of how God created a brain to retain and retrain. The neuroplasticity of the brain has been a hot topic over the past number of years; Ken and Jeanne bring the science of this in a style that is informative and understandable. With their trademark transparent style they share their experience, bring Truth, give foundations, and equip. I want to applaud you for this immensely engaging read. Thanks.

KATIE WIEDRICK
Wiedrick and Associates Apostolic Ministries.

What a brilliant approach to detoxing the Body of Christ. This is a much-needed revelation for anyone who is ready to leave the past behind and embrace the present mind of Christ.

MICHAEL DANFORTH
Mountain Top International
Yakima, Washington

This book is a labor of love created by Ken and Jeanne through the Grace of God. It will enrich the lives of the readers and put them on the road to healing that we all need so desperately. I have read their three previous books and this work is in a realm all by itself in the depth of revelation and research that it contains. It has changed my life and I am sure it will change yours.

PAUL COLLINS
Chairman of the Board, Collins Industries
Past President, Wild Rose Party of Alberta
Director, Treasure Chest Ministries

It is not very often you get to actually see the results of teaching put into action or the pages of a book change lives before it is out in book form. Since Ken taught the truths and principles shared in his book, *Deliverance from Toxic Memories,* at a "Calling All Men" retreat in Guatemala for us in February, 2012, we have received countless testimonies of how the lives of the men who attended have been changed and the relationships with their spouses greatly improved. These testimonies did not come from the men, but from their wives! Now if this isn't a testimony that real change happened I don't know what is. The truths in this book, if applied, will change you; they will set you free from the bondage of the past and present memories that are killing you and your relationships with the ones you love the most.

KIM WEILER
Founder of Fe Viva World Missions
Guatemala

Deliverance from Toxic Memories is a book that will set you free from past traumas, start the healing process both mentally and physically, and set you on the path toward your destiny. Ken and Jeanne have laid out the necessary tools to develop thought patterns that will prevent your past from dictating your future. Understanding the mystery of the mind/body/spirit connections opens fascinating possibilities to bring wholeness to broken lives. Read it; it will change the way you think about thinking.

STACEY CAMPBELL
Prophet
Co-founder and Director, RevivalNOW! Ministries,
BE A HERO, and Praying the Bible International
Founder and Facilitator, Canadian Prophetic Council
Kelowna, British Columbia
www.revivalnow.com
www.beahero.org

Ken and Jeanne illuminate with confidence and authority, using scripturally based principles, the significance of renewing our minds, which offers victory over negative thinking and toxic memories. They unpack concepts of cognition, behavior, and emotions and reconstruct by welding faith and God's word, bringing a fresh perspective for those seeking godly counsel and wisdom.

LAURA HEAL
M.A. Counseling Psychology

Ken and Jeanne do it again with this new book. Both are gifted to speak to the Body of Christ on how we can live the practical Christian life. Their chapter, "Is Stress Killing You," should be read by every person in ministry, since our profession is high on the list with health issues.

JERRY HELMAN
Senior Pastor, Brookside Ministries Church
Shamokin Dam, Pennsylvania

DELIVERANCE
from toxic memories

DESTINY IMAGE BOOKS
BY KEN AND JEANNE HARRINGTON

Designer Genes

Shift! Moving from the Natural to the Supernatural

From Curses to Blessings

DELIVERANCE
from toxic memories

Weapons to Overcome Destructive
Thought Patterns in Your Life

Ken and Jeanne Harrington

DESTINY IMAGE® PUBLISHERS, INC.

P.O. Box 310, Shippensburg, PA 17257-0310

"Promoting Inspired Lives."

This book and all other Destiny Image, Revival Press, MercyPlace, Fresh Bread, Destiny Image Fiction, and Treasure House books are available at Christian bookstores and distributors worldwide.

For a U.S. bookstore nearest you, call 1-800-722-6774.

For more information on foreign distributors, call 717-532-3040.

Reach us on the Internet: www.destinyimage.com.

ISBN 13 TP: 978-0-7684-0361-9

ISBN 13 Ebook: 978-0-7684-8491-5

For Worldwide Distribution, Printed in the U.S.A.

1 2 3 4 5 6 7 8 / 17 16 15 14 13

ACKNOWLEDGMENTS

It isn't the mountain ahead that wears you
out; it's the grain of sand in your shoe.
—ROBERT W. SERVICE (1874-1958)

The Bible says that it is *"the little foxes that spoil the vines"* (Song of Sol. 2:15 NKJV), those little nagging things that we carry around inside us that wear us out. This book is about teaching us to remove those things inside us that keep us in a constant state of stress. But when it comes to external burdens, we all need the help of others to share the load.

We would like to thank Brenda G. Smith, our administrator and friend, who has been invaluable to this project. She transcribed all our sketches and scratches and turned them into charts and graphs. She helped with the initial editing and gave advice when we couldn't make our computers obey. Without her, portions of this project would have been a burden instead of a joy.

Thanks also to the many people whom we ministered to, experimented on, and used as a sounding board until we were able to grasp the tools that God was unveiling for the healing of His Body. Without you, this would have just been an academic treatise instead of a life-giving weapon, able to destroy the lies hiding inside all of us.

I have to acknowledge the wisdom and expertise of Dr. Caroline Leaf and the insights in her book, *Who Switched off My Brain?* Her knowledge of the brain tweaked something in us that led us to examine the connection between the brain, the body, and the spirit. We also drew on the

soul: thoughts, intentions, feelings.

marvelous truths that Joseph Prince has revealed concerning God's answer for our guilt and pain. Their perceptions and the analysis of numerous scientific studies helped us unlock the revelation examined in this book.

Thanks to Acquisitions Director Ronda R. Ranalli and her patience persistence in encouraging us to finish this book despite several delays. Thanks to Terri Meckes who took on the project management for this book. She was willing to work with us and was not afraid to use some of our suggestions when it came to design and layout. Thank you to Destiny Image Publishers, who in partnership with its authors, like Jesus, go about doing good and healing all who are oppressed of the devil (see Acts 10:38).

CONTENTS

FOREWORD

It is quite common to see people expressing stress by saying, "I have a sore shoulder," a "headache," or a "stomachache." Most physical pain is a result of some mental pain or problem.

Modern society experiences excessive, chronic stress starting from a stressed mother's womb before progressing to the present world's survival of the fittest, competitive environment. As a result, metabolic syndromes such as high blood pressure, diabetes, hyperlipidemia, and obesity are present in epidemic proportions. Not only have physical diseases become prevalent—such as adrenal gland fatigue syndrome, dementia, and cancer—but mental illnesses such as depression and personality disorders are common as well. Despite the fact that there is an increase in psychotherapists both in the medical and Christian world, we are experiencing a sharp increase in the suicide rate.

What is the cause of this stress that is making peoples' lives so difficult? I believe that originally Adam and Eve lived in absolute peace in Eden, which God created and perfectly protected. I also believe that stress entered when they had to be separated from God due to their disobedience. From that moment on, in painful toil human beings had to hunt or cultivate food. Now they faced many stressors, such as the danger of starvation or sudden encounters with fierce animals from which they had to flee. What about stress in these modern times? Today, people easily get stressed by heavy traffic going to work in the morning, by relational problems at the workplace, through business problems, problems with our children, marital problems, and so on. The worst part of these problems is that they are continuous and thus create chronic stress, which develops into mental and physical illnesses. Globally, *healing* is becoming one of the buzzwords to deal with stress. People are exhausted from the rapid changes and complexity of the world and their energy is drained as they try to adapt.

Ken and Jeanne marvelously reveal the source of this epidemic, using the Word of God and science to explain how toxic memories are formed and the impact they have on the brain, both in the physiological and biochemical realms. Not only do they explain the roots but they give solutions for handling this issue. I was impressed by Ken and Jeanne's revelation and their knowledge of the Word of God when I attended their conference three years ago and read their first book *Designer Genes*. This book, *Deliverance from Toxic Memories*, not only impressed but astonished me as a medical doctor.

Brain scientists study not only the mysteries of the brain but also examine the correlations between the intellect and its sensitivity to conscious and subconscious inputs. I have been studying stress for a number of years, but I was deeply challenged by the knowledge Jeanne and Ken had concerning stress in both the natural and the spiritual.

Brain science is one of the most difficult subjects in the field of medicine. It is hard to imagine how non-medical persons could explain the causes of stress and toxic memories, not only by the Word of God, but in scientific terms. The more we know about the reasons behind stress, the more we will have the power to manage it. My sincerest desire is that the readers not only understand the relationship between the brain, which God created to function perfectly, and stress, but that they comprehend their own true destiny and identity within God.

I firmly believe that those who are interested in seeking healing from toxic memories and stress will be informed and healed as they read this book. Therefore with confidence, I highly recommend *Deliverance from Toxic Memories*.

DR. DONGHO SONG, M.D.
Director of I-Leg Hospital
Seoul, South Korea

PREFACE

In Asia, captive baby elephants are chained every day to stakes in the ground from the time they are very small. The trainers are trying to imprint in the elephants' minds the fact that they cannot escape from that stake. The result? At first they struggle and try to break free from the chains. They will lurch and jerk; they will pull with their legs and trunk until they are exhausted and finally resign themselves to their fate. Once that reality is fixed in their minds, they relax and wait till the trainer comes to work them. No more efforts are wasted as they lower their expectations concerning their existence. They know they are doomed to remain chained to that stake; that is the fact they must live with.

But elephants grow larger and they grow stronger. They eventually become powerful enough to push over and lift whole trees, strong enough to destroy walls and break down fences. There is almost nothing that can keep them from roaming freely except one thing—that little stake. That lesson, which they absorbed as a small elephant—that you cannot escape that peg and chain—has grown even stronger over time. Though they could flex their leg and in a second be free from that stake, they don't because they know they can't. Perception is often more real than the truth.

In reality, our perception is our truth and it will dictate our responses to whatever facts we encounter that fall within the realms of those perceptions. We have the very same mechanism operating in our thought life and we are just as much bound by our own chains as these poor "dumb" beasts. But our chains are structures of our own construction. It is not the stake and chain that holds the elephants, but rather their thoughts concerning the chain. So it is with us; our perceptions, our thought patterns, the neuro-pathways, the ruts in our brains, our prejudices, and our fears make up the chains of our demonic bondages and strongholds.

These strongholds began just like the baby elephants' did, in infancy or even before. To understand the process of memory building, we must have an appreciation of both the spiritual and the physiological aspects of our nature. This book is designed to give you an oversight of how the various components of your brain, your heart, and your spirit interact to form the strongholds that lock you into destructive, debilitating, toxic thinking.

We have discovered, in our own lives, hundreds of these "chains" tying us down just like Gulliver, staked down in the land of the Lilliputians. Even though these chains are actually just tiny threads of thoughts, their cumulative effect will immobilize us and we will be paralyzed to arise and move in the direction God has for us. Thus we will look at some of the specific methods we use to build these strongholds and, more importantly, the biblical mechanics to tearing them down and rebuilding healthy, godly foundations.

This book is not designed to be a one-time "deliverance," intervention, or sanctification experience. It took most of us decades to fabricate these prisons and no quick fix will successfully dismantle them. This is rather to be a tool by which each individual can learn to continually walk out the fullness of the virtues that Jesus purchased for us on the cross. Healing and walking in health are both processes that require an open ear, an obedient heart, and an expectant spirit to access the position Christ has called us to.

Our hope for this book is that all who read it will take these principles from the Word and not only avail themselves of the power that Jesus said we could walk in but also to become able ministers of that gospel, empowering them to release others whom they find bound because of fear, tradition, or bad experiences.

Stone walls do not a prison make,

Nor iron bars a cage;

Minds innocent and quiet take

That for an hermitage;

I have freedom in my love

And in my soul am free,

Angels alone, that soar above,

Enjoy such liberty.

—RICHARD LOVELACE,
"To Althea, from Prison." (1618–1658)

INTRODUCTION

I walked up the stairs toward our bedroom. Reaching out, I and grabbed the handle to our bedroom door only to find it locked. Suddenly a rage welled up within me. This urge to break down the door almost overwhelmed me as I felt the adrenaline surge through my body. My stomach knotted as I fought to control the anger. I could feel the blood pressure and heart rate rise. Finally I banged on the door and demanded, "Why is this door locked?"

Almost immediately, I heard the toilet flush in the en suite and the sound of my wife walking toward the bedroom door.

"Oh, the door must have gotten locked somehow; sorry," she exclaimed, and with a sweet smile she walked past me as if nothing had happened. A locked door was nothing but a momentary inconvenience to her; it was a direct attack and an affront to me.

I stood there trying to calm my mind down and release the tension convulsing in my body while my spirit was talking to me. "What just happened?" I asked myself. "Why did I react; why did I get so angry; why was I ready to fight with my wife; why was I out of control; what was controlling me?" Within seconds, I recognized it as a toxic memory.

When I was young, we lived on a farm and my brother and I were forever dragging mud and dirt into the house. My mother decided that on the days she was cleaning, she would lock the door and force us to stay outside until she had regained some semblance of order. For her it was a solution to keep ahead of the mess; for me it was rejection. Perception is king as far as memories are concerned; it matters not the truth of what happened or why, but only what I perceived had happened and why.

I had to go to God and forgive my mother (even though she had done nothing amiss) for locking me out. This proactive step freed me from rejection at every other locked door that I would encounter. I needed to rewrite that memory and see God in the picture. I was not rejected and alone at that point, but rather He was there and I was loved.

I (Jeanne) awoke with a start in the middle of the night. I was sobbing and fear was pounding in my heart. The neighbors were fighting again, and the noise had awoken me as we had left our windows open on this lovely summer's night. They were fighting, but why was I crying? I prayed for them and went back to sleep as I mulled over the question that had arisen in my mind—why was I crying? I knew that there was more underneath my reactions.

I recognized that if I was jarred awake by a loud noise, I would always sob or draw a deep breath as if I was letting something out. As I continued to pray about it, the Holy Spirit brought up a memory of an event that had happened when I was about eleven.

It was close to Christmas and my dad, who had been out of town working, was finally home. He had been drinking with his buddies and was emotionally upset. I remember waking up to the sound of yelling. My mother was crying and my father was hitting her. My first reaction was fear for my mother and I frantically called the police, even though he had never done anything like that before. He spent the next week or two at my grandma's house before he finally returned home. He never hit her again, but the fear that he would went deep inside me.

The loud noises that woke me in the night brought all the emotions of that night to the surface though the memories of the event stayed hidden. I needed to get healed from the past and have those memories dealt with. I forgave my parents, particularly my dad, for fighting. I released my dad, in intercession, for causing me to involve the police and for the resulting guilt and shame that I felt for doing it. I then asked God to come into the memory and to help me see the situation as He saw it. Finally, I asked God to heal my heart and erase the toxic memory.

When I am the only one in the room who gets offended by some word or action, then I am the one with the problem. When I am the only one who reacts negatively to someone's ideas, then I am the one with the problem. When I am the only one who gets taken out by some emotional interaction, then I am the one with the problem. It is not the words or actions or situations that are the problem; it is our reactions to these that are causing our problems.

The normal reaction when we get injured is to blame the person who hurt us. God wants us to change that reaction to a response that will bring healing, not further offense.

No longer should we complain, "That hurt me; stop it!" when someone bumps into our wounds. Rather, we should respond to a hurt by asking, "Why did that hurt me? What wound in me allowed that to hurt me? Where do I need healing?"

We all have wounds. If I have a boil or an open sore, you will not hurt me from five feet away. You can love me from there and I will be happy. But if you try to get closer and give me a hug, you might accidently touch that tender area. My disproportionate reaction to that touch is the clue that there is something wrong with me, not something wrong with your action.

Touchy people push others away, not because they don't want people around, but because they don't want people to hurt them. They use walls as a defense mechanism so that people won't get too close and hurt them further. If we have a wound, the closer we let people get, the more guaranteed we are that they will touch the wounded area. Many of those areas, like Jeanne's and mine, have been unhealed for decades. They become a part of our lives, just like a limp or arthritis does. If we don't know that we can be healed, we just learn to live with the "problem" and believe that's just life.

God intended that that we might have life, and that we might have it more abundantly (see John 10:10). Pushing people away and building walls of protection is not abundant life. That was my (Ken's) way of coping. Rather than letting anyone lock me out, I chose to offend everybody to keep them at a distance. It worked; I ended up with no friends, no one who could get close enough to hurt me, except my wife, Jeanne, who would not be pushed away.

Love is the most powerful force in the universe, but I couldn't love as long as I was in protection mode. Jeanne was given to me so that I could love her and to let her love change me. I have heard it said that every woman marries a man hoping that he will change, and every man marries a woman hoping that she will never change. Both are usually disappointed; but with God all things are possible (see Matt. 19:26).

The memories and resulting mindsets, which may have taken years to build, can be dismantled in a matter of days. God has created our brains in such a way that we can speak healing into ourselves and rewrite the memories. We will look at both the physical and spiritual components of memories, see how they are formed, retrieved, and processed. Through the healing Jesus purchased for us on the cross and the authority He has given us, we are able to literally "change our minds." Jesus said, *"Behold, I make all things new"* (Rev. 21:5 NKJV), even our toxic memories.

The last third of the book will explore how to create change—change in our thought patterns, change in our emotional responses, change in our circumstances, and eventually change in our world. Jesus is coming back, but in the meantime He said, *"...Occupy till I come"* (Luke 19:13). He purchased a Kingdom for us, but we must be transformed by the renewing of our minds, so that we *"may prove what is that good and acceptable and perfect will of God"* (Rom. 12:2 NKJV). If we are not healed and transformed, we will not reap the benefits of His sacrifice.

Our desire as you explore this book is that you will not just find a bunch of principles, which will help you overcome your present emotional baggage; though following the principles will help. We are not trying to give you techniques or facts that will enable you to remove toxic memories; though if you follow the techniques you will come into more freedom. Our desire is to bring us into the fullness of the grace and truth which came through Jesus Christ (see John 1:17). It is the person of Jesus, not His principles, that has the power to change us.

> *And God shall wipe away all tears from their eyes; and there shall be no more death, neither sorrow, nor crying, neither shall there be any more pain: for the former things are passed away. And he that sat upon the throne said, Behold, I make all things new* (Revelation 21:4-5).

Our past will not dictate our future if we can view the past from God's perspective. Let's go back to the future and step into our glorious destiny.

Lovingly yours,

KEN AND JEANNE HARRINGTON

SECTION A

PHYSICAL ASPECTS
OF MEMORY

Chapter 1

MEMORY FORMATION

The two offices of memory are collection and
distribution. —Samuel Johnson

A retentive memory may be a good thing, but the ability to
forget is the true token of greatness. —Elbert Hubbard

Memory is a complicated thing, a relative to truth,
but not its twin. —Barbara Kingsolver

WHAT IS A MEMORY?

According to Merriam-Webster, memory is: "the power or process of reproducing or recalling what has been learned and retained, especially through associative mechanisms," and, "the store of things learned and retained from an organism's activity or experience as evidenced by modification of structure or behavior or by recall and recognition."

Those definitions sound cerebral and colorless, devoid of the real crux of a memory—our emotions and feelings connected to the events that we remember. We are not just a computer with circuits and switches, though we have those in abundance. We are more than a machine, though many of our functions are mechanical in nature. We are the crowning achievement of a loving God, *"In whom are hid all the treasures of wisdom and knowledge"* (Col. 2:3).

At any one moment, your brain is creatively performing about 400 billion actions, of which you are only conscious of around

2,000. Each of these harmoniously regulated actions has both a chemical and an electrical component that is responsible for triggering emotions.[1]

I (Ken) jolted upright in bed; my heart was racing, I was sweating profusely, my breath came in almost convulsive bursts, and panic filled my chest. "I have a midterm today and I didn't study. I don't even remember where the room is located to write it," I cried in anguish. I grabbed the clock. It was 2:00 A.M. Then, slowly, I realized that I was no longer in university. In fact, I had graduated ten years earlier. There was no test; there was only the terrifying memory of the many tests I had not prepared for; it was all a dream. My mind was still sorting out the stress of those days which still seemed so near and so real. As I lay back down, I was amazed that so distant a memory could still frighten me and break through into the present as if it were reality. I began to fathom the overwhelming stress I had put myself under while at university. My emotions slowly calmed down as I drifted back to sleep, thankful that that phase of my life was over.

STRESS

It's emotions that either elate us or stress us out. Happy thoughts may give us a momentary lift but stress can have long-term deleterious (destructive) effects if it is not eliminated quickly from the body. It has been estimated that 87 percent of our sicknesses are psychosomatic in their origin.[2] The Holmes-Rahe Life Event Scale[3] demonstrates the connection between stress and sickness. This scale can predict with 80 percent accuracy whether or not you will get sick in the near future. (See Appendix A.) Stress is fast becoming the most insidious killer in modern society.

It is nothing less than an epidemic rampaging through Taiwan. Some 5.4 million people in Taiwan—equivalent to 31.7 percent, or nearly one-third of everyone above the age of 20—show signs of generalized anxiety disorder (GAD), according to a survey by the Taiwan-based Chinese Holistic Health Association.

Those sharing this condition have had at least three of the following chronic symptoms for six months or more: restlessness or impatience, fatigue, concentration difficulties, frayed emotions, muscle tension, and problems falling asleep or sleeping.

Based on a 2009 survey, the Mental Health Foundation estimated that roughly 2 million people in Taiwan felt heavy stress in their daily lives, lacked warm interpersonal interaction, and were depressed to the point of having once considered suicide.[4] (See Appendix B.)

It is our response to the events—our thoughts about the events, not the events themselves—that cause the problem. Our thoughts, multiplied by our memories of similar events and situations, release "molecules of emotion"[5] into our limbic system and start a cascade of stress chemicals that flood our bodies at the cellular level. If these cellular membranes become overwhelmed by these toxic chemicals, their natural, selective barriers break down and open the cells to viral and bacterial agents. This, along with the changes in blood pressure and heart rate, opens the door to all kinds of ailments.

THE NATURE OF OUR THOUGHTS

We form our thoughts from the information that we assimilate through our senses. We have five senses in the natural realm, which is our most familiar plain of existence, but we also have spiritual senses. Just as we can hear someone yelling at their kids next door, we can hear conversations in the spirit. As the sound of someone's anger may create tension in our own bodies, so hearing an accusation in the spirit may trigger a similar unease.

I (Jeanne) have often laid hands on a person when ministering to them, only to hear negative, belittling, or berating words showering down on them. Invariably, when I ask if they have encountered a lot of negativity toward themselves, they answer, "Yes." Usually a parent or a teacher or perhaps a coach used strong, harsh, negative words in an attempt to manipulate their behavior or performance. If we passively receive these negative words, they will go into our memories and fashion a picture that will affect how we perceive ourselves.

Jesus often discerned the judgments that were leveled against Him. Once a paralytic man was lowered through the roof to be healed and Jesus said:

> …"Son, your sins are forgiven you." Some of the scribes were sitting there and reasoning in their hearts, "Why does this Man speak blasphemies like this? Who can forgive sins but God alone?" But immediately, when Jesus **perceived in His spirit that they reasoned thus within themselves**, He said to them, "Why do you reason about these things in your hearts? Which is easier, to say to the paralytic, 'Your sins are forgiven you,' or to say, 'Arise, take up your bed and walk'? (Mark 2:5-9 NKJV)

Jesus could pick up the accusation in the atmosphere though nothing had been spoken.

Though we may not be sensitive enough to discern the exact nature of the accusations floating around, like a radio we will pick up the spiritual dis-ease from the accusations. Many of us have walked into a room or a house and sensed the tension in the air or had a "strange feeling" that something was not right.

A church once asked us to visit a couple whom we didn't know personally. As we got close to their house, Jeanne started to feel uneasy and said emphatically that she didn't want to visit them. When I asked her why, she could not give a specific reason, only that she felt strongly to avoid contact with these people. She overcame her resistance and we did visit them, but later we discovered the source of the agitation. The mother had a huge issue with anger and actually broke her own son's arm in a fit of rage. Jeanne felt the tension of that anger but could not put a name to it. We prayed for this family as God had alerted us secretly to the root of their problem.

When we cannot pinpoint the source of the tension that we feel, it is difficult to prevent that tension from affecting our mood. Moods are relatively long-lasting emotional states. Moods differ from emotions in that they are less specific, less intense, and less likely to be triggered by a particular stimulus or event.[6]

It is not just people but spirit beings who broadcast accusations against people. Satan is known as *"…the accuser of our brethren…which accused them before our God day and night"* (Rev. 12:10). Because these accusations come out through the spirit realm, they don't require words to convey them; even our thoughts may solicit a response. We are told:

> *Do not curse the king, even in your thought; do not curse the rich, even in your bedroom; for a bird of the air may carry your voice, and a bird in flight may tell the matter* (Ecclesiastes 10:20 NKJV).

Literal translation: *"…For a fowl of the heavens causes the voice to go, and a possessor of wings declareth the word"* (YLT). These demonic agents broadcast our accusing thoughts and many people pick up the message or at least the emotion connected with it. That is why we are told to guard our attitudes:

> *…In order that no root of resentment* (rancor, bitterness, or hatred) *shoots forth and causes trouble and bitter torment, and the many become contaminated and defiled by it* (Hebrews 12:15 AMP).

We are all like radio stations, broadcasting and receiving signals that are in the atmosphere. We must learn to discern the source of those inputs in order to accept or reject them into our thought life.

I (Jeanne) was in a good mood as I walked along the paths behind our house, when suddenly a lot of negative thoughts about a certain person popped up in my mind. The strange thing was that a fly started pestering me about the same time. I continued walking, but that fly and those negative thoughts kept following and nagging me. Finally, in the spirit I realized that the fly represented lies. I took control of my thoughts and commanded the lies or negative thoughts to leave. Immediately both the thoughts and the fly were gone. The rest of the walk was pleasant, joyful, and best of all peaceful. We may not be able to keep birds from flying over our heads, but we don't have to let them nest in our hair.

Much of what we feel is absorbed through some of the senses that we are not accustomed to operating in. Though we may not recognize the source of these unsolicited words and the emotions connected to them, they will still be stored in, and often recalled from, our memories. They will color the way we think about people and how we perceive events that we encounter. I (Jeanne) often find that men who have a hard time accepting me usually have a bitter root of judgment against their mothers. Anyone who is a mother type will trigger resentment. These reactions give us a clue that calls out, "Dig here!" so that they can be healed.

The problem is that many such people do not want their wounds touched or healed and won't let anyone correct them. They become stubborn and rebellious as God tries to touch them and love them. This attitude causes them to push the counsel of God away along with the people who try to bring it. Once they are set in their way to resist God's influence, they open the door for lies to influence them. The biblical story surrounding King Ahab's death illustrates this perfectly.

God was looking to bring judgment on this rebellious, evil king. The Lord convened a council in heaven and entertained various suggestions from both angelic and demonic hosts. God laid out His plan to lure Ahab into a battle in which he would be killed. God asked for ideas that would persuade Ahab to enter this battle. Various plans were being considered when one spirit offered a suggestion saying:

> *...I will go forth and be a lying spirit in the mouths of all his prophets. [The Lord] said, You shall entice him and succeed also. Go forth and do it. So the Lord has put a lying spirit in the mouths of all these prophets...* (1 Kings 22:22-23 AMP).

Ahab listened to the voices of his false prophets, who were now prophesying lies, and died in the battle. Many of our memories contain lies put there by the enemy, and these lies are also destroying us. It behooves us to understand how we receive the information that dictates our moods in order to learn to filter the bad from the good.

TRI-PART NATURE

Below is a schematic that portrays the tri-part nature of our being and the connections and interactions between our body, soul, and spirit.

Body, Soul, and Spirit Schematic[7]

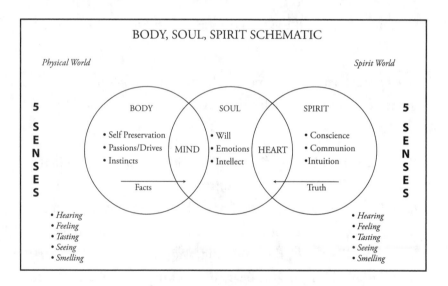

PHYSICAL SENSES

We are familiar with our four senses of hearing, feeling, tasting, and seeing, because we operate these gateways through our conscious or cognitive state. However, the sense of smell does not first go to the cerebral cortex (the center of reason), as do the other senses, but goes directly to the amygdala (the seat of our emotions) and affects us more through the subconscious or meta-cognitive state.

This routing closely links smell and memory. Smell evokes powerful memories and may be the major source of a *déjà vu* experience. In patients with damage to the temporal cortical region of the brain—the site of memory—their ability to detect smell is not affected, but only their ability to identify the odor. We must first remember a smell before identifying it.

What we know about smell and memory:

- Memory—odor memory falls off less rapidly that other sensory memory.[8]

- Smell is 10,000 times more sensitive than taste.[9]

- The "Proust effect"—the odor associated with an experience can vividly recall the memory; smell is better at this memory cue effect than other senses.[10]

Marcel Proust lent his name to the phenomenon of memory recall in response to a specific smell (after his description of such an event in *Swann's Way*).[11]

But when from a long-distant past nothing subsists, after the people are dead, after the things are broken and scattered, taste and smell alone, more fragile but more enduring, more immaterial, more persistent, more faithful, remain poised a long time, like souls, remembering, waiting, hoping, amid the ruins of all the rest; and bear unflinchingly, in the tiny and almost impalpable drop of their essence, the vast structure of recollection.[12]

The olfactory neurons reach deep into the limbic system, the ancient part of your brain shared by other warm-blooded critters, the part that deals with levels of consciousness we uncomfortably recognize as "animal." The parts sound comically ominous— the amygdala, the hippocampus, the uncus. Here is where the heart truly lies, the center of passion, lust, fear, and pleasure.

Here is where the deepest memories lie, hidden from the cortex. The limbic system transfers information into memory, and the information is colored by emotional input.[13]

Whole memories, complete with all associated emotions, can be prompted by smell. This is entirely unconscious and cannot necessarily be prompted voluntarily, although countless studies have shown that recall can be enhanced if learning was done in the presence of an odour and that same odour is presented at the time of recall.[15]

Our friend Brenda says, "The smell of warm milk always brings up an image of my grandfather's milk-house. The smell alone brings up many detailed recollections of that milk-house." I (Ken) used to feel a sense of excitement in the fall, when I would smell grain dust as the combines harvested it in the fields. That smell brought back all kinds of longings and memories about the farm and harvest time. Smells are more strongly connected to emotions than they are to events.

SPIRITUAL SENSES

The senses in the spirit don't come through our physical being and thus are often discarded as random thoughts or feelings. Remember Ebenezer Scrooge in Dickens' *A Christmas Carol* when he encountered the ghost of his old partner Marley? Jacob Marley's ghost asked him, "Why do you doubt your senses?"

Ebenezer Scrooge answered, "You may be an undigested bit of beef, a blot of mustard, a crumb of cheese, a fragment of underdone potato. There's more gravy than of grave about you, whatever you are."[16] Scrooge did not believe in the spirit realm and thus dismissed what he was experiencing as if it were some quirky physical reaction or just a conjured up memory instead of a real apparition. If we are in touch with our spiritual side, we will be able to discern if the input is real or just a figment of our imagination.

As the "Body, Soul, and Spirit Schematic" showed, there are three vehicles for information to influence us from our spiritual side. Later we will investigate and distinguish the sources of this information flow, but for now we will just examine the process through which the body and mind assimilate it.

ASPECTS OF OUR SPIRIT

1. Conscience

1. The Latin (*consciencia*) means "a joint knowledge."

2. Internal self-knowledge, or the judgment of right or wrong or principles within a person; deciding on the lawfulness of his actions and affections, approving or condemning them.

3. Consciousness—knowledge of our own actions or thoughts.[17]

Our spirit, though it is an integral part of us, has a voice of its own. We all have heard that little voice inside that argues with us about a particular course of action that is on the edge of acceptability. A properly-functioning conscience will not just condemn you when you do something wrong, but will warn you beforehand that this action is not right—that it will violate your conscience. It is designed to be our inner chamber of sober second thought. I (Jeanne) have often had a warning in my spirit not to trust someone or some situation that everyone else is enthralled with. That unction in the spirit has saved us thousands of dollars when reason says invest but the spirit says no.

Having a good conscience reduces our stress level and helps us to stay healthy and happy. The Bible says, *"A merry heart doeth good like a medicine: but a broken spirit dries the bones"* (Prov. 17:22). *"The spirit of a man will sustain him in sickness, but who can bear a broken spirit?"* (Prov. 18:14 NKJV). Continual or constant attacks of sickness are good indications of a slumbering or non-functioning spirit.

The conscience is often the vehicle that God uses to speak to us in our own private time with Him. Internal self-knowledge is the consciousness of our thoughts, and is the vehicle through which God is able to speak directly into us. When Jesus was tempted by the devil in the wilderness, *"Jesus answered by quoting Deuteronomy: 'It takes more than bread to stay alive. It takes a steady stream of words from God's mouth'"* (Matt. 4:4 MSG). That stream of words coming through our conscience keeps us connected with the mind of God and is the power to overcome evil.

2. Communion

1. The Latin (*communio*) means "fellowship."

2. The Greek (*koinonia*) means "partnership, common union."[18]

Communion is the aspect of the spirit that allows us to connect with God and with other people. It creates our ability to participate in a social intercourse that is much deeper than just discussing the weather, sports, families, or our jobs. It is the spirit-to-spirit connection. Many people are so shut down in their spirits that they are only able to operate at a trivial, surface level and push away in fear anyone who tries to touch them deeper. It is this aspect of our spirit that allows us to designate some people as friends and others, whom we may have more contact with, as just acquaintances.

I listened to a man giving out New Year's greetings on a radio and was intrigued by his insight. He said, "I would like to wish Happy New Year to all my friends. I will even greet my enemies with a Happy New Year. And to those who neither impressed me enough to be either my friends or my enemies, a Happy New Year to all my acquaintances."

Jesus had the deeper kind of connection in mind when He prayed that we *"...all may be one, as You, Father, are in Me, and I in You; that they also may be one in Us..."* (John 17:21 NKJV). We were designed for real connections or communion that reaches to the heart and spirit of another. Adam was created *"a living soul"* (1 Cor. 15:45)—literally a living, breathing spirit.[19] Our core is spirit, and only an awakened spirit can make that real spirit-to-spirit connection with another person.

Jesus always functioned out of His spirit and not His soul. That is what He meant when He said, *"...I tell you, the Son is able to do nothing of Himself (of His own accord); but He is able to do only what He sees the Father doing, for whatever the Father does is what the Son does in the same way [in His turn]"* (John 5:19 AMP). He wasn't seeing with His natural eyes but through His spirit. That knowing allowed Him to sleep during a storm that panicked His disciples (see Luke 8:23-25) and pass *"through the midst of them"* when a mob tried to throw Him off a cliff (see Luke 4:28-30).

Jesus knew the difference between the senses in the spirit and those from His flesh. He healed a woman in the middle of a crowd jostling Him because He felt a different kind of contact. He felt the draw on His spirit when:

> *She slipped in from behind and touched the edge of Jesus' robe. At that very moment her hemorrhaging stopped. Jesus said, "Who touched me?" When no one stepped forward, Peter said, "But Master, we've got crowds of people on our hands. Dozens have touched you." Jesus insisted, "Someone touched me. I felt power discharging from me"* (Luke 8:44-46 MSG).

She had touched His spirit; the rest of the crowd had just touched His body.

This ability of the spirit to intimately touch others also allows us to connect corporately to people in groups and bigger settings. That is the essence of corporate worship—the ability of many to become one before the Lord. If we are not corporate and connected in those settings we are easily distracted. Our minds wander and though we are there in body, our being is somewhere else.

Or we simply become observers, unable to enter into what the group is trying to accomplish. As we watch, we may even wonder what others are doing or thinking. If our spirit are not one with others, our soul will take over. It is our soul that gets distracted, for thoughts or musings belong to the realm of the soul not the spirit. The corporate connection in the spirit only happens as we become awake in our spirit.

This spirit connection/communion is most deeply felt in the intimacy of marriage. God created sex to be more than just a physical union. It was designed to connect a husband and wife at a deep spiritual level. The Holy Spirit uses the husband's spirit to sing into his wife's spirit and hers into his as they join physically. No "one night stand" can connect this way because the Holy Spirit will not participate in unholy actions.[20]

True oneness between husband and wife comes as they experience the glory of sex, embracing each other with their spirits as well as their bodies and souls.[21] It is the wife who tells the husband who he is (and he, her) by connecting with him spiritually during sexual union. Anyone else will both defile and confuse his soul, bringing him a lie about his identity.[22]

I (Jeanne) was not raised as a Christian but Ken led me to the Lord when we were dating. As soon as we were married and were intimate, it was as if I stepped through a new door. Everything was different; my spirit was alive and colors and beauty exploded everywhere. When my spirit joined with Ken's, everything in the spirit realm intensified for me.

3. Intuition

1. The Latin (*intuition*) means "to regard or look at."

2. Perceived without the intervention of argument

3. Seeing clearly, vision

4. Having the power to discover truth without reasoning

Intuition is the ability to discern in the spirit. Jesus operated differently than the scribes and Pharisees because He drew on the sensitivity of His spirit while they depended on the abilities of their souls. As mentioned earlier, when Jesus was ministering to a paralytic man, He first forgave his sins before He healed him. The Pharisees silently reacted with an accusation in their minds, *"Who is this who speaks blasphemies? Who can forgive sins but God alone?"* Jesus could hear the accusation in His spirit. The Bible says, *"The scribes and the Pharisees began to **reason**...but when Jesus **perceived** their thoughts..."* (Luke 5:21-22 NKJV).

Reasoning involves thinking, which is a soulish activity; perceiving involves discerning, which is a spiritual activity. Discerning is just accurately hearing in the spirit realm. I (Jeanne) will often think that I need to urgently pray for someone even when I have not thought or talked to them for some time. Later I discover that some crisis was occurring at the same time I felt the need to pray for them.

We just heard a story from a Baptist pastor in Summerland, British Columbia who was taking pictures of his family on a lake shore. There was a second lake only one hundred yards behind them with a highway dividing them. The pastor suddenly heard a voice telling him to drop the camera and run to the other lake. He said that the voice was so urgent that he took off without saying anything to his family. As he ran the voice told him to run faster. Because he was quite heavy, this was not his usual gait, but he felt compelled to sprint as fast as he could.

When he got to the other lake he spotted a body floating in just a few feet of water. He dashed into the lake and pulled the limp body of a three-year-old boy from the water. He waded back to the shore and started to perform CPR. An off-duty lifeguard, seeing the rescue, rushed over to assist and between the two of them they revived the boy. The toddler had been left in the care of his seven-year-old brother who had gotten distracted, but the pastor's sensitivity and quick obedience to the voice in his spirit saved a tragedy.

We all have this ability to hear if our spirits are awake. This ability to hear what Jesus (God) is doing is the essence of prophecy (see Rev. 19:10). The Bible is teeming with examples. Once the king of Syria was attempting to trap the king of Israel in a battle, but each time he would invade:

> *The man of God sent to the king of Israel, saying, Beware that you pass not such a place, for the Syrians are coming down there... and thus he protected and saved himself there repeatedly* (2 Kings 6:9-10 AMP).

The king of Syria suspected that a spy in his camp was warning the king of Israel, but his own spies told him that *"...Elisha, the prophet who is in Israel, tells the king of Israel the words that you speak in your bedchamber"* (2 Kings 6:12 AMP). God is always talking; we are not always listening.

Once, as we ministered to a man, Jeanne brought up the adultery that he had been involved in years ago. He was shocked.

"Who told you?" he demanded.

"You did," Jeanne replied.

"No one knows, not even my wife. I have never breathed it to anyone."

Jeanne had thought that she had heard him say it, but later realized that she had heard it from the Spirit.

Elisha could hear in the spirit what the king of Syria was planning, because there is no time or distance in the spirit realm. He could also see in the spirit. Earlier, Gehazi, his servant, had pursued after Naaman, the leper, to grab a reward for himself, cashing in on Elisha's healing of Naaman. Elisha challenged him, saying:

> *...Where have you been, Gehazi? He said, Your servant went nowhere. Elisha said to him, Did not my spirit go with you when the man turned from his chariot to meet you? Was it a time to accept money...?* (2 Kings 5:25-26 AMP)

Like Elisha, we also need our spirits awakened to hear and see what God wants us to hear and see in the spirit realm.

Inspiration is also a function of our intuition. *Inspiration* literally means "to blow or breathe into."[23] God, through our intuition, blows on us and suddenly we know what to do or how something works; the light goes on in our brain. The Bible declares of itself that *"all scripture is given by inspiration of God"* (2 Tim. 3:16). It was not a matter of thought, *"For the prophecy came not in old time by the will of man: but holy men of God spake as they were moved by the Holy Ghost"* (2 Pet. 1:21). God communicates as the Holy Spirit breathes revelation into our spirits.

George Washington Carver, called the "father of the peanut," operated by revelation under the influence of the Holy Spirit. He freely gave his hundreds of inspirations and inventions to the world. "God gave them to me," he said of his ideas, "How can I sell them to someone else?"[24] He stated, "I never have to grope for methods. The method is revealed at the moment I am inspired to create something new...Without God to draw aside the curtain I would be helpless."[25] He said that God would take the peanut apart and reassemble it in new arrangements that George used to produce new products that transformed the economy of the South after the Civil War. That is the inspiration of God—communicating through our intuition.

The ability to transcend time is another function of our spirit. John and Paula Sandford express this reality best:

> Two kinds of couples come to our office for marital counseling. The first possess awakened, functioning spirits. They are not confined to the pain of the moment. Their spirits enable them to remember lovely memories of the past and to think of happy times to come. They have roots and hopes. They reach beyond present time to nourishing events of the past and dreams of the future. But the second class are dead to all that. Their spirits cannot project them backward or forward. They are enmeshed and confined to the pains of the moment. Present afflictions are all they can think about and they want to flee.[26]

We worked with two different couples in which the husbands had committed adultery. One of the couples was restored; the other was not. The husband in the failed marriage could not let go of the past or envision a future with his wife. He was stuck in a time warp of the present problem because his spirit was slumbering.

This inability to transcend time and plan for the future is at the root of the world's debt problem. An article on the Bloomberg business news states that:

The household balance sheet is in worse condition than at any other point in history since the Great Depression. From 2001 to 2007, debt for U.S. households increased to $14 trillion from $7 trillion, and the ratio of household debt to gross domestic product was higher in 2007 than at any time since 1929 (and we know how that turned out).[27]

We had neighbors who spent their money freely on new cars, boats, and holidays when things were going well. They were self-employed and made good money, but seemed unable to see that taxes came along with that income. They were always scrambling to find cash that could cover the inevitable bills and taxes.

The lack of the intuitive sense of time (inability to see consequences) in the individual households will eventually translate into the same structure in the nation.

A little-noticed event occurred at approximately midnight on Monday, October 31, 2011: The national debt of the United States exceeded, for the first time since World War II, the country's gross domestic product. The website USDebtClock.org showed the gross domestic product crossing the $15 trillion mark for the first time on Monday, while earlier in the day the numbers from Trea-suryDirect showed the total public debt outstanding at $14.993 trillion and growing by more than seven billion dollars a day.[28]

Michael Tanner, a senior fellow with the Cato Institute…estimates the nation's total debt—including unfunded liabilities for Medicare and Social Security—is $119.5 trillion—$400,000 per capita. But Senate Majority Leader Harry Reid, D-Nev., continues to insist Social Security is just fine. A couple of weeks ago he said it is an "outright lie" to say Social Security is "headed toward bankruptcy." He called the entitlement program "the most successful social program in the history of the world." "Let's worry about Social Security when it's a problem," Reid said. "Today it's not a problem."[29]

The inability to see disaster coming is the sign of a dysfunctional spirit. To paraphrase Solomon:

The wise watch their steps and avoid evil; fools are headstrong and reckless (Proverbs 14:16 MSG).

Sloth makes you poor; diligence brings wealth. Make hay while the sun shines—that's smart; go fishing during harvest—that's stupid (Proverbs 10:4-5 MSG).

It is through these functions of the spirit that we are able to receive inputs from the realm of the spirit that give insight beyond the cognitive state and influence our memories in ways we don't often comprehend. Most of these foundational thought patterns were laid down when we were infants, before we could even reason.

CONSCIOUSNESS

From the "Body, Soul, and Spirit Schematic," we see that the spirit man is not directly connected to the mind, which is the interface between the body and the soul. As a result, the spirit is not dependent on the development of the body but is fully mature at conception. The testimonies of survivors of comas and near death experiences (NDE) prove that the spirit remains functional even when the body temporally dies or enters a comatose state.[30]

The question has been asked:

Presuming there is a separation of conscious from the physical body during an NDE, how is it possible then that the mind (physiologically the brain) remembers what occurred during the NDE, when it remained in the physical body all the time?

Dr. Bruce Greyson responded:

There have many relatively recent studies on consciousness. The current theory is that consciousness is where the memories are stored, not the brain. Many scientists have postulated that as an information storage unit, the brain cannot possibly hold all the information. Therefore, the brain is more of an accessing unit much like a radio receiver. Additional findings have shown that the way we remember is not as a computer disk drive, but rather we store a core memory attached to an emotion and then file it in a concept area in the brain or even in the body. When we retrieve our memories, we are programmed to "fill in the gaps." Therefore brain memories rarely are 100% totally accurate.

However, that being said, the NDEs report 100% life reviews of every thought, deed, and how we made others feel. This is the computer hard drive—the consciousness that survives death. When consciousness returns to the body, it takes typically 7 years to have those intense memories of the NDE to funnel through the brain. My guess is that it is such an intense experience that it may create in the brain what is known as a "flashbulb moment." These are times that the brain takes a picture of a particular instance, usually occurring in times of heightened sensory and emotional input or life-threatening moments. These memories are ingrained in the brain and the person can recall like it happened yesterday.[31]

"Brain chemistry does not explain these phenomena," said Dr. Bruce Greyson. "I don't know what the explanation is, but our current understanding of brain chemistry falls short."[32] Our understanding of the spirit does permit us to explain what is happening. As with all questions on the spirit realm, the Bible has the answer. We are not just a physical being, thus the real you does not cease to exist or stop functioning just because the body is not able to function.[33]

PRENATAL LEARNING AND MEMORIES

Recent studies prove that babies start learning long before they are born.

> "Diversity of different kinds of music is essential and can be useful for the baby's future writing, reading, and language skills," says Dr. Philip A. De Fina, chief neuropsychologist and director of neurotherapies at the NYU Brain Research Laboratories.[34]

Early experiences such as prenatal stress significantly influence the development of the brain and the organization of behavior. In particular, prenatal stress impairs memory processes.[35]

Because babies share the placenta with the mother, she can transmit her molecules of emotion to the baby. A study of fetal responses to the mother's mood while watching various types of movies found that the baby's emotions directly matched the mother's.

> Researchers have no idea how the babies pick up on their mothers' emotions, but suspect that the rush of hormones triggered by an emotional film is transmitted indirectly to the fetus. The findings, reported in New Scientist Magazine, add to the evidence that a pregnant mother's mood and stress levels can affect her unborn child.[36]

They are saying that babies hear and react to emotions! They are aware of their environment long before they have the cognitive ability to understand or assess it. A lady who had become pregnant out of wedlock told us about her boyfriend's pressure to have her get an abortion. Contrary to his wishes, she decided to keep the baby. The boyfriend continued to harangue her at every opportunity to get rid of the baby. She said that every time the baby heard the threats, he stopped moving in her womb.

Eventually the boyfriend accepted his responsibility and they got married. Unfortunately, the baby and the father were never able to bond. Even as a toddler, the child often hid when his father entered the room. Was the memory of threatened murder still dictating the child's responses? Did he subconsciously think, "If I am quiet, I will not be seen and he will not kill me"?

When I (Jeanne) realized that I was pregnant with our last child, I was surprised. I was aware that my reactions could affect the baby and always said that I was happy to be pregnant, just not happy to be fat. Out of the three boys, he is the only one who has never commented about my being overweight. Babies hear and their spirits discern what is being said and felt.

The Bible relates an interesting story about the meeting between Mary and her cousin Elizabeth. Mary was pregnant with Jesus, and Elizabeth with John the Baptist.

> *Mary arose in those days and went into the hill country with haste, to a city of Judah, and entered the house of Zacharias and greeted Elizabeth. And it happened, when Elizabeth heard the greeting of Mary, that the babe leaped in her womb...* (Luke 1:39-41 NKJV).

John the Baptist was three months shy of his birth date at this time, and his brain was not yet fully developed or aware. Yet his spirit jumped when God, in the form of baby Jesus in the womb, entered the room. His spirit was aware, teaching his mind how to respond. Thirty years later, John saw Jesus for the first time but immediately recognized Him as the Lamb of God (see John 1:29). John's memory, deposited before he was born, gave him a confirmation to his revelation of who Jesus was.

Many stimuli can affect our brains in the prenatal state:

Music

> We also encourage you to listen to all kinds of music during and after pregnancy. This will help stimulate baby's senses and improve his brain development. Exposure to different sounds and scenes is essentially what helps establish connections from one set of neurons—the nerve cells of the brain—to another. This is how we all learn. These neural structures are shaped like a tree and

root system. A baby's brain is extremely plastic, meaning that it can constantly adapt and make new connections between trees.[37]

Stress

When a mother is extremely stressed during pregnancy, she produces hormones called glucocorticoids that cross the placenta to the baby and can alter the development of its kidney and heart.[38]

We heard a man share about his congenital kidney disease. He was praying about the roots of his disease and God showed him a picture of when he was in his mother's womb. He could hear his father's angry outburst against his mother. In his heart, he felt her say, "As soon as I have this baby, he will start to beat me again." That picture helped to identify the fear he had of his father. He quickly forgave his father and commanded the fear to leave. He then claimed his healing and today his kidney is completely restored. Roots will produce fruit; bad roots produce bad fruit.

> Pre-natal stress hugely growths the likelihood of a child having attention-deficit hyperactivity disorder, cognitive delay, anxiousness and depression. Stress during pregnancy as well increments the risk of the child being autistic and, in rare cases, schizophrenic. Stressed mothers also produce babies with lower birth weight, which can be an indicator for coronary heart condition in later life.[39]

Drugs

> Consumption of two drinks per day or more, on the average, by pregnant mothers was related to a 7-point decrement in IQ in 7-year-old children even after statistically adjusting for appropriate covariates.[40]

There is a growing body of data showing that fetal exposure to cocaine, phencyclidine hydrochloride (PCP), and other CNS-active drugs results in infants and children with abnormal brain wave patterns, short-term neurologic signs, depression of interactive behavior, and poor organizational responses to environmental stimuli.[41]

I (Jeanne) had a relative whom one of our families adopted. Both of his biological parents were drug addicts. He unfortunately went through withdrawal as an infant, which caused a mental disorder as he grew. Even today he struggles with the simplest tasks in life. Many things affect babies before they leave the womb.

Food

> Flavors from the mother's diet during pregnancy are transmitted to amniotic fluid and swallowed by the fetus. Consequently, the types of food eaten by women during pregnancy and, hence, the flavor principles of their culture may be experienced by the infants before their first exposure to solid foods. Prenatal and early postnatal exposure to a flavor enhanced the infants' enjoyment of that flavor in solid foods during weaning.[42]

These very early flavor experiences may provide the foundation for cultural and ethnic differences in cuisine.

Michael, our middle son, was introduced to blueberry ice cream when he was little. That purple, creamy mess slid down his chin and bib as he shook with delight at each taste. He even ate cumquats that were so sour that he vibrated when he tried them. He would shake his head and then come back for more. As an adult, he still loves intense flavors.

All these inputs come through the meta-cogitative or unconscious state in the fetus. Ninety percent of what we learn comes through that state.[43] All those unseen and largely unrecallable memories are embedded in the baby's brain and make up part of the foundation of later mindsets.

> There are some 100 billion brain cells in a human, a number that is reached by just five months gestation in the womb. So there are literally some quadrillion synapses or connections in a child's brain, each of which can be altered by a child's experiences.

Synapses can be gained or lost, strengthened or weakened, as a result of their own electrical activity. There are a couple of useful phrases to describe this process: "Cells that fire together, wire together," which means that synapses that are highly active will be preserved and strengthened. On the other hand, synapses that are underactive will be pruned away, according to a "use it or lose it" rule, forever threatening the child's ability to do a task.[44]

All in all, the brain is a marvelous tool that God put at the discretion of the mind. *"I will praise thee; for I am fearfully and wonderfully made: marvelous are thy works; and that my soul knoweth right well"* (Ps. 139:14). We will next look at the actual progress of a thought as it works itself through the brain into the cells of the body.

KEYS

- Memories are built from both physical and spiritual inputs.

- We are tri-part beings.

- Our spirit communicates through conscience, communion, and intuition.

- Our spirit hears, tastes, feels, speaks, and smells in the spirit realm.

- Our ability to function successfully depends on the degree that our spirit is awake.

- We start building memories in the womb and are affected by the prenatal environment.

Chapter 2

MEMORY PHYSIOLOGY

*You do not really understand something unless you can
explain it to your grandmother.* —ALBERT EINSTEIN

*Nothing is more responsible for the good old days
than a bad memory.* —FRANKLIN P. ADAMS

We have looked at the many types of inputs that affect memory and
we now want to look at the way these inputs are stored, organized, and
retrieved. Neurons and glial cells make up the majority of the mass of
the brain. Though the estimates of the number of cells in the brain vary,
the average number of neurons is approximately 100 billion. The number
of glial cells present in the brain may be 10 times that many, though
estimates vary.

Neurons seem to be the brain's workhorse cells, carrying out all the
crucial electrochemical communications. The majority of the rest of the
brain's cells, called glia, were long considered little more than scaffolding.
But one kind of glial cell, the star-shaped astrocyte, actually appears to
take an active role.

In a report published in *Science*...British and American researchers showed that when rats inhale excess carbon dioxide, astrocytes
(a type of glial cell) in the brain stem sense the resulting increase
in blood acidity. The team tagged these astrocytes with a protein
that fluoresces in response to cellular activity and saw that the
cells signaled the neurons that influence breathing. The rats then

breathed more deeply, taking in more oxygen. "These guys are even more sensitive than neurons," says Sergey Kasparov, a University of Bristol molecular physiologist.[1]

The following is a table containing some of the neural/glial cell estimates.[2]

BIBLIOGRAPHIC ENTRY	RESULT (W/SURROUNDING TEXT)	STANDARDIZED RESULT
Glencoe Health 2nd Edition. Mission Hills: Glencoe Inc., 1989:252.	"Weighing around three pounds (1.35kg), the brain contains nearly 100 billion cells."	100 billion
World Book 2001. Chicago: World Book Inc., 2001: 551.	"The human brain has from 10 billion to 100 billion neurons."	10–100 billion
Magill's Medical Guide Revised Edition. Salem Press, 1998: 221.	"It has been estimated that the adult brain has around one hundred billion neurons and an even larger number of glial cells."	100 billion
The Science Times Book of the Brain. New York: The Lyons Press, 1987: 150.	"The human brain holds about 100 billion nerve cells."	100 billion
The Scientific American Book of the Brain. New York: Scientific American, 1999: 3.	"An adult human brain has more than 100 billion neurons"	> 100 billion

Memories are stored in multiple sites in the brain rather than in one specific area. Different aspects of a memory—visual, emotional, or factual information—are stored and recalled from different areas of the brain. That is why some parts of a memory are vivid, while we are unable to recall other information associated with it. The method of learning also affects the ability to retain and recall information.

There are three differing types of memory:

- *Sensory memory* is like a flash bulb going off. It is stored for only a fraction of a second, just long enough to develop a perception.

- *Short-term memories* (STM) last 20 to 30 seconds, or as long as they are rehearsed. This is what we access when trying to remember a telephone number while we are scrambling for a pen. As long as we keep repeating the number over and over, we can retain it. The capacity of STM also seems limited to a maximum of seven items. It is like the CPU of a computer that can hold a limited amount in its cache as it processes it.[3]

- *Long-term memory*, which we will refer to as just memory, is the emphasis of this book. It is permanently stored, though our ability to retrieve it can be lost.

We may be looking for a name or a word and though we know that we know it, we can't seem to bring it up. It might be "right on the tip of our tongue" or flash by just as we are about to say it and yet disappear until some other connection triggers its recall. Even remembering the context of the memory or our mood when the event happened may help trigger the recall.

I (Ken) have gone back to the physical location where I lost a memory only to find it still there. Actually the memory wasn't there—it was still in my short-term memory—but the triggers were. Once the brain had access to other sources of the incident, the memory was able to be forged again.

Memories are often reconstruction projects—as we remember a little, the rest suddenly reappears as other neural pathways are reactivated. However, our memories can be skewed by failing to remember the source of the memory. Our thoughts and perceptions can cloud the accuracy of our memories, as can hearing others "gossip" about it. We have all been absolutely positive about what we recalled only to discover that what we thought we had seen or heard was wrong. Unfortunately, the perception of an event becomes our reality once a memory is set.

The mind is adept at creating realistic scenarios by sewing together facts, suggestions, and perceptions and filling in the gaps with imagination.

Because memories are transmitted by electrochemical packets, the mind sometimes has a hard time keeping all the components straight. It can be a problem with the initial encoding, storage, or the retrieval. Freud suggested that we also have motivated forgetting: "We may tend to forget things that we do not wish to remember."[4] As we shall see later, this ability to forget is vital to our healing of our toxic memories.

I (Jeanne) once placed my father's beautiful ring of alexandrite and gold in a ring cleaning solution only to forget it. It was only later that I discovered it. By that time, the gold had mottled and the ring was ruined. I was so upset. Just recently, my sister Laura told me the story of how she had ruined Dad's ring. She had heard the story, identified with the emotional loss, and integrated the pain and the blame into her own memory.

She couldn't believe it was me even though I was the one who worked at the jewelry store and not her. Charlie Kaufman identified with what my sister felt. He said, "I think you just assume that your memory is just sort of a video playback of your experience, but it's nothing like that at all. It's a complete re-fabrication of an event and a lot of it is made up, because you're filling in spaces."

THE STRUCTURE OF THE BRAIN

Neurons

The brain contains 100 billion nerve cells or neurons, out of which extend axons. These axons are the wiring of the brain. The axons, which are like tree trunks, terminate at synapses that connect the neurons to other synapses and thus to the entire network of the brain. The adult human brain is estimated to contain from 100 to 500 trillion synapses. Every cubic millimeter of cerebral cortex contains roughly a billion of them. That is approximately 7,000 synapses for each neuron cell,[5] each of which can grow 70,000 branches or dendrites that store our memories. The word *dendrite* comes from the Greek word meaning "tree" and perfectly describes the dendrite's structure. Dr. Marion Diamond calls them the "magic trees of the mind."[6] Within this vast array of interconnected neurons, our memories are stored. It is estimated that as little as eleven of the hundred billion neurons would be sufficient to contain all the memories necessary to graduate from high school.[7]

Structure of a Neuron[8]

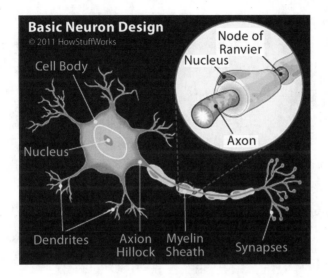

Photograph of a Neuron

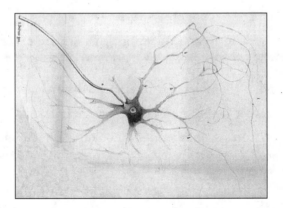

Hemispheres of the Brain

The brain is divided into two hemispheres that are designed for synergy (combined action) and perspective of thought. The right hemisphere processes from the big picture to small details and is the deductive reasoning side. The left side goes from small detail to big picture and is the inductive reasoning side. We need to involve both sides to form and fix a memory.[9] Both physiological evidence and connectionist theory seem to support the notion that in the brain, learning involves modifying the strengths of connections between neurons.[10] The more we think, meditate, or dwell on a thought, the more synergy between the two hemispheres of the brain, and thus the stronger the memory either for positive or negative.

This musing on a thought develops more dendrites and synapses, thus forming stronger neural pathways allowing easy access to the memory. "In order for you to remember an experience, that experience must change something inside your body. If it did not, you would be unaffected."[11] Most of those changes occur in the communicative capacity of the neurons by increasing their synaptic connections.

To *meditate* literally means to mutter or speak to yourself.[12] By speaking things out loud, we allow another input, sound, to make a different connection in the brain. Though the brain can learn through a one-time stimulus, it learns better and faster if there are multiple pathways. This is why multimedia presentations are better at disseminating ideas than a lecture—they make use of more synaptic connections. To fix a memory so it is not lost, we must concentrate on what we are experiencing. Some exceptional individuals have photographic memories, but most of us have to make an effort to fix a memory or else it will vanish into thin air.

My (Ken's) brother and I practiced remembering lists of items—everything from cats to tools—numbering 100 objects. The method was simple: assign a consonant to each number in the list using a B for the number 1, C for number 2 and so on. By only using consonants, we were able to fill in any vowel we wanted and thus create simple words that we could visualize. For example, the number 12 would be a word that was framed with the consonants B and C. Such words as bac, bec, bic, etc. could be used. Bic could be a Bic pen. By visualizing a Bic pen and weaving a story that would tie the object to be remembered to a giant Bic pen, we would be able to fix a memory of not only the object but also its place in the list.

This seems now to be an impossible task, but we were easily able to remember that 100-item list and recall every item and its place in the list. The principle was to actually think, muse, or concentrate long enough to form a mental picture—the more outlandish the better—and thus fix a memory. Memories are never lost, only our ability to recall them. Creating unusual and bizarre pictures allowed us easy access and recall.

Remember the times when you did something while you were preoccupied with other thoughts. Like the time the phone rang just as you came into the house. You tossed the car keys down and rushed to answer the phone. Later, because you weren't thinking about it, you couldn't find where you put the keys. Or the time you were introduced to that unassuming person only to discover 15 seconds later that you could not recall their name. No real thought to setting a memory, no establishing of a neuroconnection, no recall. Why?

Glial Cells

Because when we give only cursory or slight attention to a thought there is less synergy, the dendrites are more loosely connected, and we will not have access to the memory; thus we lose the thought. We have all done this when cramming for an exam. If we are not interested in or don't quite understand the subject then we can't muse or meditate on the material. We hear it or read it but are unable to connect it to any other thoughts, as my brother and I did with the lists. That is why we can remember for the exam the next day but completely forget three weeks later. When we don't develop neural pathways, the information is left isolated, unconnected, and is never assimilated in our memory. That is why a strange language that has no roots in your own tongue is so hard to learn; there is nothing to connect the new thought or sound to.

Because the new thought is never moved off the "ram drive" (our short-term memory) by tying it to existing thoughts or sounds, it never makes it to the hard drive (the permanent memory) and is soon deleted by the glial cells. Disconnected information can only last 24 to 48 hours before it is replaced with more relevant material. This ability to forget is facilitated by glial cells, which are the regulating cells of the brain. Glial cells literally vacuum up all the random or dissociated thoughts and dispose of them.

This is not the only function of glial cells. They are also designed to surround the neurons and hold them in place, to supply nutrients and oxygen to neurons, to insulate one neuron from another, and to destroy pathogens and remove dead neurons. They are also used to modulate neurotransmission. It was initially thought that the glial cells had no part in the "thinking" of the brain. The fact that these cells make up 90 percent of the brain mass gave rise to the popular misconception that we only use 10 percent of our brain.

Glial cells, as organizers and auditors of the brain, also control sleep. Glia interact with ATP (Adenosine-5'-triphosphate), a small chemical best known as an energy source for cells, to produce SRS (Sleep Regulatory Substances). ATP is often called the "molecular unit of currency" of intracellular energy transfer. ATP transports chemical energy within cells for metabolism. Thus when neurons transmit electrical signals to each other, they also release ATP. The ATP causes the glial cells to produce SRS, which in turn enters nearby neurons and activates a cascade of other chemicals that affect how the neurons respond to neurotransmitters.[13] The more synaptic activity (thinking/remembering), the more ATP; the more ATP, the more SRS and thus more signals to sleep, which allows the glial cells to reorganize and rejuvenate the brain. That is why mental activity is just as tiring as physical activity.

PROGRESSION OF A THOUGHT THROUGH THE BRAIN

As the brain is made up of 100 to 500 trillion synapses or connections, there is no simple route that a thought or a memory needs to take on its passage through the brain. The strength of the synaptic connections determines the access various areas of the brain have to information. The main routes or superhighways of the brain are made of the connections that have the most lanes and thus carry the majority of the traffic. But for every thoroughfare there are multiplied millions of minor pathways. Here we will only deal with the most traveled routes, even though some of the lesser traveled may better reveal some of the mysteries concerning the mind.

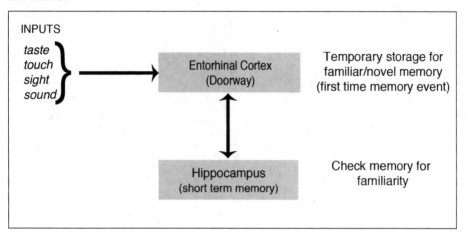

Information enters the brain and is immediately converted to a stream of electrical impulses. These impulses first pass through the entorhinal cortex (see "Brain Schematic" below), which is the doorway to the brain. The entorhinal cortex is involved in the consolidation of memories, particularly during periods of sleep, and supplies the hippocampus, through the thalamus, with the information garnered by the senses (excluding smell). Apart from this role as a conduit, the entorhinal cortex retains these sensory experiences while the hippocampus determines whether the stimulus conditions are novel or familiar. That is, the hippocampus determines whether the sensory experience retained in the entorhinal cortex has previously been represented in memory.[14]

Brain Schematic

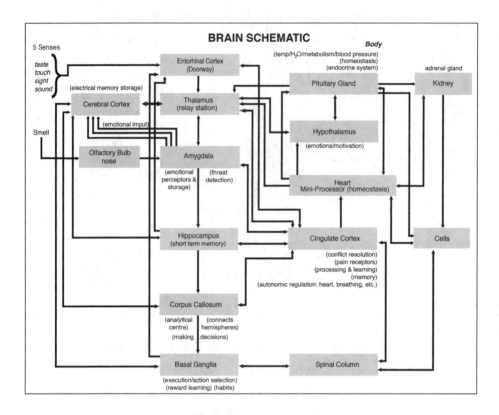

The information then moves to the thalamus, which is a relay station, before going out to both the cerebral cortex and the hypothalamus. This incoming impulse activates the recall of memories electrically stored in the dendrites of the cerebral cortex, which then returns the new information and the related memories, along with the beginnings of an attitude, to the thalamus. The hypothalamus adds a chemical component to these thoughts, and through these chemicals, connects to the nervous system and the limbic and endocrine systems.[15] These chemical inputs become the emotional and motivational components of the thought.

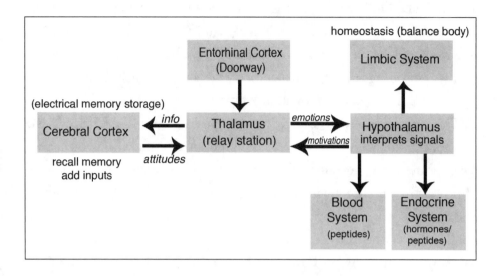

From this point on, the entire body, in addition to the brain, begins to engage in the interpretation and activation of these thoughts and memories. The hypothalamus, through the endocrine system, activates the pituitary gland. The pituitary gland is often referred to as the "master gland" of the body, because it regulates many activities of other endocrine glands. The hypothalamus decides which hormones the pituitary should release by sending it either hormonal or electrical messages.[16]

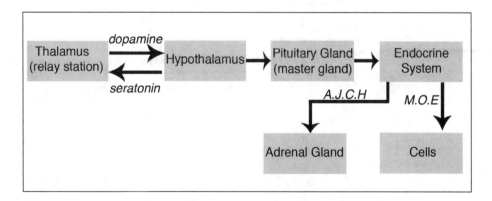

The thoughts are contained in the neuropeptides, steroids and peptides, which are the molecules of emotion (MOE)[17] that flood the body at the cellular level, while adrenocorticotropic hormone (ATCH) activates the adrenal glands that sit on the top of the kidneys. Simultaneously, the hypothalamus adds neurotransmitters (mainly noradrenaline, dopamine, and serotonin) to the thoughts and routes them back to the thalamus. As this is transpiring, the hypothalamus is regulating the body's homeostasis in response to the new information.

The inputs are now in electrochemical packets when they arrive at the amygdala, which is the library of the emotional memories of the brain. One of the main purposes of the amygdala is to prepare the release of chemicals to enhance memory building. It is rife with emotional receptors and has a strong connection to the cerebral cortex, by which it has the ability to overwhelm the reason with emotions and feelings. Three times as many neural pathways flow from the amygdala as come back from the cerebral cortex, which is the cause of our emotional overreaction to various thoughts and memories.[18]

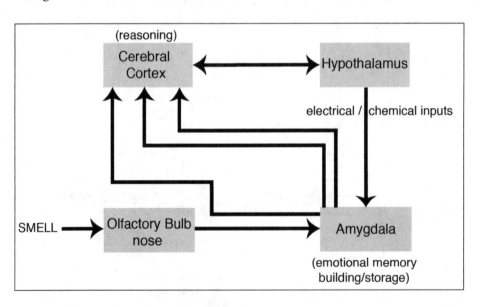

The sense of smell, through the olfactory bulb, enters the mix here at the amygdala. Since it has never passed through the cerebral cortex, these smells are connected more with emotion than reason. This is one of the main sources of what we call a *déjà vu*, or a sense that we have experienced a situation or are overly familiar with something that we cannot quite remember. These odor-based memories are very strong, though they may be elusive unless we concentrate on remembering the smell rather than the situation related to it. Pleasant or unpleasant reactions may spring up to a new situation on the basis of a memory connected to a smell which itself may not be related to the new scenario.

We bought our present house partially because it had the smell of a root cellar, which discouraged potential buyers from even exploring for the cause. They made up their minds, not based on the value of the house, but on the unpleasantness of the odor. That allowed us to buy it cheaply and pour concrete over the dirt floor of the attached atrium, which eliminated the smell. The other buyers could not make a logical decision because their emotions, dictated by their sense of smell, overruled and connected them to an unpleasant memory. If we don't understand how we think, we will not understand how we arrive at different conclusions.

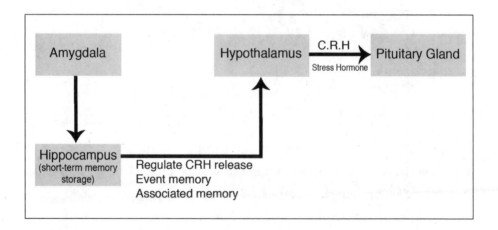

From the amygdala, the memories and thoughts drop into the hippocampus. This acts as a short-term memory storage unit, holding the memories for 24 to 72 hours maximum, or until they are analyzed by the corpus callosum. The hippocampus is also involved in emotional regulation as it inhibits cells in the hypothalamus from generating corticotrophin-releasing hormone (CRH). This hormone reduces the concentration of glucocorticoids, a manifestation of the stress response. The hippocampus also underpins episodic memory (memory of an event), allowing individuals to bind distinct features to form a single unit, called associative memory (memories associated with a pattern or a key). When we retrieve a memory, such as the name of someone, activation of the hippocampus increases. Researchers thus know that memory is distributed, not localized just in the dendrites. There are thousands upon thousands of sites that hold vital information that the brain draws on when making a decision.[19]

Vertical Section of the Brain[20]

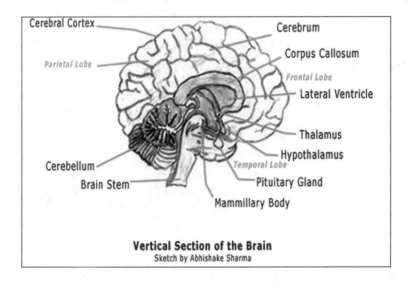

Vertical Section of the Brain
Sketch by Abhishake Sharma

If the information is accepted by the corpus callosum, it is returned to the entorhinal cortex to be acted upon; if it is rejected, the glial cells expel it as energy or hot air. The corpus callosum also connects the two hemi-spheres of the brain so that they can communicate and thus is the best organ to make informed decisions and regulate emotional responses. The amount of synergy or connection between the two hemispheres dictates the strength of a memory—the ability of the dendrites to grow and form synapses. The corpus callosum is also vital to the regulation of physiological processes, such as blood pressure and heart rate.

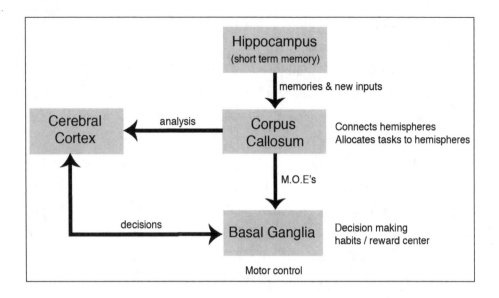

Finally, the electrochemical packets of memory (MOE) enter the basal ganglia, which is the activation or execution center. It is responsible for procedural memory or habits and addictions. It also processes different emotional and cognitive stimuli and is the reward and reinforcement center. In the basal ganglia, there is interplay of motivation, emotion, cognition (knowing and perception), and motion inputs on a neuronal level. Because it has many dopamine receptors, it is the main reward and aversion organ and initiates and executes behavior once the emotional and cognitive information has been integrated.[21] It is here that habits and addictions are instituted.

EFFECTS OF THOUGHTS AND MEMORIES ON THE HEART

The resulting signals from the brain pass down the spinal column, through the nodes that exist there, and are distributed to various organs and individual cells to activate even more hormonal and electrical responses. Each cell has hundreds of shape-specific receptors that are designed to accommodate the matching biochemical hormones. These chemicals fit like a key into a lock to open the cell membranes to individual neurochemical stimuli. These messengers activate the cells to initiate things like cell division, manufacturing of protein, or the release of other chemicals, which will communicate similar activities to other cells. Every activity is encoded in that cell which then literally has a part in remembering and responding to the brain's thoughts and memories. Cancers begin, for the most part, when cells lose their memories and divide incorrectly or uncontrollably and forget the apoptosis (cell suicide) response that should kick in in these circumstances.[22]

These biochemicals, more specifically the peptides, are the physical substrates of emotion, the scaffolds that provide the molecular underpinnings of feeling (love, hate, anger, bliss, courage, contentment, sadness, joy, etc.), sensations (pleasure and pain), and thoughts and drives (hunger and thirst). Peptides are in effect the true "molecules of emotion" because they actually activate or inhibit memory building and recall to flow through the brain and the body.

Peptides also create what researchers have called the body's "music," a secondary or parallel system where chemical information substances, the substrates of emotion, travel an extracellular fluids highway. These are the fluids outside the cells that circulate through the body to reach specific target cell receptors. As peptides trigger receptors on the cells, they initiate a cascade of cellular processes and changes.[23]

These signals, especially the ones from the adrenal glands, are shunted through the heart via the bloodstream. Your heart has its own nervous system that is composed of approximately 40,000 neurons. These neurons are connected differently and more elaborately than elsewhere in the body, and while they're capable of detecting circulating chemicals sent from the brain and other organs, they operate independently in their own right. Having its own "mini-brain" is the reason why heart transplants work, given the fact that severed nerve connections do not reconnect in a different body. Furthermore, this elaborate nervous center in the heart has more functions than simply regulating the electrical activities of the heart to keep it pumping.[24]

For example, while the heart can be influenced by messages sent from the brain, it doesn't necessarily obey it all the time. Furthermore, the heart's "mini-brain" can send its own signals to the brain and exercise its influence on it. To give one illustration: oxytocin, which is typically referred to as the "love hormone," has been shown to be released not only from the brain, but also from the heart. Oxytocin is not only important for love and bonding, especially for pregnant and lactating mothers, but it also has roles in social behavior, wound healing, learning, memory, and empathy. In short, it's one hormone that affects a very wide variety of important functions.

It's generally assumed that learning and memory are a central nervous system function. Meaning, this is a function for that organ inside our heads. However, due to some bizarre, controversial, and anomalous observations, there is a growing push toward a systemic memory mechanism. In other words, thought and memory processing is not limited to intelligence functions of the brain. This came from observations in organ transplant patients—more specifically, heart-transplant recipients.[25]

It is also a general assumption that learning is restricted to neural and immune systems. However, the systemic memory hypothesis predicts that all dynamical (active) systems that contain recurrent feedback loops store information and energy to various degrees. Sensitive transplant patients may evidence personal changes that parallel the history of their heart donors. A study recorded in the Journal of Near-Death Studies (2002) discovered that personality changes that paralleled the heart donor's personality occurred in the recipients following transplant surgery. They suggest that cellular memory, possibly systemic memory, is a plausible explanation for these parallels.[26] In other words, the heart, as a feedback or decision-making organ, retained some of the memories of the donor's decisions in the fibers of its neurons.

This study is only an example of many others. Overall, the researchers here found that, on average, the heart recipients picked up two to five parallel traits of their donors per case from the ones they investigated. This is a very high transfer of personality traits that the use of immunosuppressant drugs, the stress of surgery, and statistical coincidence cannot explain. The interview transcripts are beyond astounding to read.

There was one case of a militant, gay, McDonalds-loving recipient who became straight, vegetarian, and health-conscious after the transplant, matching her donor's preferences. Another case concerned a young donor who was a violin musician. His donated heart made the older, classical-music-hating recipient suddenly want to listen to hours of it after surgery. A third case was of a young "hell-raising" woman, who immediately picked up her donor's love for music and poetry. She was even able to finish the words to his songs, which she never heard before. Mohamed Ghilan asks, "Is the heart our organ of intelligence, while the brain is our organ of cognition?"[27]

The Bible says, *"Keep your heart with all diligence, for out of it spring the issues of life"* (Prov. 4:23 NKJV). Jesus said

> *But those things which proceed out of the mouth come from the heart, and they defile a man. For out of the heart proceed evil thoughts, murders, adulteries, fornications, thefts, false witness, blasphemies* (Matthew 15:18-19 NKJV).

He also said that people can *"understand with their hearts and turn,"* or change their minds (Matt. 13:15 NKJV). In fact, understanding seems dependent on the attitude the heart holds. The disciples *"had not understood…because their heart was hardened"* (Mark 6:52 NKJV). Jesus went on to contrast the reasoning of their brains with the perception of their hearts. *"Jesus…said to them, "Why do you reason…? Do you not yet perceive nor understand? Is your heart still hardened?"* (Mark 8:17 NKJV). The Bible also seems to suggest that the heart is our organ of intelligence, while the brain is our organ of cognition (processing information).

Dr. Caroline Leif feels even more certain that the heart has control of much of the decision-making in the body. She says:

> Neurologically speaking, your heart is over sensitive to what you think and feel—thoughts directly affect the state of your heart. Science is discovering your heart's brain is a real "intelligence force" behind the intuitive thoughts and feelings you experience.

The "heart's brain" produces an important biochemical substance known as ANP (atrial natriuretic peptide) or ANF (atrial natriuretic factor), the balance hormone that regulates many of our brain functions and motivates behavior.

Your heart is in constant communication with your brain to relax your body in three scientifically documented ways: neurologically (transmission of nerve impulses), biochemically (the hormones and neurotransmitters), and physically (through pressure waves). A growing body of scientific evidence also suggests that your heart communicates with the brain and the body in a fourth way: energetically (through electoral magnetic field interaction).

Through all these biological communication systems, the heart is a significant influence on the function of your brain and all your other bodily systems. The signals the heart sends to your brain influence not just perception and emotional processing, but higher, cognitive functioning as well. New scientific evidence on the heart's neurological sensitivity points to feedback loops between the brain and heart that check the accuracy and integrity of our thought life. [28]

That is why we make "heartfelt decisions" and find that when we don't trust a prescribed action we can't do it "with all our hearts." We can love "with all our heart" or get "heartbroken." Terrible disasters make us "heartsick." The heart is a truth analyzer; it checks the congruency of what we think and what we feel. When a thought makes its cycle from the brain to the adrenal glands, where stress hormones are released (cortisol, adrenaline, corticosteroids), and finally to the heart, a feedback loop is being formed.

If a thought is accepted by the heart, and it is positive in its emotional component, a signal will be sent to the brain and complete the feedback loop. The brain will sync with the heart and adjust its brain (alpha) wave activity to match the heart's rhythm. Studies done by the Institute of Heartmath show that the brain's activity is naturally synchronized to that of the heart, and also confirms that intentionally altering one's emotional state, through heart focus, modifies afferent neurological input from the heart to the brain. Results indicate that the brain's electrical activity becomes more synchronized during psycho-physiologically coherent states. Implications are that this increased synchronization may alter information processing by the brain during the experience of positive emotions. "States of increased heart rhythm coherence are associated with improvements in cognitive performance."[29] In layman's terms, we think better and make better decisions when we are not stressed.

If the thought is negative, it will return to the entorhinal cortex, fix a toxic memory, and complete the negative feedback loop, which will add further stress to the body. As long as the thought is allowed to freely flow it will continue to produce toxic chemicals that attack the body's health. Paul Rosch, M.D. estimates that 75 to 90 percent of all visits to primary care physicians result from stress-related disorders.[30]

If the heart decides that the thought is incongruent with the truth it feels, it can refuse to connect with it and stop the feedback loop, returning the body to a homeostatic (calm or balanced) state. To accomplish this, the heart emits ANP (atrial peptide) to lower the heart rate and the blood pressure and directs the glial cells to absorb the negative MOEs. These chemical stressors that had previously been dumped into the bloodstream, the endocrine system, and the limbic system are reabsorbed by the body, allowing normal learning and memory recall to resume.

We have looked at the physiology of the thought and memory processes, but there is more to our body than just our brain. Our organs and even individual cells respond to our thoughts and memories, which in turn affects our moods and our health. We will look at these interconnections in the next chapters.

KEYS

- The brain is mainly made up of glial cells and neurons.

- Neurons store and transport information, thoughts, and memories.

- Glial cells mainly support, organize, feed, and clean up neural activity.

- Thoughts move down neural pathways, adding chemical and emotional components.

- Feedback loops monitor and modify the effects of thoughts and memories.

- Memories are stored throughout the body, not just in the brain.

- The heart checks and modifies the integrity of thoughts.

- The heart is our organ of intelligence, while the brain is our organ of cognition.

Chapter 3

THE HEART

Follow your heart, but be quiet for a while
first. Ask questions; feel the answer. Learn to
trust your heart. —AUTHOR UNKNOWN

There are many things in life that will catch your eye, but only a
few will catch your heart...pursue those. —AUTHOR UNKNOWN

If your head tells you one thing, and your heart
tells you another, before you do anything, you
should first decide whether you have a better head
or a better heart. —MARILYN VOS SAVANT

The heart is the first feature of working
minds. —FRANK LLOYD WRIGHT

The heart has reasons that reason cannot
know. —BLAISE PASCHAL

The Bible says that as a man *"thinks in his heart, so is he"* (Prov. 23:7 AMP). Science is now discovering that the heart's neural processor is an active participant in the thinking process. It is like a mini-brain that not only influences perception and emotional processes but higher cognitive functions as well. New evidence indicates that part of the heart's role is to influence the brain by checking the accuracy and integrity of thought life.[1]

The most neurologically sensitive system in the body is the heart and circulatory system. It responds quickly to both electrical and chemical stimuli. As mentioned earlier, the heart monitors and influences the thoughts in the brain and is capable of storing many of the inputs that come through the sensory organs. In a startling study of heart transplant recipients, it was discovered that memories of events, not just the personalities of the donors, were transferred with the organ. In one case a policeman, who died in the line of duty, became a heart donor to another man. Vivid memories from the policeman donor were evidently transferred to the recipient.

The donor's wife commented:

> What really bothers me is when Casey (the recipient's wife) said offhandedly that the only real side effect of Ben's surgery was flashes of light in his face. That's exactly how Carl died. The bastard shot him right in the face. The last thing he must have seen is a terrible flash. They never caught the guy, but they think they know who it is. I've seen the drawing of his face. The guy has long hair, deep eyes, a beard, and this real calm look. He looks sort of like some of the pictures of Jesus.

The recipient reported:

> If you promise you won't tell anyone my name, I'll tell you what I've not told any of my doctors. Only my wife knows. I only knew that my donor was a 34-year-old, very healthy guy. A few weeks after I got my heart, I began to have dreams. I would see a flash of light right in my face and my face gets real, real hot. It actually burns. Just before that time, I would get a glimpse of Jesus. I've had these dreams and daydreams, ever since: Jesus and then a flash. That's the only thing I can say is something's different, other than feeling really good for the first time in my life.[2]

Apparently the donated heart had received and stored the images of the final few seconds of Carl's life and was depositing those images into Ben's brain. The dreams became an attempt by Ben's brain to sort out the information that it had received internally and was treating it like any other memory. That is the preeminence that the heart has in controlling and balancing information received and stored in the body.

Things can get even weirder when the heart comes from the opposite sex. A 14-year-old female gymnast, who had trouble with bulimia, died and her heart was donated to Gus, a 47-year-old male.

The recipient reported:

> I feel like a teenager. I actually feel giddy. I know it's just the energy of the new heart, but I really feel younger in every way, not just physically. I have this annoying tendency to giggle that drives my wife nuts. And there's something about food. I don't know what it is. I get hungry, but after I eat, I often feel nauseated and that it would help if I could throw up.

His brother reported:

> Gus is a teenager. No doubt about that. He's a kid—or at least he thinks he's a kid. Even when we're bowling, he yells and jumps around like a fool. He's got this weird laugh now. It's a girl's laugh and we tell him that. He doesn't care. His appetite never did bounce back after the surgery. He's pretty much nauseated almost all the time. After Thanksgiving dinner—and he loved it—he went upstairs and vomited.[3]

Other cases reported feeling that the donor seemed to be with them and would communicate to them. Some recipients would feel the donor's pains, fears, or ambitions. Though much of the research can only be anecdotal, the volume of evidence strongly indicates the ability the heart has to influence moods, habits, and preferences.

In 1995, Mr. Graham had been on the verge of death due to congestive heart failure. He had less than six months to live when the call came through from the Medical University of South Carolina telling him that a heart had just become available. It belonged to Mr. Cottle, 33, who had committed suicide by shooting himself in the head. A year later, Mr.

Graham contacted the organ donation agency wanting to thank the man's family for the gift of life. He began writing to Mr. Cottle's young widow Cheryl, a mother of four. The couple later met, fell in love, married, and moved to Georgia. Twelve years after the successful transplant operation, Mr. Graham shot himself dead, leaving his wife a widow for the second time in strikingly similar circumstances. After his suicide, friends of Mr. Graham said he had not shown any signs of being depressed.

Scientists say there are more than 70 documented cases of transplant patients having personality changes as they take on some of the characteristics of the donor. An example is Cheryl Johnson from Lancashire who claimed her literary tastes changed radically following a kidney transplant.

> Cheryl Johnson used to enjoy celebrity biographies and best sellers such as *The Da Vinci Code*. But now she prefers classics such as Jane Austen's *Persuasion* and Dostoevsky's *Crime and Punishment*. Character changes in transplant recipients are known as cellular memory phenomenon.[4]

There is another body of research that is looking not at the electrochemical inputs that the mind or heart receive but at the intuitive or future inputs or stimuli that the heart is able to detect. Though this would seem to enter into the paranormal realm, experiments have proven this is a common event in many organisms and across many disciplines. In the following experiment, the evidence shows that the discernment of the heart drives the response of the brain before its cognitive reasoning can assess the pictures.

That capacity to process information about distant events appears to be a property of all physical and biologic organization, and is likely due to nonlocal communication via coherent oscillations in the energy field that interconnects everything in the universe.[5] A Star Wars buff would simply say that they felt a "tremor in the Force." Perhaps we need to change our definition of what "alive" means.

Even at the subatomic level, physicists have shown in such famous experiments as the "double-slit" experiment that subatomic particles (photons) behave as if they "know" the outcome of future events before these events actually happen.[6] At the elementary level of biologic organization, cellular structures appear to have immediate knowledge of remote actions in their system. This enables the emergence of spontaneous long-range cooperative organization in biomolecules and membranes,[7] in dendritic networks of cortical neurons,[8] and in colonies of single-celled organisms such as bacteria.[9]

At the level of multicellular organisms, a pre-stimulus response has been experimentally demonstrated in earthworms.[10] At higher levels of life, accurate premonitions of natural disasters by animals have been documented throughout recorded history,[11] and there is recent experimental evidence that pets appear to "know" the moment their owners decide to return home, despite being separated by many miles and not on a regular schedule.[12] In short, this capacity for processing information about future and nonlocal events is an ability that is not peculiar to humans, and neither is it a capacity solely of the brain alone.

In their research, McCraty, Atkinson, and Bradley used the following procedure to test for intuitive responses of the heart.

Experimental Protocol

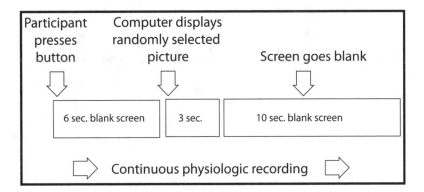

Participants watched a computer monitor and pressed a button to begin each trial. Once they pressed the button, the monitor would remain blank for six seconds, and then the computer would show them a randomly selected image for three seconds. The image would be from one of two picture sets—either a calm or emotional image. Then, the screen would go blank again for ten seconds before a message appeared on the monitor to start the next trial.

The experiment gathered data which indicated that, on average, the heart received the information about the future emotional stimulus approximately 4.75 seconds before the stimulus actually appeared on the screen. On the chart below, this is where the slope of the heart rate deceleration curves split. The slope for the emotional trials plummets much faster than the slope for the calm trials. This suggests that the heart responds to an unknown stimulus in the same way as when it knows what is coming. This shift indicates when the brain "knew" whether the stimulus would be calm or emotional. The time difference between these two events suggests that the heart received the information about 1.3 seconds before the brain.[13]

Temporal Dynamics of Heart and Brain Pre-stimulus Responses

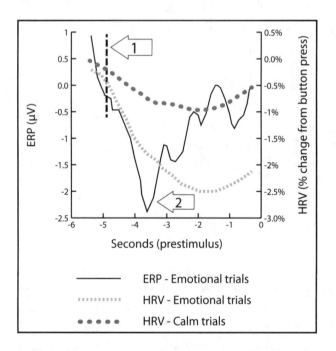

This study has provided evidence of an "intuitive effect." We've heard of this before; we called it "precognition" and "presentiment," but those terms might not be appropriate. Normally, "precognition" implies that cognition (knowing) is involved, whereas the evidence from this study of the pre-stimulus response suggests that the body is aware of a future event without the aid of conscious cognition.

Overall, it seems that anticipating future emotional events is a system-wide process, involving the heart as well as the head. The heart plays an important role in processing intuitive information—the brain doesn't do it alone. Because of the differences in the heart rate deceleration curve between the calm and emotional trials, it seems likely that the heart received the intuitive information before the brain.

Recent research in neurocardiology has also shown that the heart is a sensory organ. It is an information encoding and processing center with an intrinsic huge internal nervous system—it can learn, remember, and make functional decisions independent of the brain. This nervous system not only adjusts the heart's rhythms on a beat-to-beat basis, but it can even override inputs from the sympathetic and parasympathetic nervous systems.[14] There is also a great deal of evidence that the impulses conveyed toward the central nervous system from the heart not only balance cardio-vascular regulation, but that they also modulate the activity of subcortical and cortical regions of the brain—those involved in processing emotions and perceptions.[15] In simpler terms, the heart was able to affect, override, and regulate the thoughts and emotions coming from the brain.

The Bible has 970 references to the heart, which include such things as thoughts of the heart, speaking to the heart, saying in the heart, imagi-nations of the heart, laughing in the heart, having integrity in the heart, deceiving the heart, and strengthening the heart. All these are in the book of Genesis. In later chapters the heart is hardened, turned, has God's name put in it, gets sick, is compelled, is wise, is willing, and is lifted up—all in Exodus. Though we may be tempted to think that this is just literary license, God obviously sees the organ as the actual heart or core of an individual. Jesus said, *"Those things which proceed out of the mouth come forth from the heart; and they defile the man"* (Matt. 15:18). The Holy Spirit cautions, *"Keep thy heart with all diligence; for out of it are the issues of life"* (Prov. 4:23).

Both neurophysiologic and behavioral data indicate that inputs going to the central nervous system from the heart and cardiovascular system influence how sensory information is processed. For instance, studies have documented that cardiac-related input governs a wide range of processes such as visual perception,[16] reaction times,[17] pain perception,[18] electrocortical activity, and cognitive functions.[19] Given the complex contribution of inputs from the heart which influence how the brain processes sensory information, it is reasonable to say that *information from the heart may also inform intuitive perception.*

The fact that the heart is involved in the perception of a future external event is a surprising, even astounding result, especially from the classical perspective that only the brain has that role. These are quite amazing electrophysiological results which, if confirmed and extended by future research, will contribute to a new understanding of how the body receives and processes information about objects and events ahead in time or distant in space.

These psychophysiological effects are strong evidence that intuitive processes involve the body accessing a *field of information* that is *not limited by the constraints of space and time.* More specifically, they provide a compelling basis for the idea that the body accesses a field of potential energy that exists as a *domain apart from space-time reality* into which information about "future" events is spectrally enfolded. The investigation of intuitive perception promises a rich harvest for humankind—an enlarged scientific understanding of human perception and consciousness, and even a new view of us and of our relation to the material and nonmaterial worlds.[20]

The research is just confirming what the Bible has said all along—that God is not bound by time or space and we also can enter these realms as He wills. In the Old Testament, Elisha the prophet told the king of Israel everything the king of Syria said, even what he whispered in his bedroom (see 2 Kings 6:12 MSG). In the New Testament, *"...the Spirit of the Lord caught Philip away, so that the eunuch saw him no more...but Philip was found at Azotus"* (Acts 8:39-40 NKJV). Phillip was instantaneously transported almost thirty miles. There are obviously laws and principles that work in the cosmos that we are still unaware of.

Being sensitive allows the heart to readily interact with the body but also places it directly in the path of any "disturbance in the force" or shift in the cosmos. In Christian terms, the heart of man is connected to the heart of God, and what touches God touches us. Jesus was one with His Father, and He prayed that we would be one with them (see John 17:22). Jesus said:

> *The Son can't independently do a thing, only what He sees the Father doing. What the Father does, the Son does. The Father loves the Son and includes Him in everything He is doing* (John 5:19-20 MSG).

Jesus and the Father were so in sync that Jesus was able to do everything He saw the Father doing.

There is also growing scientific proof that there is a spiritual realm that is not constrained by time and space. David declared:

> *I can never escape from Your Spirit! I can never get away from Your presence! If I go up to heaven, You are there; if I go down to the grave, You are there. If I ride the wings of the morning, if I dwell by the farthest oceans, even there Your hand will guide me...You saw me before I was born. Every day of my life was recorded in Your book. Every moment was laid out before a single day had passed* (Psalms 139:7-10,16 NLT).

Paul said:

> *For since the creation of the world His invisible attributes are clearly seen, being understood by the things that are made, even His eternal power and Godhead...* (Romans 1:20 NKJV).

God is displaying His awesome nature, but He has hidden it in plain sight—in His creation and especially in us because we are *"the image and glory of God"* (1 Cor. 11:7 NKJV). The more we explore in the depths of our nature, the better picture we have of God. When we enter the "domain apart from the space-time reality," we enter His realm—the realm of the eternal. God wants us to discover more about Him for, *"It is the glory of God to conceal a thing: but the honour of kings is to search out a matter"* (Prov. 25:2). The heart is the interface between the spirit and the soul, which is the core of our being, and we are just discovering its importance.

The heart is vulnerable to any and all fluctuations and stresses that the body comes under. Those imbalances cause numerous chemical and hormonal reactions that can flood the bloodstream and cause major damage to the heart and the circulatory system. The heart can perceive the stress, but the brain must decide to agree to nullify and avoid that stress. Listen to your heart; it has eternity embedded in its essence. Einstein once said that imagination is more important than knowledge as knowledge is limited and imagination is not. He also said the difference between stupidity and genius is that genius has its limits. I know this is true because some of the smartest people I know are the most stressed out.

KEYS

The heart has a mini-processor that aids in the thinking and decision-making process.

The heart stores memories which are passed on even if it is transplanted.

The heart is intuitive and senses future events.

The heart is the interface between the soul and the spirit.

The heart controls the rhythm of the body.

Chapter 4

IS STRESS KILLING YOU?

*God will never give you anything you can't
handle, so don't stress.* —KELLY CLARKSON

It's not stress that kills us; it is our reaction to it. —HANS SELYE

*Stress is nothing more than a socially acceptable
form of mental illness.* —RICHARD CARLSON

*The greatest weapon against stress is our ability to
choose one thought over another.* —WILLIAM JAMES

*Be anxious for nothing, but in everything by prayer
and supplication with thanksgiving let your requests
be made known to God.* (Philippians 4:6 NASB)

Health in any system is determined by the efficiency of the communication lines within that system. When the communication in the marriage
union stops, a silent divorce begins. When its lines are down, a telephone
system cannot function. When army headquarters can't contact the front,
the battle plan plunges into disarray. A business's prosperity depends on its
capacity to connect their customers with their products and services.

We knew a couple who decided not to communicate anything negative
to each other. They would never fight, discuss problems, or express any
negative feelings they had. They thought that they could remove strife by
ignoring it. This started a time of limited communication with each other.
If something bothered one, it wasn't discussed so that "peace" would reign
in the relationship. But something else crept in as everything became only

surface, as feelings and hurts were stuffed. Anger began to grow, but it had to remain hidden with no outlet.

When Ken and I heard about their arrangement, we knew instantly that it was wrong. We use each other to speak into situations that we have wrong concepts about. By discussing things, we work them out and gain a better understanding of the truth. This was a sincere couple who thought that they knew the correct way to deal with strife in their marriage, but they were wrong. Feelings, even negative ones, are part of our early warning system, warning that danger is near. Just because only one senses the problem doesn't mean it doesn't exist. I rely on Ken to see things that I can't and vice versa; we walk as a team.

Needless to say, marriage for that couple did not succeed. The husband eventually ran off with a 16-year-old girl who shared things with him. We can't be spiritual if we're not practical. The silence between him and his wife was his idea, but destruction of the marriage was satan's idea. At one time he had been a man of faith, but through a mistaken idea that communication wasn't important he lost everything. He abandoned a confused and distraught wife with five children, some the same age as the girl he left with. Communication is vital for the health of any system, especially a marriage.

For each structure the vehicle of communication may be different and the pathways accessed may vary, but the essence is the same—move the information or the goods from the source to the destination, or face disaster. A traffic jam, a logjam, or losing your Internet server can all be equally disruptive and destructive. The same holds true in the body; if the cells aren't connected and able to communicate, the body's health is endangered. One simple miscommunication often cascades into multiple miscommunications, which will lead to sickness or even death if not corrected. Health in any system requires efficient communication. Jesus said, *"My sheep recognize My voice. I know them, and they follow Me"* (John 10:27 MSG).

Without connecting to God we lose our source of life. At one point, Jesus made some statements that offended and confused many of His followers. When many abandoned Him as a result, He asked His remaining disciples if they were going also. Peter replied, *"Lord, to whom would we go? You have the words that give eternal life"* (John 6:68 NLT). Offense stopped the communication between Jesus and His followers; stress stops communication among our body's cells and organs.

The body's mechanism for overcoming any break in the internal communication is through multiple feedback loops. They are designed to monitor and correct any aberration that may appear. Stress, which by its nature is designed to interrupt the homeostasis of the body in reaction to a threat, overrides these feedback loops and prioritizes a new set of paradigms—fight or flight. However, a continual heightened threat awareness and the corresponding neglect of the nonessential (for the battle) elements of the body can only be maintained for a brief period of time without compromising the health of the individual.

That stress response is good when you encounter a bear or if you need to cram for an exam, but becomes counterproductive when there is no enemy to fight or flee from. When I (Ken) was young we were once putting up some silage in a distant hay field. Because it was so far from the feedlot, we just dumped it on the ground and packed it with a tractor, planning to move it later. The hired man was driving the tractor over the growing pile when he got too close to the edge and tipped over. The tractor landed upside down and he got pinned under the seat with his leg jammed across his chest.

My friend and I desperately attempted to roll the tractor off of him, even pushing with a truck but to no avail. We got frantic in our efforts as he could not breathe and was turning blue. Finally I grabbed the seat and heaved on it with all my strength as my friend pulled the trapped man out. It came off so easy that I thought, "Why didn't we do that at the beginning and avoid all the agony that he suffered." Later, after the ambulance had left and the excitement quieted down, we managed to right the tractor. The seat that I had lifted so easily was supported by a two-inch channel iron that was now bent at almost 90 degrees. It took three hours, a tiger torch, and a come-a-long rated at several tons to straighten it out. Stress empowered me to react strongly to a threat of the man's death, but I could not live with that amount of adrenaline continuously flowing in my body.

Without its feedback loops functioning properly, the defence mechanisms of the body intensify even when there is no perceptible enemy such as a virus, bacteria, or germ. Take for example cytokines, which are one of the molecules that the body produces to combat the stress of invasion or infection. (The word *cytokines* comes from the Greek *cyto,* meaning "cell," and *kinos,* meaning "movement.")

Cytokines are substances that are secreted by cells in the immune system. They are a category of signaling molecules, and they carry information between cells. Cytokines are critical to the immune system, although they function in other systems as well. However, they are most often secreted by immune cells that have encountered a pathogen; they then activate other immune cells to respond to the attack.

Some dangerous situations, such as trauma or infection, can stimulate cytokine production to increase up to a thousand-fold.[1] If there is no real infection, only the appearance of one, then these high concentrations of cytokines will often attack healthy cells. This is the situation that stress creates—increased immune response with no enemy to respond to. The cytokines become like a leaderless, undisciplined, rouge army—they harass ordinary citizens.

Adverse effects of stress produced by high cytokine concentrations lead to many diseases and conditions including major depression, Alzheimer's disease, and cancer.[2] Over-secretion of cytokines can trigger a dangerous syndrome known as a cytokine storm.[3] A cytokine storm is a potentially fatal immune reaction, which highly elevates cytokine levels in response to a pathogen. This immune response caused many of the deaths in the swine flu and SARS epidemics. In these cases, a healthy immune system may have been a liability rather than an asset, as it overreacted and attacked healthy cells.[4]

The body normally responds to high levels of cytokines with a feedback loop that initiates apoptosis or cellular death. This cellular death is crucial to immune homeostasis. It is designed to balance the lymphocyte expansion by activating cells to self-destruct, sometimes in enormous numbers. This prevents the toxic effects of massive lymphocyte expansion.[5]

If low-grade stress persists through fear, anxiety, or pressure, then we are continually dripping toxic chemicals into the bloodstream. That breaks down the communication as the feedback loops are overridden, allowing overproduction or inappropriate production of certain cytokines that result in disease. For example, it has been found that interleukin-1 is produced in excess in rheumatoid arthritis where it causes inflammation and tissue destruction.[6] Similarly, if we are disconnected from God, then our thoughts will also be disconnected. It then becomes difficult to think good, positive thoughts. The Bible says that God *"...observed the extent of human wickedness on the earth, and He saw that everything they thought or imagined was consistently and totally evil"* (Gen. 6:5 NLT).

God's solution to counter the natural way of thinking is to purposely do the opposite.

> *For the rest, brethren, whatever is true, whatever is worthy of reverence and is honorable and seemly, whatever is just, whatever is pure, whatever is lovely and lovable, whatever is kind and winsome and gracious, if there is any virtue and excellence, if there is anything worthy of praise, think on and weigh and take account of these things [fix your minds on them]. Practice what you have learned and received and heard and seen in me, and model your way of living on it, and the God of peace (of untroubled, undisturbed well-being) will be with you* (Philippians 4:8-9 AMP).

I (Jeanne) was diagnosed years ago with fibromyalgia and suffered with it for several years. It was so bad that I could barely comb my hair and had to spend a day or two a week in bed. Knowing that healing was part of my inheritance, I decided to change my way of thinking. I began to speak more positively and to focus on what God was saying more than what my body was saying. We need to continually speak to ourselves that we are wonderfully loved by God, completely forgiven, and that He has a plan and a purpose for our life. I no longer have fibromyalgia or any of its symptoms. Now I am at peace with my body and with God.

A lack of peace brings depression. Studies suggest that major depression is also accompanied by immune dysregulation and activation of the inflammatory response system.[7] That is also why depression is accompanied by various aches and pains. We need to hear positive words to counter depression.

> Come quickly, Lord, and answer me, for **my depression deepens**. Don't turn away from me, or I will die. Let me hear of your unfailing love each morning, for I am trusting you... (Psalms 143:7-8 NLT).

In the book of Job it saids, *"[God] has redeemed my life from going down to the pit [of destruction], and my life shall see the light!"* (Job 33:28 AMP). Fixing our eyes on Jesus removes our thoughts from concentrating on our problems to embracing His solution.

Continual exposure to stressful situations will create havoc, even in healthy individuals. Career-oriented women, especially those with no children, have a much higher rate of deadly ovarian cancer than the average woman. Single working women have fourteen times the average risk of ovarian cancer than a matched group of homemakers. Job stress itself may be a factor, sometimes because of overt and covert sexual harassment.

David prayed, *"May those who try to destroy me be humiliated and put to shame. May those who take delight in my trouble be turned back in disgrace"* (Ps. 40:14 NLT). We must aggressively resist coming under accusation and abuse. When Paul got attacked by a snake, he did not cringe and cry; *"he shook the creature off into the fire and suffered no harm"* (Acts 28:5 NASB). Likewise, words from people in the past can come up and bite us. These words were often stuck on us like labels—dummy, lazy, stupid, worthless, useless, etc. We need to disavow these words, removing them from our memories, if we want to remove the labels. If we would just shake off all the negative verbal and mental thoughts that assail us, we, like Paul, would suffer no harm from them.

Canadian physician Sir William Osler noted that the course of tuberculosis depended more on "what the patient has in his head than what he has in his chest." Ishigami in Japan came to a similar conclusion in his paper. He found that some stable patients deteriorated and died after learning of the loss of a loved one. In other, more severe cases, a surprisingly complete recovery came about, despite the fact that no specific therapy was available. He noted that these patients were optimistic and not easily worried.[8] The psalmist David often experienced devastating situations but he rescued himself by going to God.

> I waited patiently and expectantly for the Lord; and He inclined to me and heard my cry. He **drew me up out of a horrible pit** [a pit of tumult and of destruction], out of the miry clay (froth and slime), and set my feet upon a rock, steadying my steps and establishing my goings. And He has **put a new song in my mouth**, a song of praise to our God. Many shall see and fear (revere and worship) and put their trust and confident reliance in the Lord (Psalms 40:1-3 AMP).

I (Jeanne) recently went for a routine mammogram, and they discovered something in the left breast and under the arm. I was sent for an ultrasound to confirm the diagnosis. There was a lot of fear in the room and I said out loud, "It is nothing! It is nothing!" After the test, the doctor decided to wait before doing anything and retest again later. It is six months later and my words have prevailed over the early test results; I am completely free from any lumps. God is both good and faithful to His word. Praise God!

A firm faith and a feeling of social support from family and friends all appear to be powerful stress buffers. It is not surprising, therefore, that such attributes have also been reported to be associated with a lower risk of cancer. *"A father to the fatherless, a defender of widows, is God in His holy dwelling. God sets the lonely in families, He leads out the prisoners with singing…"* (Ps. 68:5-6 NIV). God promised that He *"will never leave you nor forsake you"* (Heb. 13:5 NKJV).

A lack of emotional support, as well as certain other traits, was convincingly demonstrated by Grossarth-Maticek to be highly predictive of cancer. More importantly, they have shown in extensive, long-term prospective studies that stress reduction strategies were effective in reducing malignancy by 50 percent in individuals assessed as being cancer prone. The following table delineates the irrefutable evidence that *enjoying life and experiencing pleasure increased longevity and general health.*

Number and Percent Alive and Well vs. Pleasure and Well-being Index

[1]PWI score	<1.5	2	2.5	3	3.5	4	4.5	5	5.5	6	6.5	7
# Subjects	80	121	138	172	199	487	536	382	330	298	200	112
# Healthy	2	3	8	25	38	147	155	167	188	150	148	84
% Healthy	2.5	2.4	5.7	14	19	30	29	44	57	50	74	75
% Alive	5	14	20	27	35	56	64	70	75	74	80	78
% with Cancer	49	47	43	25	14	11	8	7	9	6	3	4.6
[2]SRI score	1.8	1.6	2.0	2.6	3.0	3.6	4.1	4.6	4.9	5.6	5.4	5.3
Avg Age test start	56	57	57	58	60	59	58	59	60	59	58	59
Avg Age now	77	78	78	79	81	80	79	80	81	80	79	80

[1]PWI (Pleasure & Well-being Index) (Measurement of Enjoyment & Feeling Good)

[2] SRI (Self-Regulatory Index)   (Measurement of Flexibility or Adaptability)

PWI stands for "Pleasure and Well-being Index" and is a measurement of enjoyment and feeling good. SRI stands for "Self-Regulatory Index" and is a measurement of flexibility or adaptability. This table is the results 21 years after the original test.[9]

Note how the percentage of healthy people increases as both the PWI and the SRI increase, and how the cancer percentage decreases. The *self-regulatory index* described how people felt as they monitored and adjusted the results of their behavior to better suit their lives. In other words, *how flexible and adaptable* they were. This test group shows how much being adaptable and enjoying life prolongs that life. Only 5 percent of those who enjoyed life the least were still alive 21 years after the first testing, compared to 78 percent survival for those with the highest enjoyment and adaptability ratings. Of those still living, 49 percent with the lower scores had cancer versus only 4 percent for the happy people. Those are dramatic results and can be life-changing if we are wise and change our ways and words.

I (Ken) have not always been the most adaptable person. I had five instances in one day when I let my emotions boil over into anger. My PWI and SRI score took a decided dip as I fumed over each situation. The Bible says, *"Do not be eager in your heart to be angry, for anger resides in the bosom of fools"* (Eccl. 7:9 NASB). (See Appendix C for an anger inventory.) When I looked at all these instances, I discovered that every one of them was a result of my plans getting changed. I needed wisdom to overcome my foolish reactions.

As I pondered what I had discovered, God spoke to me. He said, "Your inability to adapt to a new set of circumstances is my definition of an old wine skin." When I heard that I quickly repented of my resistance to change and asked for His grace to not get angry but get excited when my plans conflicted with His plans. Jesus said:

> *No one pours new wine into old wineskins. Otherwise, the wine will burst the skins, and both the wine and the wineskins will be ruined. No, they pour new wine into new wineskins* (Mark 2:22 NIV).

God is stretching us, but if we are not adaptable and flexible He cannot give us new revelation because it will just stress us out and cause us to have a breakdown.

As I have a tendency to be a workaholic; Jeanne counterbalances me by making us enjoy a little R and R on a regular basis. Even a short, one- or two-day vacation breaks the drudgery of having to work. We have learned that rest and relaxation is vital to our well-being. Even mini-vacations in your mind offset the pressures that life throws at us. Norman Cousins calls laughter "internal jogging." Cousins had been diagnosed with a life-threatening illness, an experience that led him to question Western medicine. Cousins found the treatments suggested by his doctors to be totally lacking, so he checked himself out of the hospital and checked into a hotel. From there on, he literally laughed himself back to health. He immersed himself in only funny movies and television shows. He enjoyed every one of the Charlie Chaplin movies, and watched *Candid Camera* episodes until his sides hurt from laughing. His illness disappeared.[10]

> This is the actual scientific definition of a laugh right here. It's a psycho-physiological reflex, a successive, rhythmic, spasmodic expiration with open glottis and vibration of the vocal chords often accompanied by a bearing of teeth and facial grimaces. That's the medical definition of a laugh. Oh wait, no, that's actually a description of rabies.[11]

Good friends and a good laugh will cure much of what ails us. A study by Spiegel similarly demonstrated that metastatic breast cancer patients who participated in group social support activities had an 18-month increase in survival compared to controls who received only routine treatment.[12] Fawzy and coworkers found that if a six-week stress management intervention was added to the treatment for early stage melanoma, it enhanced immune system function when compared to controls. After six years, the stress management group had less than half the rate of recurrence and deaths.[13] We need people to support us for *"A friend loves at all times, and a brother is born for a time of adversity"* (Prov. 17:17 NIV). (See Appendix A for a stress test.)

CANCER

Good health depends on good communication; good communication within our internal environment as well as with our external environment preserves homeostasis in our bodies. Essentially, the basic problem with a cancer cell is that it does not communicate properly with the body. "Cancer can be regarded as a rebellion in an orderly society of cells when they neglect their neighbors and grow autonomously over surrounding normal cells."[14] We are living in a physical world that mirrors the supernatural world. The macrosystems such as the galaxies also mirror the microsystems such as our bodies and even our cells. Just as the gravity and energy of one planet affects all the celestial bodies around it, so each cell and organ interacts and directly or indirectly affects all other organs and cells.

> *What we have is one body with many parts, each its proper size and in its proper place. No part is important on its own. Can you imagine Eye telling Hand, "Get lost; I don't need you"? Or, Head telling Foot, "You're fired; your job has been phased out"? As a matter of fact, in practice it works the other way—the "lower" the part, the more basic, and therefore necessary* (1 Corinthians 12:20-22 MSG).

It would seem silly for the hand to say, "I want to wear those shoes now," or the eye to say, "That ring would look good on me." (Though with today's piercing craze some of the strangest body parts are wearing bizarre ornaments.) Each of us, like our body parts, is specially designed with unique functions and purposes.

Intercellular communication plays an important role in maintaining an orderly society, but it is disturbed or blocked in the process of carcinogenesis—cancer. While we cannot define stress, the sense of being out of control is always distressing. That also happens to be the best definition of the cancer cell—it is essentially a cell out of control, because it does not communicate by giving or receiving instructions from adjacent cells.

Behavioral factors and inappropriate responses to stress must also be considered along with genetic factors in attempting to understand why some individuals develop cancer. Science is beginning to appreciate the endemic roots of cancer—those influences emanating from within us. These root causes may be equally as significant as any external forces, but they are potentially under our control. William Osler said, "It is much more important to know what sort of a patient has a disease than what sort of a disease a patient has." The Bible tells us how to respond to people or situations that irritate us.

> *Go ahead and be angry. You do well to be angry—but don't use your anger as fuel for revenge. And don't stay angry. Don't go to bed angry. Don't give the devil that kind of foothold in your life* (Ephesians 4:26-27 MSG).

De-stress yourself right now. Close your eyes, take a deep breath, and let it out slowly. Forgive the person who made you angry; let go of the offense and release the tension. Be good to your body and mind by releasing every judgment that is choking you. Forgiveness works because then we're no longer a prisoner of the past. Through the act of forgiving others, we actually heal ourselves.[15]

HPA AXIS

Though hyper people may be more prone to external stress, everyone has internal stressors. We all have fears and phobias that were built into us as memories from childhood. When these memories are activated, they often initiate a flow of stress chemicals disproportionate to the anxiety that we suddenly feel. The magnitude of our stress response is dictated by the sensitivity of our Hypothalamic-Pituitary-Adrenal (HPA) axis. Constant, low-level stress reduces the threshold required to activate a system-wide response. If the concentration of the stress hormones cycling among these three glands and the heart is too high, the feedback loop will be shut down and you will feel overwhelmed.

In university I (Ken) did an experiment to measure the electrical charge required to make a frog leg contract. The frog's leg responded when 10 mV (millivolt = 10^{-3} volts) were applied. If the leg was allowed to relax for 30 seconds, it required another 10 mV to have the leg contract again. However, if I only allowed 10 seconds between the shocks, I only needed 7 mV to get the same reaction. If I did not allow enough time for the tension to leave the leg, smaller and smaller voltages would make the leg contract. Eventually, only one mV would get a full reaction. We are the same; if we don't de-stress, less and less pressure will cause us to react. Our median stress level will dictate how much additional stress we can normally handle.

A major stressor—such as a near car crash, the boss yelling, the kids screaming, or a big test—will cause the hypothalamus to release CRH, which flows to the pituitary gland, stimulating it to release another hormone called ACTH (see the chart below). ACTH drips into the bloodstream and signals your adrenal glands, on the kidneys, to release the stress-response hormones cortisol and adrenaline.

Adrenaline will immediately increase your blood pressure and heart rate. Cortisol releases sugars, in the form of glucose, to fuel the muscles and the mind, readying them for a response to the stress. The heart receives theses stress chemicals and releases ANF and ANP, which are neuropeptides that bind to receptors in the adrenal cortex and the hypothalamus. They are designed to regulate the body's fluid balances, the blood pressure, and other behaviors.[16] These chemicals, along with the cortisol, eventually flow back to flood the hypothalamus and complete the feedback loop. The cortisol will reduce the production of CRH in the hypothalamus and the feedback loop allows the body to begin to return to normal.

LOCATION	ORGAN	CHEMICAL RELEASED	RESPONSE
Brain	Hypothalamus	GRH[i]	↑Stress/Negative ↑Emotions
Bottom of the Hypothalamus	Pituitary Gland	ACTH[ii]	↑Fear
Kidney	Adrenal Gland	(Stress Chemicals) Cortisol Adrenaline Coricosteroids	↑Blood Pressure ↑Heart Palpitations ↑Sugar in Blood ↓Immunity to Infection ↓Memory & Creativity
Heart	Mini-Neural Precessor in heart muscle cells	ANF[iii] ANF[iv]	↓Blood Pressure ↓Heart Rate ↓Vasopressin[v]

[i]CRH: Corticotropin Releasing Hormone—stimulate ACTH production
[ii]ATCH: Adrenocorticotropic Hormone—metabolism of glucose and steroids
[iii]Atrial Natriuretic Peptide: regulates water, sodium, potassium, fat deposition
[iv]Atrial Natriuretic Factor: regulates blood flow
[v]Vasopressin: regulates water balances/thirst

However, if the stressors continue, as with the frog leg, then the CRH production will also continue at the rate of the distress the body feels, and the deleterious (destructive) effects of these hormones will begin to accelerate. The stress hormones work throughout the body to influence everything from fear and memory to cellular activity and appetite. They also interact with the hormonal system that controls reproduction, metabolism, and immunity. Hormones are good and necessary in short spurts, but when they overload your system they become destructive, which is why high stress is correlated with bad health.

"A cheerful heart is good medicine, but a broken spirit saps a person's strength" (Prov. 17:22 NLT). Our son, who has been fighting schizophrenia, likes to laugh a lot. He will start and go for several minutes. We jokingly told him that he should apply for the position of a Yoga Laughing Instructor as this seems to be the new craze. And I thought that only comedians could make money off humor. We need to take in a funny movie or read a joke book to turn off our internal stressors.

- An overactive HPA (Hypothalamic-Pituitary-Adrenal) axis means the body is unable to turn off its stress response, which will lead to anxiety and depression.

- An overactive HPA axis will lead to increased bad cholesterol, increased appetite, elevated sugar levels, diabetes, and obesity.

- Cortisol prevents the release of immune chemicals and decreases the body's ability to fight infection, opening it up to various diseases such as cancer. Cortisol, which is produced when we have heated arguments, remains in the male for only about one hour but in the female for over twelve hours. This is why women still feel the emotional undertones of a fight the next day long after the man has forgotten it.

- CRH will reduce ovulation, sperm counts, and libido.

- Stress reduces the release of growth hormone, which counters aging.

- The continual presence of stress will produce an exhaustion that makes us feel wiped out when the next real stressor comes.[17]

HPA (Hypothalamic-Pituitary-Adrenal) Axis Interaction

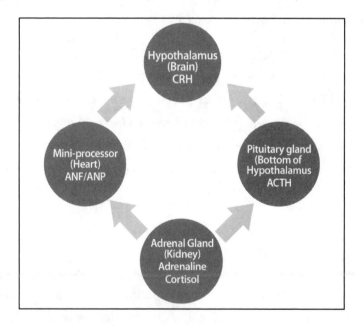

The stress chemicals, adrenaline and cortisol, also wreak havoc on the artery walls, causing them to require repair with a substance called collagen. Even this repair is subject to problems. Because collagen is the critical component in repairing damaged arteries (atherosclerotic lesions), extra collagen accumulation at the repair sight (plaque) leads to a narrowing of the arteries (arterial stenosis). If that excessive collagen breaks down, it will float in the arteries and further clog them. Collagen constitutes up to 60 percent of plaque, so too much collagen leads to narrow arteries, while not enough collagen produces hardened arteries (atherosclerotic), which are prone to rupture and cause strokes.[18] With too much stress, often the cure is worse than the disease. This is a major problem, as we can see from the number of people taking cholesterol medicine.

We are a marvelously complex creation.

> *[God] made all the delicate, inner parts of my body and knit me together in my mother's womb. Thank You for making me so wonderfully complex! Your workmanship is marvelous—how well I know it. You watched me as I was being formed in utter seclusion, as I was woven together in the dark of the womb. You saw me before I was born* (Psalms 139:13-16 NLT).

God created us; therefore we should learn to relax and not stress out, for *"if God be for us, who can be against us?"* (Rom. 8:31). God commanded Joshua just before his first battle, *"Be strong and of good courage; do not be afraid, nor be dismayed, for the Lord your God is with you wherever you go"* (Josh. 1:9 NKJV). Stressful situations do not have to engender a fear response if we know that no matter what happens we are in God's loving hands.

FEAR

The root of stress is fear. Fear is a negative expectation of both the known and the unknown. It is the ruminations of the subconscious mind that prompt most of the emotional responses that we have. Because our emotions are so fickle and fluctuate so violently, most decisions made by them will be unreliable. Studies have shown that negative emotions, especially from bad parents, bad bosses, bad teachers, or bad feedback loops, have more impact on our decision making than the good influences. Bad information is also processed, or regurgitated, and remembered more than positive information.[19] This constant rumination of bad events evokes toxic memories and thus constantly drips toxic chemicals into the bloodstream and onto our cells and organs. God is willing to forgive and forget and calls us to do the same thing. Jesus taught His disciples to pray, *"Forgive us our debts, as we also have forgiven our debtors"* (Matt. 6:12 NASB).

This tendency to emphasize bad or evil over good seems to be a universal law. Baumeister stated that when equal measures of good and bad are present, the psychological effects of bad ones outweigh those of the good ones. This may in fact be a general principle or law of psychological phenomena, possibly reflecting the innate predispositions of the psyche.[20] It is not just a predisposition in us but a law in the universe; everything moves from a state of higher order to a state of lower order or disorder. It is that loss of order and control that creates stress in our lives.

I (Jeanne) was extremely fearful when I was younger, but over the years I've learned to trust God in all of my situations. As we started to fly to new countries, meet new people, eat strange food, and encounter new customs, I was stretched. I was accustomed to imagining everything that could possibly go wrong, but with those possibilities going exponential with all the unknowns of travel, I had to trust God or be a basket case. As almost all of what I feared never happened anyway, I learned to rest in God. What can I say? *"If God be for us, who can be against us?"* (Rom. 8:31). He has proven so faithful that when I know I am in His will, I no longer stress over the "what ifs."

Gottman in his research proposed that in order for a relationship to succeed, positive and good interactions must outnumber the negative and bad ones by at least 5 to 1. If the ratio falls below that, the relationship is likely to fail and break up.[21] This is in reality the outworking of the Second Law of Thermodynamics, which states that every system runs down and tends to disorder. The stress chemicals that our bodies produce and store in our organs and cells accelerate that disorder. The ultimate disorder in any person or system is death and destruction.

The Bible speaks of the law of the Spirit of life in Christ Jesus setting us free from the law of sin and death (see Rom. 8:2). Without life, death will reign in our thoughts, actions, and relationships. The law of death is always working and must be aggressively resisted in our thought life or it will take over not just our mind (negativity), but our entire physical being. Our toxic memories are constantly assailing us with negative thoughts about our character, motives, and the outcome of our endeavors. God wants us to *"know that all things work together for good to those who love God, to those who are the called according to His purpose"* (Rom. 8:28 NKJV).

Since we started traveling, we have encountered many situations where we are not in control. We are subject to the whims of the weather, flight delays, cultural differences in time management, and confusion over expectations. We are learning to be flexible and to enjoy the adventure. Once when flying through Seattle, we were asked if we would take another flight because the weather at our destination was iffy. The backup airports along the route either had ice or fog, forcing the airlines to use Portland as the emergency airport. That was the opposite direction to where we were traveling, so they needed to take on extra fuel and get rid of some passengers.

We accepted the airline's offer of a night's free accommodation with meals and tickets to anywhere they flew. We had a year to use the new tickets. Within that year, they added Hawaii as a destination and we got a free trip and a great vacation. Be flexible; God is in control and He knows how to make even the bad times good. You will just wear yourself out trying to micromanage even your own life.

Vince Lombardi, while coaching the Green Bay Packers, stated that "fatigue makes cowards of us all." That is what stress does; it wears us out and makes us vulnerable to doubt and fear. It is interesting that the Bible agrees saying, "[satan] *shall speak great words against the most High, and shall wear out the saints of the most High, and think to change times and laws...*" (Dan. 7:25). It is not our situations that stress us and wear us out; it is our reactions of worrying and fretting about those situations that wear us down. An attitude of joy, rather than dread, will invigorate us, *"for the joy of the Lord is your strength"* (Neh. 8:10).

Jesus said:

> *Look at the birds of the air; they neither sow nor reap nor gather into barns, and yet your heavenly Father keeps feeding them. Are*

you not worth much more than they? And who of you by worry-
ing and being anxious can add one unit of measure (cubit) to his
stature or to the span of his life? And why should you be anxious
about clothes? Consider the lilies of the field and learn thoroughly
how they grow; they neither toil nor spin. Yet I tell you, even
Solomon in all his magnificence (excellence, dignity, and grace)
was not arrayed like one of these. But if God so clothes the grass
of the field, which today is alive and green and tomorrow is tossed
into the furnace, will He not much more surely clothe you, O you
of little faith? (Matthew 6:26-30 AMP)

Sage advice; as Richard Carlson says in modern vernacular: "Don't sweat
the small stuff...and it's all small stuff."

KEYS

- Good communication within the body is vital for health.

- Stress breaks the lines of communication.

- Stress results from our thoughts about our situations.

- Stress is the body's response to attack.

- Long-term stress disrupts the body's feedback loops and disrupts homeostasis (balance).

- Long-term stress reduces your overall health and will eventually kill you.

- Our attitudes can reduce stress.

- The root of stress is fear, which is a function of control.

SECTION B

DELIVERANCE FROM TOXIC MEMORIES

Chapter 5

HEALING TOXIC MEMORIES

*Nothing fixes a thing so intensely in the memory as
the wish to forget it* —MICHEL DE MONTAIGNE

*It is the peculiar quality of a fool to perceive the faults of
others and to forget his own* —MARCUS TULLIUS CICERO

*When a deep injury is done us, we never
recover until we forgive* —ALAN PATON

THE PROBLEM

Stress is killing us! The question of how to remove that stress has spawned an entire industry. Ten million Americans see psychiatrists for stress-related issues each year.[1] Of the $120 billion spent on prescription pharmaceuticals, over one third, or $40 billion, was spent on stress-related drugs—those for depression, anxiety, sleep, etc.[2] Job stress is estimated to cost U.S. industry more than $300 billion a year in absenteeism, turnover, diminished productivity, and medical, legal, and insurance costs.[3] Everyone knows there is a problem, but nobody has the solution except God. The Bible says:

> *Do all you have to do without grumbling or arguing, so that you may be God's children, blameless, sincere and wholesome, living in a warped and diseased world, and shining there like lights in a dark place. For you hold in your hands the very word of life...* (Philippians 2:14-16 PNT).

But how do we not express those irritating feelings and memories? Do we just stuff and suppress them? Research shows that attempted thought suppression has paradoxical effects as a self-control strategy, perhaps even producing the very obsession or preoccupation that it is directed against.[4] The more we try to diet, the more we think about food. The more we try to stop worrying or fretting, the more the situation or person rents space in our head.

We often work with people in counseling who seem fine until the smallest thing is mentioned, which triggers a huge explosion. That over-reaction is our key that there is a lot of suppressed anger. There is a root to that anger that some toxic memory has fed. Countless people have been brought up to believe that anger and expressing anger are wrong. This attitude does not stop the feeling; it merely stops it moving through and out of the body as a natural course of action. Over time, with habitual suppression—often with food, alcohol, cigarettes or drugs—individuals cannot express any anger naturally and it can accumulate as blocked energy. "Suppressed emotions, specifically anger, are widely accepted to be major contributors to depression, clinical stress, and all its implications including high blood pressure."[5]

> A further principle drawn from research with conditions such as obsessive compulsive disorder, social phobias, and agoraphobia indicates that the very "coping strategies" used by the patients to relieve or forestall unpleasant emotions such as anxiety, shame, and guilt often backfire; they tend to maintain the disorder. A schizophrenic patient who uses magical gestures to ward off supposed evil spells or calls the police to save him from the threatening voices of neighbors never learns how to reprocess, to test out, to correct his misinterpretation. Since judicious exposure to the threatening stimuli appears to modify the pathogenic belief, we can infer that dysfunctional information processing is not fixed but is amenable to change.[6]

Suppression and repression will not solve the problem of toxic memories. Memories are living entities and burying them does not kill them, it only blocks their natural flow. Burying a memory is like building a dam and thinking that will solve the problem of an unwanted river. The longer the dam blocks the flow of the river, the greater the pressure that builds behind it. Eventually, the dam will burst or the river will take a new course, either of which will likely be more destructive than a river contained within its banks. The solution is to stop the flow of the river (or the toxicity of the memory), not just attempt to block or repress it.

THE SITUATION

I've tried everything and nothing helps. I'm at the end of my rope. Is there no one who can do anything for me? Isn't that the real question? The answer, thank God, is that Jesus Christ can and does. He acted to set things right in this life of contradictions… (Romans 7:24-25 MSG).

The Bible tells us not to stress or complain:

Nor grumble, as some of them did…these things happened to them as an example, and they were written for our instruction, upon whom the ends of the ages have come. Therefore let him who thinks he stands take heed that he does not fall. No temptation has overtaken you but such as is common to man; and God is faithful, who will not allow you to be tempted beyond what you are able, but with the temptation will provide the way of escape also, so that you will be able to endure it (1 Corinthians 10:10-13 NASB).

God has provided, in His-story, examples for those of us who overcame situations that should have produced bitterness and hatred but didn't. The story of Joseph reveals how to overcome betrayal and evil without it consuming us.

Joseph was the eleventh son of the patriarch Jacob. He had one younger brother, an older half-sister, and ten older half-brothers. As the oldest son of the favorite wife (there were three others), Joseph enjoyed the favored position with his father. He was a bit of a know-it-all and irritated his brothers with his tattling to dad about what they were doing wrong (see Gen. 37:2). His favored position did nothing to enhance the family harmony. The situation came to a head when Joseph foolishly announced that he had a dream in which his brothers would bow down to him. *"...So they hated him even more for his dreams and for his words"* (Gen. 37:8 NASB).

Their rage boiled over one day when they were all far away from home. The brothers were going to kill him but settled on throwing him into a pit. I can imagine Joseph's consternation and anger that his brothers would treat "Daddy's pet" this way. He must have yelled and threatened them, "If you don't let me out right now I'm going to tell Dad." They ignored him and laughed as they sat down to eat. Maybe Joseph's tone changed when the threats didn't work and a more conciliatory suggestion came out. "If you let me out, I won't tell Dad."

Just then a caravan came along, and the brothers decided to sell him rather than kill him. So they sold him and disposed of their problem brother. Joseph likely didn't realize the degree of their hatred, figuring that as soon as they were done scaring him they would ride over the hill and end the joke. Reality slowly set in as that night and the next passed with no brothers and no rescue. The shock of his sudden change of status and the hopelessness of his predicament would eventually give way to anger and resentment that anyone, especially his brothers, could do this to him.

Joseph would suffer further humiliation as he was stripped and sold naked in the slave market in Egypt. But he was young and had a strong faith in God and justice. So he threw himself into his new situation. Even though he may have felt alone, God had not abandoned Joseph and whatever he did prospered (see Gen. 39:2). So much so that Potiphar, his owner, made him his personal servant and put him in charge over everything that he had.

Things might have gone that way for a long time except that Potiphar's wife had the "hots" for Joseph. She repeatedly tried to seduce him, but Joseph honorably refused. Finally, one day she got him alone in the house and forcibly tried to make him have sex with her. He fled the house, but she tore off his coat as he ran. Now rejected, her lust turned to anger. She now epitomized the saying that, "Heaven has no rage like love to hatred turned, nor hell a fury like a woman scorned."[7]

She screamed rape, and poor Joseph went from being a slave in Egypt to being a slave in prison in Egypt. *"But the Lord was with Joseph and extended kindness to him, and gave him favor in the sight of the chief jailer"* (Gen. 39:21 NASB). *"What shall we then say to these things? If God be for us, who can be against us?"* (Rom. 8:31). But Joseph was getting discouraged. The Bible says that *"...He was laid in chains of iron and his soul entered into the iron"* (Ps. 105:18 AMP).

He became depressed and hopeless. Everything he tried just got him deeper into trouble, but *"...the Lord was with him; and whatever he did, the Lord made it prosper"* (Gen. 39:23 NKJV). God prompted the keeper of the prison to put all the prisoners under Joseph's charge. Even though Joseph seemed on a downward slide from favored son to slave to prisoner, he was always promoted wherever he landed.

This slide continued for thirteen years! All the dreams and promises had faded away. A ray of hope appeared once when Pharaoh's butler ended up under Joseph's charge and Joseph was able to favorably interpret his dream. He urged the butler:

> *"Remember me when it is well with you, and please show kindness to me; make mention of me to Pharaoh, and get me out of this house."* ...*Yet the chief butler did not remember Joseph, but forgot him* (Genesis 40:14,23 NKJV).

And he continued to forget him for two full years.

By that time Joseph was not looking to him for any help, and yet God had arranged everything for the time frame He was setting up. We want things to happen now because our time is short; God has things happen in the fullness of time because He is outside of time.

> [God] has saved us and called us with a holy calling, not according to our works, but according to His own purpose and grace which was given to us in Christ Jesus before time began (2 Timothy 1:9 NKJV).

God has time in His hands, but we have to trust Him when it seems that time is running out. Joseph, like us, could only see his circumstances, not his destiny.

Then everything changed with a dream that Pharaoh could not interpret. Suddenly the butler remembered, Joseph was ushered in to Pharaoh's presence, and in ten minutes he was taken from the prison to the palace and put in charge of the entire country! Pharaoh said, *"Without your consent no man may lift his hand or foot in all the land of Egypt"* (Gen. 41:44 NKJV). I think Joseph would have asked God for forgiveness for doubting Him, after he pinched himself to make sure it wasn't a dream.

Nine years later, Joseph was distributing the grain Egypt had stored up, according to Joseph's counsel, when his brothers showed up. Joseph recognized them but they couldn't recognize him. So he tested them to see where they were at, calling them spies and putting them in prison. Their first reaction was to regretfully cry:

> Then they said to one another, "We are truly guilty concerning our brother, for we saw the anguish of his soul when he pleaded with us, and we would not hear; therefore this distress has come upon us" (Genesis 42:21 NKJV).

Their first reaction was to blame their present troubles on what they had done to Joseph 22 years earlier. I am sure this was not the first time they had declared this. They were paranoid that their treacherous actions were reaping disaster. They were so paranoid that 17 years later when their father Jacob died, they said, *"Perhaps* [now] *Joseph will hate us, and may actually repay us for all the evil which we did to him"* (Gen. 50:15 NKJV). Their toxic memories plagued them for 40 years but Joseph, who had the wrong done to him, had a completely different reaction.

When his brothers first displayed their fearful regrets of what they did to Joseph, *"They did not know that Joseph understood them, for he spoke to them through an interpreter. And he turned himself away from them and wept..."* (Gen. 42:23-24 NKJV). His heart went out to his brothers. Later, when he revealed who he was:

> *Then Joseph could not restrain himself...and he wept aloud... "I am Joseph your brother, whom you sold into Egypt. But now, do not therefore be grieved or angry with yourselves because you sold me here; for God sent me before you to preserve life"* (Genesis 45:1-5 NKJV).

He had no animosity or bitterness, though he had ample opportunity to have both. For thirteen years he woke up every morning facing the consequences of his brother's evil actions toward him. He always acted lovingly toward them, and after Jacob died, *"Joseph wept when they spoke* [fearfully] *to him. ...Joseph said to them, 'Do not be afraid, for am I in the place of God?'"* (Gen. 50:17,19 NKJV).

The truth was—he was. He had the power of life and death over them. He could have easily executed all of them and no one would have blamed him. But that was not his attitude. He was heartbroken that they would even consider that he could be so heartless. His attitude was: *"You meant evil against me; but God meant it for good, in order to bring it about as it is this day, to save many people alive"* (Gen. 50:20 NKJV).

Why was the thought of revenge so foreign to Joseph that he couldn't believe that anyone would even consider that he would hurt them? Why were his brothers stuck in their fear and paranoia for almost 40 years? What was different? Joseph had been healed from his trauma and they had not. How did he get delivered from his toxic memories?

THE SOLUTION

Forgive

Joseph had obviously forgiven his brothers because there was no bitterness toward them at all. The very thought of revenge didn't even enter his mind. It actually hurt him that they would think that way after all the good he had done for them over the past 17 years. He had entirely dismissed the past from his present and was in no way planning on having it as part of his future. So complete was his healing that he couldn't fathom his brothers' paranoia.

Forget

The secret for his healing is hidden in the way Joseph named his sons:

> *Joseph called the firstborn Manasseh [making to forget], For God, said he, has made me forget all my toil and hardship and all my father's house. And the second he called Ephraim [to be fruitful], For [he said] God has caused me to be fruitful in the land of my affliction* (Genesis 41:51-52 AMP).

He didn't forget the events, but he did forget the emotions connected with those events. He knew if he was to be fruitful (Ephraim), he must be forgetful (Manasseh). God created the glial cells in our brains to assist in that process.

Rewrite

Joseph's forgiving and forgetting allowed him to put a new take on the events that brought him to Egypt. He told his brothers:

> *Do not be distressed and disheartened or vexed and angry with yourselves because you sold me here, for **God sent me** ahead of you to preserve life. ...**God sent me** before you to preserve for you a posterity and to continue a remnant on the earth, to save your lives by a great escape and save for you many survivors. So now it was **not you who sent me here, but God**; and He has made me*

*a father to Pharaoh and lord of all his house and ruler over all the
land of Egypt* (Genesis 45:5-8 AMP).

Three times he emphasized that it was God, not them, who arranged
the trip to Egypt.

Here is the new memory that Joseph had:

- Yes, you sold me because you were mad, but God had a plan
  and used you to achieve it.

- If I hadn't been sold, I never would have gotten to Potiphar's house.

- If I hadn't gotten to Potiphar's house, his wife wouldn't have
  tried to seduce me.

- If she hadn't tried to seduce me, I never would have been
  accused of rape.

- If she hadn't lied about me, I never would have gotten thrown
  in jail.

- If I didn't get into jail, I never would have met the butler and
  interpreted his dream even though he forgot about me for
  two years.

- If he hadn't forgot about me for two years, I wouldn't have
  stayed in Egypt and been able to interpret Pharaoh's dream.

- If I hadn't interpreted his dream, I never would have been
  promoted to Prime Minister.

- If I wasn't Prime Minister, I would not have been able to
  ration the grain during the famine.

- If there was no grain in Egypt, I would not have been able to
  save you and all the people.

- I never would have thought of that. He used your anger to
  save a nation and preserve a people alive. What a great plan
  God had! Isn't He awesome!

Now every thought about his time in prison brought up thoughts of praise and thanksgiving in Joseph, not anger and bitterness. His Egyptian name, *Zaphnath-paaneah*, meant "Savior of the Age."[8] Instead of being a victim of events he couldn't control, Joseph became a major player in a grand scheme to save the world.

Paul declared that *"all things work together for good to those who love God, to those who are the called according to His purpose"* (Rom. 8:28 NKJV). If you are willing to forgive, your glial cells will help you to forget, and God will rewrite your toxic memory and give you *"…the oil of joy for mourning, the garment of praise for the spirit of heaviness"* (Isa. 61:3 NKJV).

> *For I know the thoughts and plans that I have for you, says the Lord, thoughts and plans for welfare and peace and not for evil, to give you hope in your final outcome* (Jeremiah 29:11 AMP).

Our job is to forgive and forget; God's job is to rewrite our memories and turn our disasters into victories.

THE APPLICATION

So what does that look like in our lives? How do we forgive, forget, and rewrite? The best examples are always personal, because it is our own experiences that ingrain the truth in our souls and allow us to impart that truth to others. Everything else is just theory or doctrine. Jesus said that *"if any man will do His will, he shall know of the doctrine, whether it be of God, or whether I speak of myself"* (John 7:17).

Doing what God says allows you to know the truth about what God is saying. Without experience, we just have theory or speculation or wishful thinking. That is why others' testimonies build our faith to try it ourselves. No one could argue with Lazarus, after Jesus resurrected him, about the reality of God and the afterlife; he had been there, done that (see John 11). His experience trumped their doctrine and made him impervious to fear about death. To really know the truth we must continue or abide in Jesus's words and commands (see John 8:31-32). Abiding is about walking it out, trying it ourselves to see if it works!

Jeanne and I had a situation years ago when we were first married that could have made us bitter. We did not even understand the principle of forgive/forget/rewrite yet, but we knew we needed to stay out of bitterness if we were to be of any use to God. I (Ken) had wanted to be an engineer, and in high school I took all the math, trigonometry, and physics courses to get ready for university. My father wanted me to come back and work with him on the farm and convinced me in my last high school year to switch to agriculture in university. That meant that I needed to catch up on biology, physiology, and organic chemistry to be able to graduate.

I was not the most dedicated student those first few years, and with the extra load I almost flunked out. I had to make a major lifestyle shift and move out of residence so I could concentrate more on my studies. My father could afford to assist me but he chose not to, and I had to drive taxi two nights a week to keep from starving. Jeanne and I married during my last year and her job and my taxi driving kept the wolf away from our door.

My father was not ready to have me return to the farm right after graduation and asked me to wait until the next spring. Jobs were hard to find during that time, but I landed one as a milkman for a few months. Later, Jeanne's dad got me a job in construction. During this time we moved out of our nice apartment into a basement suite with a nosy landlady. We scrimped and saved and with Jeanne's bonus from work paid off my university loans. In February, we finally went back to the farm.

The Bible says that the events that happened to the Israelites "*...happened unto them for examples: and they are written for our admonition, upon whom the ends of the world are come*" (1 Cor. 10:11). Our story is not to discredit or dishonor my father but is to demonstrate, like Joseph's story, how God works things for our good. We don't see the good during the bad times, but God gives us *"the valley of Achor* [trouble[9]] *for a door of hope"* (Hos. 2:15).

This doesn't mean, of course, that we have only a hope of future joys—we can be full of joy here and now even in our trials and troubles. Taken in the right spirit these very things will give us patient endurance; this in turn will develop a mature character, and a character of this sort produces a steady hope, a hope that will never disappoint us... (Romans 5:3-5 PNT).

Once we arrived on the farm, we began to fix up the trailer that was to be our home. For the next few weeks we paneled, tiled, and painted our new house. Since I was not officially working on the farm, I received no pay, even though we were repairing my dad's trailer. Jeanne was three months pregnant with our first child and was often feeling sick and had to stay in bed, but we were young and happy just to be together, looking forward to our new future.

When the spring work started in earnest I worked six days a week, alternating one long and one short day—one 16-hour and one 12-hour day. I was paid $300 per month, which was the same as any hired man with no education. That sum worked out to 76.5 cents an hour! Not a princely sum for four years of university and a degree, but we were looking to the future and trusted that things would soon change. But they didn't; in fact, they got worse.

Because Jeanne was starting to get very big with the baby, she didn't want people to see her in a bathing suit. One of our friends offered to let us to camp on their farm, which had a private beach. My parents had a little holiday trailer, and I asked if we could borrow it for the week. My dad came back with an offer to rent it to us at $70 for the week.

We had very little savings to fall back on, and even though we were going into debt at the rate of $30 per month—the amount of our tithe—we needed the break. The week was lovely but we started to realize that something was amiss with the farming arrangement. We first thought that it was just the pressure of another family in the same yard, and so we began looking for alternative accommodations.

Our living situation in the trailer was less than ideal. The water we used had to be pumped from the barnyard into the basement cistern of the original log house, which still stood beside the trailer. This meant that Jeanne, a city girl, had to climb the fence, walk through the muck and the cattle, redirect the water tank spout to go to the cistern, climb back over the fence, check the water level in the cistern until it was full, retrace her steps over the fence, and then reverse the flow of the water back to the watering tank. Sometimes, because of her pregnancy, she would lie down to rest and the cistern would overflow into the dirt dugout under the log house. This brought out the ire in my dad, and he would loudly display his displeasure.

The water going out of the trailer soon became a bigger problem than the water coming in. The sewage removal was a wooden cribbing, acting as a cesspool under the trailer. It finally collapsed, causing the dirt in front of the front door of the trailer to cave in. This meant that everybody who came into our home had to come through the back hall next to our bedroom. There was a real danger that the whole area under the trailer would collapse, not to mention the smell that was no longer capped. Still, my parents made no move to improve our living conditions though I, as a son, was making less than a hired man would have earned.

In our search for a new place to live, we found a half-section of land with a decent house on it for only $32,000. We hoped that my dad would help us out so that we could buy it. I had worked for the Farm Credit Corporation while going to university and knew that if my dad would cosign, we could easily afford it and have it paid for in a few short years. I offered to rent his equipment, which would have helped him, but I got a flat-out "No" to my proposal.

We were at a crossroads. If we stayed another six months, we would have no money to even put down a deposit for rent. If we left, four years of university would be down the drain. We prayed for an answer and for a softening of my father's heart.

My parents went on a holiday, leaving me behind to run the operation. I was busy as we had six quarters of cropland, hundreds of cattle in two separate feedlots, and a silage pit to excavate. I ran from sunup to sundown, and then the disaster hit—we got hailed out, five hundred acres of crops gone in one hour. Since my father was gone and could not be reached (there were no cell phones in those days), my grandpa and I decided to cut the worst of the damaged crop down, hoping the rest would make a comeback and at least produce some silage. As we talked, I knew the Lord was also talking. Grandpa was saying, "Let's salvage what we can." God was saying, "Get out while you can."

Before we even came to the farm, I had had an argument with God. I so wanted to be farming, but He had said, "I don't want you to go there."

I replied, "But I want to."

He said, "I don't want you to go."

I replied, "But I want to."

He said, "Okay, go, but you will be sorry." God was not making a threat; He was stating a fact.

That conversation flooded back to my mind as I surveyed the damage that the hail caused and realized the damage that my stubborn independence had caused. I told my grandpa right there that we had to leave, and he acknowledged that that was likely the best course of action. After talking to Jeanne, I phoned her dad and he said he had a job with the iron-workers union that I could have right away. We packed up and left before my parents came home as there was nothing left to do that my grandpa could not handle for a few days. Thus ended my dream of becoming a farmer, though I know God saved me from a nightmare.

There were lots of opportunities to get bitter and walk in judgment and unforgiveness. After all, it was my father who talked me out of my chosen engineering profession but wouldn't help when I chose what he wanted. It was my dad who refused to pay me while working on his trailer for a month, refused to fix the septic system, refused to pay me a living wage, refused to help me establish myself, and who had hardened his heart so much that he charged us a whole week's wages just to rent their little travel trailer. He had prevented me from being an engineer, and now was preventing me from being a farmer. There was no advantage to being a son, and at that point I didn't feel like one.

Anger and even hatred would have been my response, except God was teaching us a lesson—He was in charge, not my father. When I repented of my part in this fiasco, I clearly heard God speak to me. He said, "I hardened your father's heart just like I hardened Pharaoh's (it is mentioned 11 times in Exodus). I didn't want you here, and I would not let your father bless you."

It was God, not my father, who directed my steps and moved me away from both engineering and farming (see Gen. 45:5-8). God had a better plan, and since I had given Him permission to guide me, He did. *"A man's heart plans his way, but the Lord directs his steps"* (Prov. 16:9 NKJV).

Knowing this was from God, I could forgive my father. I found out later from my sisters that he thought I was the problem and that I didn't want to stay. He was oblivious to any part he might have played in our leaving. He was not trying to hurt me, but God wouldn't let him help me either.

I was able to quickly forget our hard situation and the deprivation as we soon had a new son, a new career, a new house, and a new church. God connected us with great Christians who impacted our lives in a way that would not have happened in the town close to the farm. God had bigger plans for us so that we could be impacted by the larger Body of Christ and eventually impact others.

Once God is written into the story, the events take on new and greater meaning. God promises *"that all things work together for good to them that love God, to them who are the called according to His purpose"* (Rom. 8:28). Like the ingredients of a cookie, which individually are not palatable (flour, baking powder, salt, sugar), yet when mixed together and heated become a delight. We do not have the capacity to see the whole:

> *For now we are looking in a mirror that gives only a dim* (blurred) *reflection [of reality as in a riddle or enigma], but then [when perfection comes] we shall see in reality and face to face! Now I know in part* (imperfectly), *but then I shall know and*

understand fully and clearly, even in the same manner as I have been fully and clearly known and understood [by God] (1 Corinthians 13:12 AMP).

We can honestly say that there have been no toxic memories associated with our time on the farm or in university because we were able to completely forgive, completely forget, and joyfully rewrite that part of our lives. That is the key to relationships and to productive living. End the paranoia and the bitterness. Allow God to show you the true meaning of the events you endured so that you can live with purpose, not regret, the life God has destined for you.

Joseph learned this lesson, but his brothers remained paranoid, fearing what he would do to them for what they had done to him 40 years earlier.

> *When Joseph's brethren saw that their father was dead, they said, Perhaps now Joseph will hate us and will pay us back for all the evil we did to him. And they sent a messenger to Joseph, saying, Your father commanded before he died, saying, So shall you say to Joseph: Forgive...I pray you now, the trespass of your brothers and their sin, for they did evil to you. Now, we pray you, forgive the trespass of the servants of your father's God. And Joseph wept when they spoke thus to him. ...And Joseph said to them, Fear not; for am I in the place of God? [Vengeance is His, not mine.] As for you, **you thought evil against me, but God meant it for good**, to bring about that many people should be kept alive, as they are this day. Now therefore, do not be afraid. I will provide for and support you and your little ones...* (Genesis 50:15-21 AMP).

Joseph was so upset when he realized they thought he would retaliate that he wept. He had long since recognized God's good plan for the whole family that overruled any other conflicting motives. It never entered into his mind to harm anyone, because his brothers' envy had become the tool that God used to work out His plan of salvation for their families. Joseph had the same heart as Jesus, who said, on the cross, *"Father, forgive them;*

for they know not what they do" (Luke 23:34). If we know that God is in control, we can forgive, forget, and rewrite our memories, ensuring that our toxic past will not dictate our glorious future.

KEYS

Stress is increased by toxic memories.

Toxic memories are created by unresolved issues.

The solution:

- forgive the people involved.
- Forget the negative emotional baggage.
- Rewrite the narrative, interjecting God's purposes over all others.

Application:

- forgive people as an act of will, not emotion.
- Forget any evil intentions.
- Decide not to ruminate on the situation.
- Declare your belief that any evil intentions are irrelevant.
- Disavow any judgments.
- Use the glial cells to forget.
- See what God did and is doing through the situation.
- Be thankful and rejoice that you were chosen to go through it.
- See the good coming and declare it.

Chapter 6

THINKING RIGHT

We can't solve problems by using the same kind of thinking
we used when we created them. —ALBERT EINSTEIN

There is nothing either good or bad but thinking
makes it so. —WILLIAM SHAKESPEARE

Let our advance worrying become advance thinking
and planning. —WINSTON CHURCHILL

FALSE PERCEPTIONS

People's perceptions and spontaneous thoughts about situations influence their emotional, behavioral (and often physiological) reactions to those situations. "Individuals' perceptions are often distorted and dysfunctional when they are distressed."[1] These are the findings of Aaron Beck and Albert Ellis from which they developed cognitive behavioral therapies. The heart of their research is that our reactions, physically and emotionally, are connected to our belief systems. If our beliefs are too extreme, our stress levels will spike and we will distort the truth about what is happening.[2]

Three extreme beliefs that most of us harbor are:

1. Everyone must treat me with respect.

2. I must be able to do all things well.

3. My life should be easy.

Such thoughts or cognitions ultimately determine our emotional state and behavior. Mental stresses or disorders, therefore, are maintained by faulty assumptions or attitudes that are often grossly distorted. I (Ken) believed that I was stupid because I made mistakes. It was okay for others to make mistakes; I didn't think they were stupid if they did, but I had to be perfect. The truth was that I was fairly smart, at least smart enough to get a Bachelor of Science in Agriculture. But whenever someone pointed out a mistake I had made, anger rose up within me because I was not going to accept that anyone thought I was stupid. As a result I would brag, exaggerate, embellish, and outright lie just so I wouldn't look stupid. Now that was a stupid reaction. Becoming aware of such "cognitive distortions" or "irrational beliefs" and replacing these ideas with more rational or adaptive thoughts is the first step in bringing peace into our lives.[3]

NECESSITY OF PEACE

Peace is the opposite of stress. Peace is not a passive attitude of apathy or "Que Sera, Sera" (whatever will be, will be). It is an aggressive application of the fruit of the spirit. *"The fruit of the [Holy] Spirit [the work which His presence within accomplishes] is love, joy (gladness), peace..."* (Gal. 5:22 AMP). Jesus said, *"Blessed are the peacemakers..."* (Matt. 5:9). The Colt .45, a single action revolver, was known as the Peacemaker in the Wild West, because its capacity to fire six shells without reloading was a strong deterrent to aggressive behavior.

Peace is a weapon that stills aggression. *"A soft answer turneth away wrath: but grievous words stir up anger"* (Prov. 15:1). Meeting aggression with aggression will never solve the war. The major way to combat an angry spirit is to come with the opposite spirit. The world's normal view of peace is that it is an absence of war. We call *peacetime* that period when there are no wars, but the biblical or Kingdom view is totally different. In the Bible Jesus says, *"Peace I leave with you; my peace I give you. I do not give to you as the world gives. Do not let your hearts be troubled and do not be afraid"* (John 14:27 NIV). The Kingdom's peace is intended to be exercised right in the middle of war. It is an inner peace that has power to still the storms that are swarming around us.

I (Jeanne) recall when the Y2K controversy was making people nervous. The whole computerized world was going to shut down because embedded codes only had two digits instead of the four that the new millennium required. We had bought some candles and some kerosene for lamps; we also prayed and asked if there was any danger that we should be concerned about. As we prayed, the peace of God descended and we knew that everything was going to be okay. Some our friends were anxious and tried to get us to worry with them. We had a great peace from the Spirit and refused to give it any more thought and made no further preparations. Rick Joyner said, "I'm going to get a generator just in case I need it to produce electricity, and I'm going to buy it on January 2, right after the Y2K panic, when people will be selling the ones that they never needed." As with most fears, Y2K came and went just like any other day.

Jesus is called the Prince of Peace (see Isa. 9:6), and there will be no real peace unless He is reigning over the nations and our circumstances. On one occasion, Jesus and His disciples were in the middle of a storm. The waves were starting to fill the boat and the disciples were in a panic. Jesus was asleep at the back of the boat.

> And they awoke Him and said to Him, "Teacher, do You not care that we are perishing?" Then He arose and rebuked the wind, and said to the sea, "Peace, be still!" And the wind ceased and there was a great calm (Mark 4:38-39 NKJV).

A boat is designed to ride out a storm; the problems arise when the storm gets in the boat. Jesus was not fazed by the storm in the boat because there was no storm or fear in Him. He chided His disciples, *"Why are you so fearful? How is it that you have no faith?"* (Mark 4:40 NKJV).

Before, they were afraid because of the storm; now, *"They feared exceedingly, and said to one another, "Who can this be, that even the wind and the sea obey Him!"* (Mark 4:41 NKJV). They were more afraid after the storm stopped than they were before, because they understood storms but they didn't understand Jesus. They knew what they needed to do even in a dangerous storm, but now they were in completely uncharted waters, stuck in a boat with someone who had power over what they were afraid of.

Jesus could act in faith and peace because God had told Him to go to the other side of the lake, and He was secure in the fact that if God told them to go nothing could stop them. He was at peace with the Father, and that transcended any issues or storms that tried to interfere with the word He had received. He could then use the peace He had in Him to control the storm without. He rebuked the wind as if was a spirit and then imposed His peace over the waves: "Peace, be still!"

Jesus used peace as a commodity that He could either spread out or withdraw. He told His disciples to do the same thing. *"Whatever house you enter, first say, 'Peace to this house.' And if a son of peace is there, your peace will rest on it; if not, it will return to you"* (Luke 10:5-6 NKJV). The peace that the Holy Spirit produces in a life is like oil on water—it breaks the surface tension. All strife melts away when the presence of the Lord enters a room.

We hit some strong turbulence while flying back from a trip and people were gripping their seats in fear. Suddenly, I (Jeanne) started to laugh. Surprised, Ken turned and asked, "What are you laughing about?"

"I just had a wave of peace come over me that we will be okay."

I moved from fear to faith because I had learned to sense the peace of God. When God gives that peace I no longer have doubt about the outcome of a situation.

> *Let the peace (soul harmony which comes) from Christ rule (act as umpire continually) in your hearts [deciding and settling with finality all questions that arise in your minds, in that peaceful state] to which as [members of Christ's] one body you were also called [to live]. And be thankful (appreciative), [giving praise to God always]* (Colossians 3:15 AMP).

Let God, through His peace, decide what is important for us.

When two children are battling over who is the boss, there is tension everywhere. When Mom or Dad enters the room the strife ends; everyone feels relieved because the true authority has entered the room. The peace of God is like that; problems may still remain, but they are not problems to the one who carries the peace with them. Jesus preached a gospel of peace; peace with God is the beginning of peace with ourselves and with others. With everything and everybody in our lives, we must lower our expectations if we are to avoid strife; with God, we need to raise our expectations if we are to learn to walk in peace.

ANALYZING THOUGHTS

The best way to prevent toxic memories is to reject the thoughts associated with them before they get fixed in our memories. We don't simply suppress or ignore the thoughts that arise in our minds. Rather, a conscious effort must be made not to accept wounds and offenses before they are integrated into our thoughts and memories. If we are passive in our thinking patterns, we will not filter what is coming through our minds for its toxic content. We must learn to discipline our minds by actively examining what we are thinking about. "An idle mind is the devil's playground." We must ask:

1. Is this thought good for me?

2. Is this thought good for God's Kingdom?

IS THIS THOUGHT GOOD FOR ME?

Offenses

Am I offended by this thought? Does it steal my peace? Does it make me angry? Is it good for me? These are the questions we need to ask before we let a thought into our minds. I was once told that you could be wounded in humility but you could only be offended in pride. How dare they say that, or think that, or do that. Somebody pushed one of your buttons, which only proves that you have touchy trigger points. The word *offense* is derived from the Greek word *skandalon*, which is the trigger of a trap or the bait stick.[4] It is the root that *scandal* is derived from.

If we take offense we take the bait, trigger the trap, and are caught. It is not the offender who gets caught, it is the offended. The offender goes merrily on his way, often oblivious to the seething thoughts that are left boiling up inside of us. If we fix the memory of this offense, it may stick with us for a lifetime and wreak havoc with our health and our mental stability. Jeanne had an aunt who wouldn't speak to her sister for over twenty years because of a dispute over some eggs. She got trapped and lived in bondage to the feelings evoked by that toxic memory. As Jeanne shared and prayed with her, God laid it on the other aunt's heart to phone and make peace. They remained as friends until death.

The Bible says, *"if thy hand or thy foot offend thee* [causes you to sin], *cut them off, and cast them from thee...if thine eye offend thee, pluck it out..."* (Matt. 18:8-9). The same needs to be said about a thought that brings offense and causes you to stumble or to miss God's mark. We should pluck it out and throw it away. Better to walk in peace without that thought than stay in torment with it. We need to refuse that thought, preventing it from affecting us, if it will hinder our faith or be detrimental to our health.

Wounds

People often say things that hurt us or situations arise that disappoint and wound us. How do we deal with the negative thoughts that arise about our self-worth and the strength of our relationships? What do we do when thoughts arise like, *I thought they were my friends; I'm such a fool; I'm so stupid; Why did I do that? My life sucks; They will never do that to me again;* or *If that's the way they are going to act, I'll just leave*? How do we cope when the dark clouds of depression roll over our soul and spirit and we just want to "veg out" and not answer the phone or even get out of bed?

We talk to ourselves! The feelings are real but they are not true. They are real, but they will bring death to both our physical and mental health. Jesus said, *"The thief cometh not, but for to steal, and to kill, and to destroy: I am come that they might have life, and that they might have it more abundantly*" (John 10:10). An abundant life encompasses all the aspects of health, peace, joy, prosperity, and strong relations. Satan is trying to steal and destroy those things in your life. He will use anybody or any situation he can to accomplish that. Because he operates unseen but not unheard, we don't realize he is real and that he is the initiator of the attacks coming at us. We have even been duped into thinking the opposite—that God is angry and that He initiates all the bad things in our life. The world even calls natural disasters "acts of God."

When someone does something amiss, we will never attribute evil intentions to them if we are confident that they love us and have our best interests at heart. If someone were to accuse your best friend of speaking lies about you, you would say, "I refuse to believe that. I know her better than that." But if the same accusation was brought against someone you know despises you, you would likely say, "I don't doubt that for a minute. They're always spreading gossip about me." What is the difference? Proven trust!

Trust comes from experience. Jesus is *"a friend that sticketh closer than a brother"* (Prov. 18:24). We may believe that in our heads, but our wrong perceptions kick in when things get difficult. Because we think the world should be easy and God could make it that way if He wanted to, then He must not love me enough to change things for my good. We don't trust Him. We think everything is His fault, or at least in His power to prevent if He cared enough. That was the attitude of the disciples during the storm. When they were afraid of sinking, they awoke Jesus and cried to Him, *"...Teacher, do You not care that we are perishing?"* (Mark 4:38 NKJV). The first thought, even though Jesus was asleep, was that He didn't care. That often is our misconception and our accusation against God; when He doesn't respond with the speed we think He should we decide He doesn't care for or love us.

If we are going to defeat the thoughts that satan fires at us to discourage us, we must counter those negative thoughts with words of affirmation. Affirmation about God's will for us and our worth to Him. We will all get wounded, but we can all be healed. We must *"refuse the evil, and choose the good"* thoughts if we are to keep our peace (Isa. 7:15). Fighting thoughts with other thoughts is like sword fighting in your mind. If they thrust with this argument, I will parry with that; if they strike with this fact, I will counter with that. The problem is no argument or opponent is ever dispatched with practice fencing or sword fighting in our minds. The only thing that is defeated is our peace and the only thing we learn is how to stay in strife.

We must fight thoughts with words if we are to get a victory. Jesus forced the devil to retreat from the field of battle by countering every satanic suggestion with *"it is written"* (Matt. 4:4,7,10). Three times satan thrust at Jesus and three times Jesus countered with words—God's words. *"And when he had exhausted every kind of temptation, the devil withdrew until his next opportunity"* (Luke 4:13 PNT). Jesus used God's words to force satan to back off. Jesus told His disciples to use the same technique to get a victory when they are under attack. He said:

> But when they deliver you up, take **no thought** how or what ye shall speak: for it shall be given you in that same hour what **ye shall speak**. For it is not ye that speak, but the Spirit of your Father which speaketh in you (Matthew 10:19-20).

Our own reasoning will not get us out of trouble because it is immersed in false perceptions and toxic memories that have no power in them.

False Perceptions That Cause Stress

1. Everyone must treat me with respect.

LIE: THE WORLD REVOLVES AROUND ME.

We are told not to think of ourselves too highly:

> For I say, through the grace given unto me, to every man that is among you, not to think of himself more highly than he ought to think; but to think soberly, according as God hath dealt to every man the measure of faith (Romans 12:3).

When we realize that we are not the center of the universe and every-thing is not about us, we will avoid many disappointments.

TRUTH: GOD CREATED THE WORLD FOR ME.

I may not be that important to the world but I am important to God. *"He that spared not His own Son, but delivered Him up for us all, how shall He not with Him also freely give us all things?"* (Rom. 8:32). God took the most valuable possession that He had, Jesus, and sacrificed Him for us. That is how much He valued us. Jesus said:

> *If the world hates you, you know that it hated Me before it hated you. If you were of the world, the world would love its own. Yet because you are not of the world, but I chose you out of the world, therefore the world hates you* (John 15:18-19 NKJV).

Lower your expectations about the world being enthralled with you. God, however, always has His eye on you.

> *The eyes of the Lord are upon the righteous, and His ears are open unto their cry* (Psalms 34:15).

> *Are not five sparrows sold for two farthings, and not one of them is forgotten before God? But even the very hairs of your head are all numbered. Fear not therefore: ye are of more value than many sparrows* (Luke 12:6-7).

God is watching over you and the world He made for you.

> *The heaven, even the heavens, are the Lord's; but the earth He has given to the children of men* (Psalms 115:16 NKJV).

> *...What is man that You are mindful of him, or the son of man that You take care of him? You have made him a little lower than the angels; You have crowned him with glory and honor, and set him over the works of Your hands. You have put all things in*

subjection under his feet. ...But now we do not yet see all things put under him (Hebrews 2:6-8 NKJV).

God gave you the earth, but the world is not yet ready to give it up. Unless you are willing to fight for what's yours, you will be discouraged. The battleground is in your mind and the enemies are our distorted thoughts. Resist them by forgiving, forgetting, and rewriting them with God in the scenario.

LIE: PEOPLE SHOULDN'T HURT ME.

Being blindsided by an opponent in football or hockey will result in an injury much more often than being hit with the same force when you are prepared for the hit. Why? Because your defenses are down and you are more vulnerable when you don't see it coming. The same is true in a relationship. The more we trust a person, the greater the damage he will inflict when he says or does something that wounds us. The usual response is to put our walls up to shield us from any impact. The problem is that walls not only keep people out, they lock us in.

TRUTH: HURT PEOPLE, HURT PEOPLE.

I believe the quote, "Hurt people, hurt people," is referring to those people who have chosen to not let go of their control, have not forgiven, and have not let God heal them. Rather, they have kept hold of "control" and grown bitter. Most of the time this is the easiest response and it comes naturally to us.

> In our flesh, it feels so easy to want to hold on to that pain. To make the other person "pay" for what they did. When we hold on to that pain, we hurt others because we are still feeling that pain and we are responding out of that pain. Our emotions are always close to the surface and we are ready to fight at a moment's notice.[5]

Our triggers become "hair triggers," destined to go off at the slightest touch. It becomes easy to lash out at the people around us with very little provocation.

We all have wounds or unhealed areas in our lives. If I have an open sore, you will not hurt me by loving me from five feet away. If I let you close enough to hug me, eventually you are bound to bump into that wound. The closer I let you get, the more guaranteed you are to touch some sore spot. That is what makes intimacy so hard; we will get hurt, and most of us have no solution. That is why we keep people at a distance and push them away when they get too close.

The following schematic illustrates what happens when people get too close. The Os represent those areas in our character that are healed; the Xs represent the wounded areas. When we let people past our outer shell, our personalities, and allow them to touch our soul at the character level, eventually they will encounter an unhealed area (the Xs touching). Then you have a war on your hands, each blaming the other for the offense.

Character Schematic

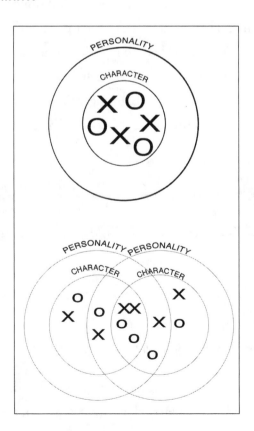

I (Ken) was that way. I would offend people, not because I didn't like them—I did like them, but they were getting too close for my comfort. I found that offense was the best defense. I found myself saying stupid, hurtful things at the most inappropriate times. Jeanne thought I was a social klutz because I would blurt out the strangest things or say inappropriate or hurtful jokes to people. At a party, I would either be a wallflower, hiding in a corner, or I would be the loudest, most obnoxious person in the room. Both methods worked; people stayed away from me. However, that tack doesn't work well in a marriage or in the Kingdom of God where we are forced to get close to others.

If someone accidently touches you on the arm, you will not likely react or even notice. However, if you have an unhealed wound or an open boil there, that touch will prompt an immediate, possibly violent response. When people bump into such wounds, the natural response is to recoil and demand, "Stop that! That hurts. Don't touch me there." Our overreaction is our key for us to recognize that we have an unhealed wound.

What we should be saying is, "Ow, that hurt. I wonder what wound in me made that hurt so much." Blaming others for their hurting of us will not get us healed; dealing with the issues that cause us pain will. We need to:

> Get rid of all bitterness, rage and anger, brawling and slander, along with every form of malice. Be kind and compassionate to one another, forgiving each other, just as in Christ God forgave you (Ephesians 4:31-32 NIV).

Expecting other people to not hurt you only prolongs the pain of unhealed wounds.

LIE: YOU SHOULD LAY YOUR LIFE DOWN FOR ME.

Only babies can expect that others will look after them; everyone else needs to grow up and start to carry their own weight. In the Bible, Paul said:

When I was a child, I spake as a child, I understood as a child, I thought as a child: but when I became a man, I put away childish things (1 Corinthians 13:11).

Children are egocentric and their worlds are very small. They don't consider anything or anybody who doesn't directly touch that realm. They often cry or have a fit if things don't go their way. We have all seen the child in the grocery store, holding the mother hostage with tears and screams, demanding some candy. Often, the mom will give in just to avoid a scene and further embarrassment.

TRUTH: WE NEED TO GROW UP.

The shock to a child comes when the rest of the world will not kowtow to their demands. Childishness or immaturity can be termed a "princess or king" attitude that demands, "You should lay your life down for me; you should serve me." Maturity and love, especially in a father or a mother, is a willingness to lay their life down for their children. Jesus said, *"Greater love has no one than this, that one lay down his life for his friends"* (John 15:13 NASB). Expecting others to cater to our wishes will eventually lead to disappointment.

2. I must do everything well.

This idea comes from:

1. A performance orientation that says:
    - I have to perform to be accepted.
    - I have to perform to be loved.
    - I have to perform to be respected.
    - I am not allowed to have fun until I have performed.

Trying to perform—to do things right—puts us under a form of law. Law is always about right and wrong. Performance requires us to strive to do it right and doesn't allow for us to rest and relax at what we are doing. It squelches creativity. When musicians are performing, they do the chords and progressions that they have practiced and can reach so that the audience hears perfection. Later, when the crowd is gone and the musicians are just jamming, they may try some crazy things. They will push to develop sounds or techniques that they have never attempted before. With no expectation to do it right, there is a freedom and capacity to be creative. Some of the best worship we ever heard came after the formal service had been dismissed, most of the people had left, and the band played on. They seemed to reach notes and sounds that they hadn't before. They were just having fun worshiping together with no audience to please but one—God.

The law of performing things exactly to the letter kills us and stresses us out (see 2 Cor. 3:6 NIV). The lie is that when I do anything wrong, I am bad. The truth is that it is not about my *do*, but about my *who*—about who I am. The Bible says that I am:

> …*Found in Him, not having mine own righteousness, which is of the law* [by doing it right], *but that which is through the faith of Christ, the righteousness which is of God by faith* (Philippians 3:9).

It was Jesus who did things right, not us, and God sees us *"hid with Christ in God"* (Col. 3:3). God looks at Jesus in us and sees Him, not us. That is why *"God commendeth His love toward us, in that, while we were yet sinners, Christ died for us"* (Rom. 5:8). If I have to be perfect but I'm not, I won't even try.

I (Jeanne) love painting with oils. I particularly love painting animals. Though I could not originally paint well, I took some lessons and improved significantly. The more I painted the better I got. Practice makes perfect, but we have to have permission to make mistakes or we will never venture further. Anything worth doing is worth doing poorly. This holds true for every field of endeavor, whether arts, sports, or work.

I listened to a radio program discussing what made one performer or player better than the next. Why would one musician play for the philharmonic and another teach music to children? Why would one hockey player make the NHL and the next play only in house leagues and pickup games? The answer was the same for both; those who practiced more than 10,000 hours became proficient in their chosen field.[6] That practice was not performance; it was done for the pleasure of reaching the goal. Paul said:

> ...*I focus on this one thing: Forgetting the past and looking forward to what lies ahead, I press on to reach the end of the race and receive the heavenly prize...* (Philippians 3:13-14 NLT).

The investigator reasoned that success was 10 percent talent and 90 percent effort and determination. You don't have to be perfect to become perfect; you just have to believe in yourself and want it bad enough.

The idea that *I must do everything well* also comes from:

2. Believing that I am just a hireling and not a son or daughter.

- A hireling works for wages but a son or daughter has an inheritance.

- A hireling works at the business; the son or daughter owns the business.

- A hireling works to obtain a position; the son or daughter possesses favor with the father.

- A hireling needs a contract to protect their rights; the son or daughter operates under a covenant with the father that guarantees their privileges.

Joseph kept sinking in position or status but he had favor *"because the Lord was with him; and whatever he did, the Lord made it prosper"* (Gen. 39:23 NKJV). The Bible says that favor is our shield, it is our life, it defeats our enemies, it exalts us, it is better than wealth, and it brings God's mercy to us (see Ps. 5:12; 30:5; 41:11; 89:17; Prov. 22:1; Isa. 60:10). These are the favors bestowed upon a beloved son or daughter.

Satan tempted Jesus, saying, *"If you are the Son of God"* (Matt. 4:3,6 NKJV). He purposely left out one word that God had spoken shortly before when He declared, *"...This is My beloved Son, in whom I am well pleased"* (Matt. 3:17 NKJV). Satan left out the word *beloved.* It was counterproductive to remind Jesus that He was the *beloved* Son. At this point Jesus had done no ministry or miracles, yet His Father was pleased with Him. It was not what He did that pleased His Father; it was the fact that He was His beloved Son.

Satan showed Jesus all the kingdoms of the earth and promised to give them to Him if He would bow down and worship. Jesus was already Lord over all! Satan often comes tempting us to work for what is already ours. He suggested that Adam and Eve could be like God if they ate from the tree of knowledge of good and evil (see Gen 3:3-5). The truth was that they were already like God, being co-creators with Him. Striving always accompanies an attempt to earn something that you already possess.

The idea that *I must do everything well* also comes from:

3. Not believing that God loves to add His *super* to our *natural.*

We are ordinary people with an extraordinary God. Peter could not walk on water, but he could walk. His part in the miracle was to get out of the boat and do what he could do—walk. God provided the miraculous ability to not sink. As long as the word he heard to "walk" was being mixed with faith, it profited Peter and he did not sink (see Heb. 4:2). When he feared, he no longer had faith and sank (see Matt. 14:30). Peter feared *"when he looked down at the waves churning beneath his feet"* (Matt. 14:30 MSG). The truth was, he couldn't walk on calm water; the storm was just a distraction that caused him to look away from Jesus who was the source of his confidence. Looking at the impossibility of our circumstances is a sure way to forget God's love and power toward us.

Our friends Clint and Karen had a difficult situation to overcome. Through a series of difficulties they found themselves with their bank trying to foreclose on a loan. The bank lumped that loan, which was a corporate loan, together with their house mortgage and their line of credit.

That was not even legal, but banks have deep pockets and can push hard. They were so determined to foreclose that at first they would not even take moneys that Clint and Karen paid to clear up the situation.

Clint and Karen and others prayed and felt that God was going to intervene and stop the nonsense. The bank was trying to take their house for a debt of around $5,000. Though they had finally taken the $15,000 that had been paid the month before, they still were pressing for foreclosure. When court day arrived, the judge was so furious with the triviality of the suit that he threw it out of court. That was exciting, but it was only the beginning. As Clint was walking into the court room, he got a phone call asking him to do a contract worth around $40,000.

When he went to do the job, he asked the man how he got his name. The man said that he found him in the yellow pages under "aggregate concrete finishers." He said that Clint's company was the first name on the list.

Clint replied, "I have never put an ad in the yellow pages, and with my company name we would never be at the front of the list."

The man then pulled out his cell phone and pulled up the page where he had seen Clint's company. The company was not there. He looked surprised and then added, "I don't know what happened, but I guess we are supposed to be together." God has a way of promoting us, putting His supernatural on top of our natural.

The children of Israel had witnessed God's power for 40 years in the wilderness and knew that no enemy could stand against them. Moses sent 12,000 men against Midian's army that was estimated at 120,000; that's a ten to one disadvantage. Israel destroyed that entire army, yet when they checked their own casualties they found not one man missing (see Num. 31:49). That is a score of 120,000 to zero; no one is that good.

Later, when they entered the land and had victory after victory, God said, "I drove them out, but not with your sword or with your bow" (see Josh. 24:12). Israel did the natural part, they swung their swords and shot their bows in the battle; God did the supernatural and gave them the victory. Both the natural and the supernatural were required. We have the authority; He has the power. He will not do it for us, but He loves to do it with us.

God will even take our mistakes and turn them into good.

In 1973, 3M scientist Art Fry was trying to mark his place in his church choir hymnbook with bits of paper that kept falling out. As he did so, he remembered attending a presentation from colleagues describing a "failed" adhesive technology—developed in 1968 by research scientist Dr. Spence Silver who was looking for ways to improve the adhesives that 3M used in its tapes.

Silver had found an adhesive shaped like tiny spheres about the diameter of a paper fibre. The spheres were very sticky individually, but because they made only intermittent contact, collectively they did not stick very strongly. Silver was convinced that there were good applications for the adhesive somewhere in 3M. For 5 years, with the support of his manager, he had presented the technology to colleagues around the company.

Fry wondered whether this failed adhesive could be used to temporarily mark pages, and working on his own time, he developed a temporary bookmark using the adhesive. However, he had a couple of problems: When he took the prototype to the marketing department they weren't interested—the market for bookmarks was too small! When he took it to the engineering and production departments, they told him there would be considerable processing measurement, and coating difficulties and production would create a lot of waste.

Fry's response to the engineering and production people was, "Really, that is great news! If it were easy, then anyone could do it. If it really is as tough as you say, then 3M is the company that can do it."

The marketing department took a little more work. Fry came up with other uses—notepaper—the marketing department still wasn't interested. Who would want to pay for something that would replace scrap paper? Undaunted Fry passed out free samples to staff around the company. He made sure to give some to the administrative assistants of key executives. This created internal demand and repeat orders. Around the same time, Geoff Nickolson—Silver's manager—convinced Joe Ramey, the division vice president, to come with him to Richmond, Virginia, and walk up and down the streets on "cold" calls to see if they could sell the product. They did. These efforts overcame the doubts from the marketing department.

As a result, in 1981, one year after its introduction, Post-it® Notes were named the company's Outstanding New Product, and Fry was named a 3M corporate scientist in 1986. Today they remain an office staple and generate over $100 million in sales.[7]

All this resulted from a mistake gone good.

"...All things work together for good to those who love God, to those who are the called according to His purpose" (Rom. 8:28 NKJV). After observing our lives, my (Jeanne's) brother said, "You win, you win; you lose, you win." Even the bad days become good when God orchestrates the outcomes. We may plan but it is God who makes it happen.

> *The steps of a good man are ordered by the Lord, and He delights in his way. Though he fall, he shall not be utterly cast down; for the Lord upholds him with His hand* (Psalms 37:23-24 NKJV).

God told Paul:

> *"My grace is sufficient for you, for My strength is made perfect in weakness." Therefore most gladly I will rather boast in my infirmities, that the power of Christ may rest upon me. Therefore I take pleasure in infirmities, in reproaches, in needs, in persecutions, in distresses, for Christ's sake. For when I am weak, then I am strong* (2 Corinthians 12:9-10 NKJV).

We don't have to do it right or perfect. If we are walking with the Lord, His grace is sufficient.

3. The world must be easy.

Many Christians were sold a bill of goods in order to entice them to come to Jesus as savior. They were promised that if they accepted Jesus, their marriage, health, finances, and relationships would be totally healed and that they would prosper in everything that they did. When the promises don't materialize as they hoped, they get discouraged and walk away from God. That would be the proper response if it was God who had duped them, but He never said those things—others did. What Jesus promised was that although *"The thief comes only to steal and kill and destroy; I came that they may have life, and have it abundantly"* (John 10:10 NASB). He went on to say, *"…Here on earth you will have many trials and sorrows. But take heart, because I have overcome the world"* (John 16:33 NLT). Therefore, recognize that an abundant life will not be void of challenges and opposition.

Though most of us thought we were signing up for a cruise with everything looked after, the ship we got on turned out to be a battleship. We ended up in a war which many of us think we are not prepared to fight. In *Lord of the Rings*, Théoden, King of Rohan, was similarly not prepared to fight. When he was challenged to meet the enemy in battle, he argued, "I cannot afford open warfare."

To which Aragorn replied, "Nevertheless, open warfare is upon you."[8]

Open warfare is upon us:

> *Then there was war in heaven…. And the dragon lost the battle, and he and his angels were forced out of heaven. …The devil, or satan…was thrown down to the earth with all his angels. … And the dragon was angry…and declared war against…all who keep God's commandments and maintain their testimony for Jesus* (Revelation 12:7-9,17 NLT).

The fight is not between God and the devil; that battle would not last a nanosecond. The fight is between satan and us. Jesus, as a man, as the second Adam, defeated satan on the cross when He bore the full judgment of God and ripped open the veil, declaring, *"It is finished!"* (John 19:30 NKJV).

That was the moment of satan's demise, the instant when *"...the accuser of our brethren, who accused them before our God day and night, [was] cast down"* (Rev. 12:10 NKJV). Now, we have *"...boldness to enter the Holiest by the blood of Jesus, by a new and living way which He consecrated for us, through the veil, that is, His flesh"* (Heb. 10:19-20 NKJV). Jesus recovered what the devil had stolen—our right to come into God's presence. He now has no access to heaven's courts, but still maintains influence on the earth.

Though the enemy was defeated in heaven, we have been granted the privilege of enforcing that defeat on the earth. God has left satan and his minions to teach warfare to those who do not have previous battle experience (see Judg. 3:2). We are engaged in that battle whether we like it or not. John prophetically heard an angel declare:

> *Woe to the inhabitants of the earth and the sea! For the devil has come down to you, having great wrath, because he knows that he has a short time* (Revelation 12:12 NKJV).

The only way satan can hurt God is to destroy His children—us. The present state of the world shows that up until now, he has been successful at that task.

Jesus said, *"In the world ye shall have tribulation: but be of good cheer; I have overcome the world"* (John 16:33). We are not trying to get a victory; we have the victory if we are in Jesus and He is in us, though there still will be a battle.

> *In face of all this, what is there left to say? If God is for us, who can be against us? He that did not hesitate to spare His own Son but gave Him up for us all—can we not trust such a God to give us, with Him, everything else that we can need?* (Romans 8:31-32 PNT)

I (Jeanne) was once sharing with a woman who was a witch about God's love and plan for her. We were in a public place, and two of her fellow witches were standing off to the side. I could tell from their gestures and expressions that they were trying to block what I was saying from influencing their friend. I silently bound the enemy and proceeded to tell the lady about Jesus and how He had died for her. I was able to lead her in a prayer of salvation, and you could see the life of Jesus had entered her.

If we are to bring that victory into reality we must learn how to fight. The fight will not be easy, but *"if we endure hardship, we will reign with Him"* (2 Tim. 2:12 NLT). *"This is the victory that has overcome the world, even our faith"* (1 John 5:4 NIV). But if we are expecting the world to be easy, we will be more discouraged than encouraged. We will triumph over satan by the blood of the Lamb and the word of our testimony, because we do not love our lives so much as to hide from death (see Rev. 12:11). Jesus established the pattern:

> *...If any man will come after me, let him deny himself, and take up his cross daily, and follow Me. For whosoever will save his life shall lose it: but whosoever will lose his life for My sake, the same shall save it* (Luke 9:23-24).

Joyce Meyer once said that we need a backbone, not a wishbone. The circumstances around us are not designed to be easy but to give us character. God says to us:

> *Fear not [there is nothing to fear], for I am with you; do not look around you in terror and be dismayed, for I am your God. I will strengthen and harden you to difficulties, yes, I will help you...* (Isaiah 41:10 AMP).

> *You are My battle-ax and weapons of war: for with you I will break the nation in pieces; with you I will destroy kingdoms* (Jeremiah 51:20 NKJV).

> *Beloved, do not be surprised at the fiery ordeal among you, which comes upon you for your testing, as though some strange thing were happening to you; but to the degree that you share the sufferings of*

Christ, keep on rejoicing, so that also at the revelation of His glory
you may rejoice with exultation (1 Peter 4:12-13 NASB).

God is not concerned when the world rises against Him. He sits in the heavens and laughs (see Ps. 2:4). We need to do the same, even when things get hard, for ours is the victory.

IS THIS THOUGHT GOOD FOR GOD'S KINGDOM?

There are two realms in this world—the Kingdom of God and *"the dominion of darkness"* (Col. 1:13 AMP). The Kingdom of God is about *"...righteousness and peace and joy in the Holy Spirit"* (Rom. 14:17 NASB). Our dark side is about fighting for our rights and controlling people and situations; it stems from fear and striving for position. There really is no kingdom of self, for we *"...are slaves of the one whom you obey, either of sin resulting in death, or of obedience resulting in righteousness"* (Rom. 6:16 NASB). Our thoughts and memories will determine our actions, which in turn will determine the kingdom we are in.

Satan comes only to steal and kill and destroy; Jesus came so that we may have life, and have it abundantly (see John 10:10). If a thought taken to its ultimate conclusion brings life, it is from God. If it will not bring life, it comes from another source. James says that wisdom which is not from above is earthly, natural, and demonic (see James 3:15). So our natural wisdom may have demonic roots and thus bring death. You can have an argument with your spouse, be 100 percent right, but bring death to the relationship. It is not about right and wrong; it is about life and death. Everything outside of God's Kingdom will ultimately result in death.

The world's pessimistic view is that death overcomes life; the truth is that life overcomes death. In the end:

When our dying bodies have been transformed into bodies that
will never die, this Scripture will be fulfilled: "Death is swallowed
up in victory" (1 Corinthians 15:54 NLT).

Jesus declared, *"...be of good cheer; I have overcome the world"* (John 16:33). Having the proper perspective—that life, not death is the ultimate conclusion of existence on this plain—removes all stress and anxiety. *"O death, where is thy sting? O grave, where is thy victory?"* (1 Cor. 15:55).

KEYS

🔑 Get free from believing that:

- Everyone must treat me well.

- I must do all things well.

- Life must be easy.

🔑 Use the peace of God to calm storms and decide matters.

🔑 Analyze your thoughts:

- Is this thought good for me?

- Is this thought good for the Kingdom?

Chapter 7

DEALING WITH TOXIC THOUGHTS

Fantasy is toxic: the private cruelty and the world war both have their start in the heated brain. —Elizabeth Bowen

The degree of one's emotions varies inversely with one's knowledge of the facts. —Bertrand Russell

Flowers are restful to look at. They have neither emotions nor conflicts. —Sigmund Freud

EMOTION-FILLED THOUGHTS

As I was writing this chapter, I got a phone call and I gave advice to a friend who was having a relational problem. The Lord gave me some insight on how he could sow seeds of love and respect into his wife. A verse of Scripture also came to mind about the power of God's word going out and accomplishing what He sent it to do (see Isa. 55:11). I shared this with Jeanne and she asked me, "Are you doing that for me? Give me an example."

I immediately thought that she was accusing me of teaching things that I myself was not doing. I thought she said, "Oh, you give great advice to others, but you don't do it yourself, you hypocrite." In fact, she was only asking me what the advice about sowing seeds and the revelation of sending a word looked like. I couldn't handle the emotions that rose up and I snapped back at her. My reaction made it obvious that I had a wound connected to any correction or any suggestion that I did anything wrong.

In any conflict, we must not succumb to that first wave of emotion that crashes into our mind; it is not truth. That wave is the summation of years of toxic memories connected to the moment. It is like the straw that breaks the camel's back; the straw wasn't that heavy, but when added to all the other weight that was being carried, it caused the collapse. We need to remove and forget all the baggage we are carrying so that one little incident will be treated as it should be—as nothing.

I had to walk away for 15 to 20 minutes so that the chemicals of emotion could dissolve and dissipate from my bloodstream. Then I could calm down and properly respond to my wife. After that I went back and asked God why I reacted so poorly. I saw a picture of my father telling my mother, "Just leave me alone until my work is done. I don't have time to deal with that now." I realized that I was under the tyranny of the urgent and thus was not willing to deal with the responsibility of the necessary. That's like constantly changing burnt out light bulbs while ignoring the mold growing in the walls; what's in your face to do is usually less important than what's in your heart to do.

I repented and received God's forgiveness. I then dealt with my judgment that I had to finish my work before I could relate to my wife. According to the Bible, a judgment institutes a law that:

> *In posing as judge and passing sentence on another, you condemn yourself, because you who judge are habitually practicing the very same things [that you censure and denounce]* (Romans 2:1 AMP).

In sowing that judgment against my father, I guaranteed that I would reap the same thing (see Gal. 6:7).

Jesus said, *"Think not that I am come to destroy the law, or the prophets: I am not come to destroy, but to fulfil"* (Matt. 5:17). When we do things that impose a law, repenting and asking for forgiveness will not abolish the law. Suppose that I were to climb to the top of the Sears Tower in Chicago and jump off in an attempt to commit suicide, but halfway down I decide that this had been a bad decision. At that point I can repent and ask for forgiveness and God will forgive me, but that will not stop the law of gravity that is pulling me to my doom. A law works all the time and does not respond to repentance, but God does. He will not suspend the law, but He sent Jesus to fulfill or take the consequences of my actions. That is the gospel: Jesus gets what I deserve and I get what He deserves. That is the divine exchange of the cross where both mercy and justice are satisfied.

That exchange only works as we take up our cross and go to Jesus to exchange it for His payment. We have the authority to apply the blood to our situations by removing the judgment.

BREAKING A JUDGMENT

Renounce the lie that is associated with the judgment.

In my case, it was that all the work has to be finished before I can be relational. The work is never done, so there is never time for relationships. There is always a lie connected to a judgment. Any time we use the words, *always* or *never*, a judgment will be present. Nothing is *always* or *never*. The events judged may have occurred, but our perception of what happened is skewed and thus not the truth.

Disavow the words and thoughts that made the judgment and break off the judgment.

I had to break the judgment that all the work needs to be done first. The truth is that my wife is higher on the priority list than my work.

Ask Jesus to take the reaping of what I have been sowing.

I asked God to bear the consequences of my neglect of my wife and restore my marriage's joy and fellowship. Jesus came to bear the consequences of our sins in His body. *"He canceled the record of the charges against us and took it away by nailing it to the cross"* so that we are free (Col. 2:14 NLT).

Ask God to take away the structures, mindsets, thought patterns, neural pathways, or ruts in your brain that allow us to believe the original lie that created this stronghold.

I needed my priorities reset and the lie removed that work trumped my wife's needs.

Ask God to give you a new heart that believes the opposite of the original judgment.

I needed to believe that my wife was next to God in my priorities and that if I had my top priorities right, He would order everything else. True, work has to be done, but I would rather be without a job than without a wife. It is her needs, not her wants that must be met first. If she is okay, then the needs of the job will be met in proper order. So I prayed:

> *Dear Lord, I repent of believing the lie that I had to finish all my work before taking time for my wife. I repent of believing the lie that my work takes precedence over my wife.*
>
> *I disavow these thoughts and words that I have spoken and break this judgment.*
>
> *I put the cross between what I have been sowing through these words and the reaping of it. I ask you to reap the consequences of my sin, in your body, on the cross.*
>
> *Put to death all the thought patterns, mindsets, neural pathways, and lies that have made up this stronghold.*
>
> *Give me a new heart to believe that my wife has precedence over my job and that if I live in right order and love her first then You will ensure that my job situation will not suffer.*
>
> *In Jesus's name, amen.*

Removing judgments is the quickest way to engage our glial cells to remove the lies that are embedded in our subconscious. Once the lies are dismantled and removed, the stress from the situation dissipates.

WHAT IS TRUTH?

Many of us confuse what we think with what is the truth. We idolize our own thoughts and feelings. We are really saying that what I feel is what I feel; my mind is made up; don't confuse me with the facts. If we try to attach truth to these emotions, we will be like *"children, tossed to and fro and carried about with every wind of doctrine"* or belief (Eph. 4:14 NKJV). Every new idea will blow our emotions around and cause us to feel and respond differently. In fact, even facts don't constitute the truth. Facts are just data about a subject, not the reality of that subject. Our perception of reality, of what is real is usually limited to just that—our perception. Any magician or stock promoter can tell you that perceptions can be easily fooled.

We call this book *real* because we can see and touch it. But what was this book a hundred years ago—a tree, some dirt? What will this book be in another hundred years? What we call *real* is just the arrangement of the facts or the molecules in a in a particular pattern for a slice of time. Whatever we can see is in a state of transition. It is neither what it was, nor what it will be. The real things are the unchanging things, *"...for the things which are seen are temporal; but the things which are not seen are eternal"* (2 Cor. 4:18). The things we can't see don't change and are more real, more true, than what we can see.

The truth is actually a person—Jesus, who never changes. He said, *"I am the way, the truth, and the life..."* (John 14:6). He didn't say, "I know the way and the truth and the life"; He said, "I Am." When the mob approached in the garden to arrest Him, Jesus used that phrase *"I am He,"* and they drew back and fell to the ground (see John 18:6). Just using the name of God, "I Am," brought such an impact that the words literally knocked them down (see Exod. 3:14). The truth always has the power to change situations. Until we see things the way God sees them, we will not know the truth and will be locked into lies. Jesus said, *"If you abide in My word...you shall know the truth, and the truth shall make you free"* (John 8:31-32 NKJV). The truth will help us get rid of our toxic thinking.

Jesus called the Holy Spirit *"the Spirit of truth"* who would guide us into all truth (see John 16:13). But we can operate under both the spirit of the truth and the spirit of the error (see 1 John 4:6). Peter made the declaration, *"You are the Christ, the Son of the living God"* (Matt. 16:16 NKJV). Jesus got excited and proclaimed that Peter had received that by the Spirit.

He said, *"...Flesh and blood has not revealed this to you, but My Father who is in heaven"* (Matt. 16:17).

Immediately after, Peter began to rebuke Jesus, whom he had just declared divine; go figure. Jesus recognized the source of this rebuke and said, *"Get behind Me, Satan! You are an offense to Me, for you are not mindful of the things of God, but the things of men"* (Matt. 16:23 NKJV). Which spirit we are operating in determines the amount of truth we can absorb. Jeanne and I have agreed that we will pray when an argument or a dispute arises between us. We joke that the one who is too distraught to pray is the one with the demon. That joke usually allows the "demonized" one to shake off the negative thoughts of the enemy and receive the truth.

David write to God: *"Behold, You desire truth in the inward parts, and in the hidden part You will make me to know wisdom"* (Ps. 51:6 NKJV). Yet our hearts can fool us, for *"The heart is hopelessly dark and deceitful, a puzzle that no one can figure out..."* (Jer. 17:9 MSG). We need Him to give us:

> *The spirit of wisdom and revelation in the knowledge of Him, the eyes of your understanding being enlightened; that you may know what is the hope of His calling, what are the riches of the glory of His inheritance in the saints* (Ephesians 1:17-18 NKJV).

The spiritual forces of the unseen realm affect us more than most of us realize. That is why we need more than our feelings or our thoughts to discern truth.

> *...The Holy Spirit teaches, comparing spiritual things with spiritual. But the natural man does not receive the things of the Spirit of God, for they are foolishness to him; nor can he know them, because they are spiritually discerned* (1 Corinthians 2:13-14 NKJV).

Lack of discernment is like looking through a veil—we only see in part (see 1 Cor. 13:12). A veil was put over the Jew's faces when they were given the law, so that they could not discern the Spirit. Their minds were blinded. *"...For until this day the same veil remains unlifted in the reading of the Old Testament, because the veil is taken away in Christ"* (2 Cor. 3:14 NKJV). Without Jesus removing that veil, none of us can see. The Bible is clear—the wiser we are in our own eyes, the blinder we are to the truth. Jesus said:

> *I praise you, Father, Lord of heaven and earth, because You have hidden these things from the wise and learned, and revealed them to little children. ...No one knows who the Son is except the Father, and no one knows who the Father is except the Son and those to whom the Son chooses to reveal Him* (Luke 10:21-22 NIV).

> *Do not deceive yourselves. If any of you think you are wise by the standards of this age, you should become "fools" so that you may become wise. For the wisdom of this world is foolishness in God's sight. As it is written: "He catches the wise in their craftiness"; and again, "The Lord knows that the thoughts of the wise are futile"* (1 Corinthians 3:18-20 NIV).

> *"For My thoughts are not your thoughts, neither are your ways My ways," declares the Lord. "As the heavens are higher than the earth, so are My ways higher than your ways and My thoughts than your thoughts"* (Isaiah 55:8-9 NIV).

Pilate asked Jesus, *"What is truth?"* and then walked away from the One who was truth (see John 18:38). If we refuse the truth, especially when it is staring us in the face, we will not prosper. What God thinks and speaks is the truth. If we are to prosper in all areas of our lives, especially in our mental health, we must learn to embrace His words as the plumb line of truth. We need to ask God for His perspective on everything that we do.

> *Roll your works upon the Lord [commit and trust them wholly to Him; He will cause your thoughts to become agreeable to His*

will, and] so shall your plans be established and succeed (Proverbs 16:3 AMP).

DON'T USE EMOTIONS AS ARBITRATORS OF THOUGHTS

Moses led the children of Israel for 40 years, but was never able to remove from them their emotional attachments to Egypt and the fanciful, romantic memories that they yearned to return to. Their emotions recalled the good but dismissed the bad. They forgot that they were slaves, that their baby boys were killed, that they were beaten, and that the Egyptians *"set over them taskmasters to afflict them with their burdens"* (Exod. 1:11). At that time, they cried out and *"God heard their groaning, and God remembered His covenant with Abraham, with Isaac, and with Jacob"* (Exod. 2:24). But once they were in the desert, they complained, *"We remember the fish, which we did eat in Egypt freely; the cucumbers, and the melons, and the leeks, and the onions, and the garlick"* (Num. 11:5). Perception will override fact when emotions are connected to that perception.

Moses told them, *"Remember that the Lord rescued you from the iron-smelting furnace of Egypt in order to make you His very own people and His special possession"* (Deut. 4:20 NLT).

> *See, I have set before you this day life and good, and death and evil. ...But if your [mind and] heart turn away and you will not hear...I declare to you today that you shall surely perish...I have set before you life and death, the blessings and the curses; therefore choose life, that you and your descendants may live* (Deuteronomy 30:15,17-19 AMP).

It is not about right and wrong, remembering or forgetting; it is about life and death. I have had arguments with Jeanne and been 100 percent right but still brought death to our relationship. Our success depends on discerning life, not on being right. The original deception came when Adam and Eve chose to rely on the tree of the knowledge of good and evil and cut themselves off from the tree of Life (see Gen. 3). Jesus had a conflict with some Pharisees: *"When Jesus perceived their thoughts; He answered and said to them, 'Why are you reasoning in your hearts?'"* (Luke 5:22 NKJV). Our thoughts must work with our spirits so that we can choose life; reason alone is not sufficient.

We are looking to discern if our thoughts are good for us or not; whether they have life on them or death. Jesus said, *"The words that I speak unto you, they are spirit, and they are life"* (John 6:63). In another place He said:

> **You are already clean because of the word which I have spoken** to you. *Abide in Me, and I in you. As the branch cannot bear fruit of itself, unless it abides in the vine, neither can you, unless you abide in Me* (John 15:3-4 NKJV).

Our ability to live out a fruitful life comes through the words that we allow to influence our life. If we believe that we are losers and unclean then we are in direct opposition to Jesus who says that we are already clean. Our thoughts and feelings are not the truth; what Jesus says is the truth. If we idolize what we think and feel, elevating them to the stature of truth, then the Word says that we are worldly or carnal.

> *The carnal attitude sees no further than natural things. But the spiritual attitude reaches out after the things of the spirit. The former attitude means, bluntly, death: the latter means life and inward peace. And this is only to be expected, for the carnal attitude is inevitably opposed to the purpose of God, and neither can nor will follow His laws for living...* (Romans 8:5-8 PNT).

Thoughts that are not in alignment with God's perspective will always cause us stress because they are incongruent with life.

The entire cosmos has been running down ever since satan fell and introduced death into God's creation. That is seen in the entropy of material objects and atrophy in biological organisms; things rust and people die. One of the projections of the second law of thermodynamics is that the ultimate fate of the universe will be a state of entropy, without thermodynamic energy. In this state, the universe can no longer sustain motion or life.[1] However, the Bible declares that *the law of the Spirit of life in Christ Jesus hath made me free from the law of sin and death* (Rom. 8:2). This is the difference between a pessimist and optimist—one sees death and destruction, the other sees life and abundance.

> *Death and life are in the power of the tongue, and they who indulge in it shall eat the fruit of it [for death or life]* (Proverbs 18:21 AMP).

> *For to be carnally minded is death; but to be spiritually minded is life and peace* (Romans 8:6).

DON'T GO THERE

One of the best ways to de-stress your thought life is to consciously decide to refuse a negative thought. Simply change the channel, much like you would if you did not want to view something on television. Recently, on a flight to Korea, I watched the interplay between two children sitting in front of me. The younger brother got mad at his sister, and in a fit he hit her and yelled at her that he hated her. The older sister seemed to ignore her brother's assault and continued to play the video game they were engaged in. Within 30 seconds, her brother was laughing and again asking for his sister's help, which she gladly gave. If that had been two adults engaged in this row, it would have created a major incident with possible legal and certainly relational consequences. I felt the Holy Spirit prompt me to query the Lord about what had I just witnessed. "What just happened?" I asked.

The Holy Spirit said, "Children live in the moment and not in the past." This verse sprang to my mind: *"I say to you, unless you are converted and become as little children, you will by no means enter the kingdom of heaven"* (Matt. 18:3 NKJV). To *convert* means to twist or turn quite around and reverse your thinking and actions.[2] These siblings had a different way of thinking than adults have and thus responded effortlessly to conflict resolution—they ignored it. Neither of them took offense or harbored resentment but chose rather to forgive and forget the emotionally charged incident. The older sister loved her little brother and was able to overlook his bad attitude and childish outbursts. She was the mature one and yet childlike in her forgiveness.

The apostle Paul told the Corinthians, *"Do not be children in under-standing; however, in malice be babes…"* (1 Cor. 14:20 NKJV). Malice is the evil habit of the mind, which tends toward ill will or spite.[3] Children don't use malice as a protection strategy; they believe the best about people and their intentions. They don't have the layers of injuries that would enflame a minor incident into World War III. They have not yet developed toxic memories about the ones they love. This is the childlike nature that Jesus was encouraging His disciples to regain, *"…for of such is the kingdom of God"* (Mark 10:14). Offenses are the bait that satan uses to entrap us in our emotional strongholds (see Matt. 18:7). No offenses, no strongholds; no strongholds, no bait to tempt us; no bait, no entrapment; no entrapment, freedom results. Who is more mature when it comes to refusing offenses, the children or the adults?

Your mind, which is the interface between the body and the soul, should not be the arbitrator of what it is allowed to think about. That is like the pitcher being allowed to call the balls and strikes. He is too connected to the situation to be rational. Thus our mind must learn to yield to the peace of our spirit and allow it to *"act as umpire continually"* in our hearts (Col 3:15. AMP). The spirit is not concerned about what is right or wrong but rather what brings life or what brings death. It calls you to choose life so that you may live (see Deut. 30:19). By an act of our will we must submit to the discipline of our spirit to determine what we will allow our thoughts to dwell on.

An undisciplined mind will allow any thought or image to occupy our imagination because it has no spiritual discernment (see 1 Cor. 2:14). When the mind exercises no controls over its thoughts, it allows us to conduct ourselves:

...in the passions of our flesh [our behavior governed by our corrupt and sensual nature], obeying the impulses of the flesh and the thoughts of the mind [our cravings dictated by our senses and our dark imaginings]... (Ephesians 2:3 AMP).

Dwelling on any image in our mind allows it to fix itself into our memory, much like when a picture is left frozen on a plasma screen TV for too long and a ghost image burns itself permanently onto the display monitor. We must take our responsibility and choose what we look at or our mind will choose it for us.

An undisciplined mind is like an undisciplined dog that is taken on a walk. The lack of training grants the dog permission to take the owner for the walk. He will go where he wants to go, come back when he wants to come back, and ignore all attempts to rein him in. Such a dog, depending on his temperament, will attack, threaten, molest, or jump on anyone that comes in his path. He will invade the boundaries of all he encounters as he seeks to smell out anything that attracts his attention. He will pee and defecate where and on whom he chooses, always marking off his territory with no concern or restraint. He will be an embarrassment to his owner and a source of irritation to all who cross his path.

The undisciplined mind produces the same effect as it drags us into areas and situations that later we regret. The mind is part of our flesh, and if it has unrestrained freedom it will indulge the flesh. The Bible says we are not to use our liberty as an opportunity for the flesh (see Gal. 5:13). We actually need to have the opinion that we are better than the thoughts that we are thinking.

In reference to your former manner of life, you lay aside the old self, which is being corrupted in accordance with the lusts of deceit, and that you be renewed in the spirit of your mind, and put on the new self, which in the likeness of God has been created in righteousness and holiness of the truth (Ephesians 4:22-24 NASB).

We get renewed in our mind, not by looking at what we think or feel, but by looking at what Christ has done. Self-accusations belittle our own thoughts and actions. We will continually stress ourselves as we fail to live up to our own standards. We need to take these accusatory thoughts and declare that we are not judged on our performance but on that of Jesus.

> *For the weapons of our warfare are not physical [weapons of flesh and blood], but they are mighty before God for the overthrow and destruction of strongholds, [inasmuch as we] refute arguments and theories and reasonings and every proud and lofty thing that sets itself up against the [true] knowledge of God; and we lead every thought and purpose away captive into the obedience of Christ...* (2 Corinthians 10:4-5 AMP).

It is Christ's obedience, not ours, that God is looking at. We have been taught, usually from harsh, critical fathers, that God is harsh. The fearful servant in Jesus's parable told the master:

> *...I knew you were a harsh man, harvesting crops you didn't plant and gathering crops you didn't cultivate. I was afraid I would lose your money, so I hid it in the earth* (Matthew 25:24-25 NLT).

His toxic judgments, about his inability to please the master immobilized him in fear and blocked his capacity to be innovative or even logical in his investment strategies. Our own strongholds, built on lies, freeze us out of the promises and possibilities that God has ordained for us. The biggest lies that block us from His best are that we are not wonderfully loved, truly forgiven, and that God is not really in control.

Every stress and every sin can be traced back to these three roots. All other lies are only variations of one of these three.

> *Don't copy the behavior and customs of this world, but let God transform you into a new person by changing the way you think. Then you will learn to know God's will for you, which is good and pleasing and perfect* (Romans 12:2 NLT).

God's will is that all people might believe in Jesus and through Him have salvation—a salvation that will restore their mental and physical health, their righteousness, their relationships, and their finances (see John 1:7). The Father wants you to *"...prosper in all things and be in health, just as your soul prospers"* (3 John 1:2 NKJV). Our soul will not prosper unless we are determined to think the thoughts that agree with God's thoughts. *"For I know the thoughts that I think toward you, says the Lord, thoughts of peace and not of evil, to give you a future and a hope"* (Jer. 29:11 NKJV).

THOUGHTS CREATE MOODS; MOODS CREATE ACTIONS

If we don't have any hope, we will get depressed and see everything from a negative viewpoint. Bad moods spawn bad thoughts. A mood is created by the limbic system as it subconsciously responds to the inputs from the memories which are constantly dripping molecules of emotions into the amygdala. If these inputs are fear-based, there will be an evil foreboding hanging over our minds. Our mood will be an expectation of something bad happening. Every situation will be judged from the basis of that expectation. We will be in a foul mood and project or act out that mood to all we encounter.

If my actions don't change, over a period of time my mind will adjust my belief system to mirror my thoughts to give me a reason to believe that what I am thinking or feeling is true. I may blame my anger on a situation beyond my control rather than on my fears. I will say things like, "I'm Irish, that's why I have a temper," or, "I'm German, that's why I seem so harsh." We will justify our actions by ascribing a good motive that will placate our conscience and justify our reason for ignoring our convictions. "Sex before marriage is okay for me, because technically we are already married in our hearts." These thoughts:

> *Demonstrate that God's law is written in their hearts, for their own conscience and thoughts either accuse them or tell them they are doing right* (Romans 2:15 NLT).

Accusing or excusing ourselves will not salve our conscience or relieve the stress that our sin creates. Because thoughts spawn actions, we need to change our thoughts to change our actions.

But you don't defeat thoughts with other thoughts; you defeat thoughts with words—words that speak life, not excuses. Also, we need good thoughts to get out of bad moods.

> *Don't worry about anything; instead, pray about everything. Tell God what you need, and thank Him for all He has done. Then you will experience God's peace, which exceeds anything we can understand. His peace will guard your hearts and minds as you live in Christ Jesus. ...Fix your thoughts on what is true, and honorable, and right, and pure, and lovely, and admirable. Think about things that are excellent and worthy of praise* (Philippians 4:6-8 NLT).

That is the function of faith—to remember the promises of God. We need to verbalize our faith so that we have another input for our brain. We believe what we say more than what someone else says, so we must say it. *"Let the redeemed of the Lord say so, whom He hath redeemed from the hand of the enemy"* (Ps. 107:2). We must decide that an evil mood is not good for us and use that decision to motivate our change. We can disarm the lies of the enemy that everything is conspiring against us and that disaster is coming. The world thrives on negativity, or rather dies to hear bad news. We are told to put on *"...the oil of joy for mourning; the garment of praise for the spirit of heaviness"* (Isa. 61:3).

Depressing and negative thoughts allow fears and phobias to take root in our psyche. The "what ifs" take on a reality that is unhealthy. A fear thought is not a faith or love thought. We use fear as a shield of mistrust to protect ourselves. The thought is that if I worry enough about what can go wrong, I will think of what can go wrong, and I can intercept what can go wrong before it happens. The problem is that this attitude creates stress, which will kill you faster than whatever you were worrying about.

Ninety percent of what we worry about never happens.[4] Winston Churchill said, "When I look back on all these worries, I remember the story of the old man who said on his deathbed that he had had a lot of trouble in his life, most of which had never happened."[5] There is a Swedish proverb which says, "Worry often gives a small thing a big shadow." Dean Smith said, "If you treat every situation as a life and death matter, you'll die a lot of times."[6] This echoes Shakespeare, who had Julius Caesar say, "Cowards die many times before their deaths; the valiant never taste of death but once."[7]

Joyce Meyer uses an acronym for fear that is most revealing: F.E.A.R.— False Evidence Appearing Real. Our fears are not real; they are the summation of our toxic memories which create a dread of what is coming. Jesus told us:

> Give your entire attention to what God is doing right now, and don't get worked up about what may or may not happen tomorrow. God will help you deal with whatever hard things come up when the time comes (Matthew 6:34 MSG).

These fear thoughts are not healthy love thoughts, for:

> There is no fear in love; but perfect love casts out fear, because fear involves torment. But he who fears has not been made perfect in love (1 John 4:18 NKJV).

The torment of fear can last for years if it is believed. Joseph's brothers were still paranoid that God would punish them some 40 years after they sold Joseph into slavery (see Gen. 50:15). That is a long time to be haunted by a fear of retribution, especially since Joseph had admonished them:

> Do not be grieved or angry with yourselves, because you sold me here, for God sent me before you to preserve life. ...God sent me before you to preserve for you a remnant in the earth, and to keep you alive by a great deliverance. Now, therefore, it was not you who sent me here, but God... (Genesis 45:5,7-8 NASB).

All the assurances in the world from Joseph didn't shake their fear or their torment. They had accepted their fears as the truth and it became their belief system when dealing with Joseph. We have thoughts and speculations that also are not the truth; they are just strongholds in our minds that lock us up. We need God's perspective on things. *"Then you will know the truth, and the truth will set you free"* (John 8:32 NIV). The anorexic girl looks in a mirror and sees someone fat; the unemployed man sees a loser; the mother with a wayward son sees herself as a failure. Those are virtual realities, not truths. The truth is what God says.

> *For I know the thoughts and plans that I have for you, says the Lord, thoughts and plans for welfare and peace and not for evil, to give you hope in your final outcome* (Jeremiah 29:11 AMP).

Our toxic thinking about ourselves imprisons us, but God's words *"are life unto those that find them, and health to all their flesh"* (Prov. 4:22).

"A peaceful heart leads to a healthy body; jealousy is like cancer in the bones" (Prov. 14:30 NLT). Health is a matter of the mind, not a matter of medicine. We hold the key to our health and it depends upon which thoughts we allow to influence us. A relaxed mind promotes physical healing. Relax! Don't stress! We may not know the future, but we know who holds the future.

> *Be relaxed with what you have. Since God assured us, "I'll never let you down, never walk off and leave you," we can boldly quote, God is there, ready to help; I'm fearless no matter what. Who or what can get to me?* (Hebrews 13:5 MSG)

Speaking that way removes all the tension and stress from our lives.

KEYS

Don't idolize your emotions and thoughts, they may be wrong.

Remove judgments, they will dictate what you believe.

Emotions are not reliable judges of truth.

Control your thoughts, don't let them control you.

Check your mood, it will cloud your judgment.

SECTION C

PREVENTING THE FORMATION OF TOXIC MEMORIES

Chapter 8

ANALYZING OUR THOUGHTS

There are things known and there are things unknown, and
in between are the doors of perception. —ALDOUS HUXLEY

I want to know all God's thoughts; all the rest
are just details. —ALBERT EINSTEIN

Opinion has caused more trouble on this little earth
than plagues or earthquakes. —VOLTAIRE

It ain't what you don't know that gets you into trouble. It's
what you know for sure that just ain't so. —MARK TWAIN

As [a man] thinks in his heart, so is
he. —PROVERBS 23:7 NKJV

THINKING TOO MUCH

Studies have shown that rumination or rehearsal of an injury or a transgression will result in a decrease in our ability to forgive the transgressor. In the studies, the more the injured party thought about the offense or the way it affected them, the longer and deeper was the psychological and interpersonal distress. When people thought about how depressed and angry they were, they became more depressed and angry and stayed that way longer. The more they thought about the offense, the more upset and the less forgiving they became.[1]

Forgiveness itself removes a toxic mixture of anger, bitterness, hatred, resentment, and fear of being humiliated or hurt again. "These negative emotions have specific physical consequences, including increased blood pressure, adrenaline and cortisol levels, which have been linked to cardiovascular disease, immune suppression and, possibly, impaired neurological function and memory."[2] Thus the phrases, "He makes my blood boil," or, "My blood pressure went through the roof when he did that." You may have even said, "You're driving me crazy," or, "You make me sick." These all indicate strong emotions with real physical consequences!

We must understand where our thoughts come from and analyze them, not just accept them. Are they fearful thoughts or are they faithful thoughts? Will they help or hinder our tranquility? For our health's sake, we must learn *"to refuse the evil and choose the good"* (Isa. 7:15 NKJV). Because toxic thoughts are so emotionally laden, refusing them will require dying to those feelings. We are not suppressing or repressing these feelings, neither are we denying them. We are actively refusing to respond to them. Just because I am hungry doesn't mean I have to eat; just because I am tired doesn't mean I have to sleep; just because I am mad doesn't mean I have to strike out. The Bible says:

> *Go ahead and be angry. You do well to be angry—but don't use your anger as fuel for revenge. And don't stay angry. Don't go to bed angry. Don't give the devil that kind of foothold in your life* (Ephesians 4:26-27 MSG).

Don't act out your fears. *"Yea, though I walk through the valley of the shadow of death, I will fear no evil; for You are with me..."* (Ps. 23:4 NKJV). It is only the shadow of death, not the reality of death that assails us. The reality is God with you: *"...Christ in you, the hope of glory"* (Col. 1:27). We can do it afraid. The fear is not the reality; our faith is the reality. Our thoughts are mirrors to our belief system, and our words will eventually release those beliefs into our world.

> *A good person produces good things from the treasury of a good heart, and an evil person produces evil things from the treasury*

of an evil heart. What you say flows from what is in your heart* (Luke 6:45 NLT).

We were made in God's image, and our words are designed to create just as His words do. *"By the word of the Lord were the heavens made; and all the host of them by the breath of His mouth"* (Ps. 33:6). I like to say that the reason God can't lie is because everything He says happens. How would we fare if everything we said happened? If we truly believed that, we would speak differently. In his agony Job declared, *"For the thing which I greatly fear comes upon me, and that of which I am afraid befalls me"* (Job 3:25 AMP). We need to change the way we think so that we won't regret the things we say.

I (Jeanne) remember, as a child, standing in a ravine. I was resting after pulling my sled up the hill, before taking another run down through the snow. Staring up into the starry sky, I thought about the next year, as it was New Year's Eve. I stood there in the cold wondering, "Will I even be alive in the year 2000? Will war or disease strike me down? Will I live into the next millennium?" I remember marking that place and the thoughts in my mind like they were yesterday. In 2000, I received the news that I had cancer. We fought it as a family with Christ and beat it. I have often wondered—did I open the door for attack that night through fear?

BUILD MEMORIES FROM GOD'S PERSPECTIVE

Rehearsing God's goodness allows us to change our thoughts about situations. The activity in our corpus callosum (the part of the brain that connects the left and right sides) increases as we speak out loud. This adds an additional auditory stimulus and gives us a better perspective to decide whether to accept or reject a thought.[3] Speaking God's truths helps us to build memories from God's perspective, not ours, connecting us to reality instead of our perception of reality.

The Bible is full of overcomers who chose to believe when the situation did not warrant it. In the middle of his troubles—having lost his children, his prosperity, and his health—Job said, *"Though He slay me, yet will I trust in Him"* (Job 13:15). Job was declaring his trust in the person of God no matter the outcome of his disastrous situation. Faith declarations release not just healthy hormones but angelic beings to bring to pass what we have declared. While recovering from my cancer surgery, I decided to declare that whether I live or die I am His. Speaking peace into a situation creates peace no matter what the circumstances. Peace is the opposite of stress and promotes healing.

Certain Jews, set over the affairs of the province of Babylon—Shadrach, Meshach, and Abed-Nego—refused to bow and worship the Babylonian king's image. The king warned them:

> *If you do not worship, you shall be cast immediately into the midst of a burning fiery furnace. And who is the god who will deliver you from my hands?" Shadrach, Meshach, and Abed-Nego answered and said to the king, "O Nebuchadnezzar…if that is the case, our God whom we serve is able to deliver us from the burning fiery furnace, and He will deliver us from your hand, O king. But if not, let it be known to you, O king, that we do not serve your gods, nor will we worship the gold image which you have set up"* (Daniel 3:15-18 NKJV).

The facts declared death; faith declared life.

In this case, God intervened. He didn't stop the threat, but He went into the furnace with them. That is what we really need: God walking with us in all our battles. The three men were thrown into the fiery furnace, but when the king looked in he said:

> *"I see four men, walking around freely in the fire, completely unharmed! And the fourth man looks like a son of the gods!" … Nebuchadnezzar said, "Blessed be the God of Shadrach, Meshach, and Abednego! He sent his angel and rescued his servants who trusted in him! They ignored the king's orders and laid their bodies on the line rather than serve or worship any god but their own." …Then the king promoted Shadrach, Meshach, and Abednego in the province of Babylon* (Daniel 3:25,28,30 MSG).

We know that God is able but we often doubt that He is willing to intervene on our behalf.

> *And behold, a leper came and worshiped Him, saying, "Lord, if You are willing, You can make me clean." Then Jesus put out His hand and touched him, saying, "I am willing; be cleansed." Immediately his leprosy was cleansed* (Matthew 8:2-3 NJKV).

To relieve stress, look at what God is doing, not at what the enemy is doing. The news of the day is usually negative and can promote fear, but God is love, and love casts out fear.

> *God is love. When we take up permanent residence in a life of love, we live in God and God lives in us. This way, love has the run of the house, becomes at home and matures in us, so that we're free of worry on Judgment Day—our standing in the world is identical with Christ's. There is no room in love for fear. Well-formed love banishes fear. Since fear is crippling, a fearful life—fear of death, fear of judgment—is one not yet fully formed in love* (1 John 4:17-18 MSG).

Speaking God's will is important, for our thoughts and words have substance. The Hebrew word *dabar* is translated equally as both "thing" and "word." Words are things; they are containers for power, both good and evil. Words are the vehicles that bring substance to our thoughts. We are told to *"decide and decree a thing, and it shall be established for you"* (Job 22:28 AMP). Jesus reiterated that thought, saying:

> *…Whoever says to this mountain, "Be removed and be cast into the sea," and does not doubt in his heart, but believes that those things he says will be done, **he will have whatever he says*** (Mark 11:23 NKJV).

That is why we need to encourage ourselves as David did, saying, *"Why art thou cast down, O my soul? and why art thou disquieted within me? hope in God: for I shall yet praise Him, who is the health of my countenance, and my God"* (Ps. 43:5). Jeanne and I have been speaking to various parts of our bodies and have been producing health as a result. We sum it up by saying, "I walk in divine health; I have divine healing." As we talk, the glial cells in our brain readjust our neural pathways to agree with what we say.

I was listening to a radio program discussing the main ingredient that produced a great athlete or musician. The largest component for success was practice, not talent. Repeating the same movements consistently strengthened the synapses and thus the neural pathways, allowing the person to perform with excellence. The same is true of us—if we say the right things over and over that agree with God, we will produce neural pathways of blessing and success. This is not positive thinking; this is faith speaking.

We are declaring what God has said to train our minds to believe what we say. We must believe before our confessions have power, so our first declaration is to our own heart (see Rom. 10:10). Once we are in faith, our declarations into our realms of authority will change things. We are either speaking life into our circumstances or death.

> *As he loved cursing, so let it come unto him: as he delighted not in blessing, so let it be far from him* (Psalms 109:17).

> *Death and life are in the power of the tongue, and those who love it will eat its fruit* (Proverbs 18:21 NKJV).

The fruit of death is more death; the fruit of life is more abundant life.

Our friend shared a story about her girls' experience while camping with her cousin's family at the lake. Her cousin was fussing about her kids getting head lice because they were all sharing a hair brush. Our friend spoke out loud that there was no way that her girls were going to get lice. Later, when they were all back home, she received a text message that the other kids did get lice. Our friend's daughters, with their long beautiful hair, were exposed to the same hair brush yet without any problems. God was teaching her that her words have power to protect, changing the inevitable into the impossible. That is why the Bible tells us:

...be filled with the Spirit; speaking to yourselves in psalms and hymns and spiritual songs, singing and making melody in your heart to the Lord; giving thanks always for all things unto God and the Father in the name of our Lord Jesus Christ (Ephesians 5:18-20).

Filling ourselves with light is the most effective way to drive out the darkness. We don't fight thoughts with thoughts; we fight thoughts with words—words of life. Regaling God's glory is the best way to forget our plights. Sword fighting in our minds—thinking of how we will counter any attack against us—stirs up many emotions that are counterproductive to our peace. Jesus told His disciples:

Now when they take you [to court] and put you under arrest, do not be anxious beforehand about what you are to say **nor [even]** *meditate about* *it; but say whatever is given you in that hour and at the moment, for it is not you who will be speaking, but the Holy Spirit* (Mark 13:11 AMP).

We are to come into a place of rest, not anxiety, for God *"...is able to keep you from falling, and to present you faultless before the presence of His glory with exceeding joy"* (Jude 24). We don't work to make that happen, but we just believe and rest. *"This is the work of God, that ye believe on Him [Jesus] whom He hath sent"* (John 6:29). The more we worry, the less we believe and the more stressed we are.

REMOVING STRONGHOLDS

Don't try and stuff bad thoughts. We need a catharsis or a purging of the toxic emotions, not a burying. If we stuff and deny our emotions, we will lose the ability to discern what we really feel, which will produce tension with no logical way to release it. We need to shine a light on our negative thoughts and expose them. Anything left in the dark remains under the influence of the realm of darkness. Satan can use those areas to accuse you and bring you into bondage. Expose all of your thoughts to the light of the truth. If that thought is good for you, it will have life on it. If it is negative, it will cause negative emotions to arise which will be deleterious to your well-being.

We need to take control of such thoughts and disown them even if we have entertained them for years. We are not denying that the events or situations happened; that's witchcraft. We are choosing to believe that God was there and He is always in the process of turning evil situations around for His and our good (see Gen. 50:20). We are not victims, but *"In all these things we are more than conquerors through Him that loved us"* (Rom. 8:37). *"...If God be for us, who can be against us?"* (Rom. 8:31). Anything that opposes our victorious standing in Christ must be removed.

We hang on to our negative thoughts because we value what we think too highly. There is a principle that is called the Endowment Effect that allows us to idolize our thoughts and emotions. In essence, the principle states that ownership of anything (goods, houses, stocks, or thoughts and ideas) increases its value beyond its worth in the eye of the owner.[4] We will overvalue and thus cherish our thoughts until we recognize that they are toxic and disown them. After we have refused the thought, it will lose its worth and we will wonder how we could have valued such distorted ideas.

I (Ken) experienced this a few years back when my mom was dividing most of her treasures with her children. My three sisters and I sat with my mom as she went through each item and we listened to the stories connected to them. She had organized her things in such a way that we could each choose what we wanted. Each item was prized as we gathered our hoards and set aside another for my brother. When I got home and went over all that I had collected, I realized that most of it was junk. Each article had been valuable once, but time had done its work. Some had chips out of them, some were missing lids or legs, and some were now only partial sets. What made it valuable? My mother's memories connected with each piece had increased their worth in our eyes. When I phoned my sisters they too had discovered that most of what they now possessed was worthless. The real value was connected to my mom's memories and not the articles.

SIGNS OF SUPPRESSED EMOTIONS AND TOXIC THOUGHTS

It is not hard to see the results of suppressed emotions if we are looking for them. If we are not, then all the symptoms are rejected as someone else's fault or just brushed off as us having a bad day. When we transfer the responsibility for our feelings to another's action, we are giving away our authority and allowing the other to manipulate us. My feelings and reactions are my feelings and reactions. Nobody makes us mad; we choose that response because we have programmed our brain, over a period of time, to react that way. Offense is a form of defense. Anger is designed to make people back off and get out of my space. There are signals that we need to recognize and respond to if we are going to get healed.

Touchiness

Touchiness is an indication of a wound being present. As mentioned in a previous chapter, if I casually or even lovingly touch you on your healthy arm, there will be no reaction. If I touch you in the same way and you have an open wound or an infection, that touch will hurt and you will react. That is why many of us shun intimacy. It is easy for me to love you from a distance; I will never bump into your wounds from a distance. Let me in your space and love you up close and I will eventually touch something that hurts.

God designed the people in your life, especially your spouse, to be irritating, not because they don't love you, but because they do. God wants us to get healed, and He will spare no expense to bring people into our lives who will push past our walls and love on us. Our defensive strategy of pushing people away when they hurt us is counterproductive to receiving that love because it further wounds us with perceived rejection. Touchy people repel, instead of attract, the loving people they need for their healing.

I know one lady who was so touchy that she constantly lost her friends. They would say something to her in innocence but she took it the wrong way. Once offended, she found it hard to forgive and held grudges for a long time. Eventually she would drop the relationship for her expectations of others were out of proportion to reality. As a result, she was very lonely yet unaware that she was the one who was hard to be around.

The more I prayed for this lady, the more problems she encountered and had to overcome. God was toughening her up. As the word says, *"I will strengthen and harden you to difficulties, yes, I will help you…"* (Isa. 41:10 AMP). As time went on, she began to mature and forgive others more quickly. She began to have more grace for others. She began to keep friends and even make new ones. She found that being touchy (believing the worst) was not good for her. We also must start to think healthier thoughts.

> *Finally, brethren, whatsoever things are true, whatsoever things are honest, whatsoever things are just, whatsoever things are pure, whatsoever things are lovely, whatsoever things are of good report; if there be any virtue, and if there be any praise, think on these things* (Philippians 4:8).

The proper response to being touchy is to seek out the source of the wound that caused the pain instead of alienating the ones who triggered the pain.

> *Therefore strengthen the hands which hang down, and the feeble knees, and make straight paths for your feet, so that what is lame may not be dislocated, but rather be healed* (Hebrews 12:12-13 NKJV).

It is painful to open up old wounds, but it is necessary if we want to be healed. God wants us to go back, find the source, forgive the person involved, forget and disown the wound, and rewrite the memory with the Father's purposes overruling every other intention. Your brain is designed to forget; use the mechanism God has put at our disposal for our healing. It is not somebody else's problem; it's ours. Nobody else can get into your head or make your decision for you. Passive acceptance will only produce active pain.

A Short Fuse

A short fuse on our temper indicates a high stress level. We all have trigger points or buttons that set off an anger reaction. Let's say that a tension level of ten is required before I snap. An incident that comes in at level four will not cause me to blow, but if I am already stressed at a level seven, an additional four will put me over the top. If I appear touchy—too quick to react to a perceived slight—then my long-term stress level is too high to deal with life's little problems. Since stress contributes to 85 percent of diseases, a constant low level of stress hormones circulating in my body is the receipt for disaster. As said previously, it is not the situation in our life that stresses us, but our reaction to that situation that is dangerous. (See Appendix A.)

"He who is slow to anger is better than the mighty, and he who rules his spirit, than he who captures a city" (Prov. 16:32 NASB). God is more interested in who we are than what we do. Our doing is what stresses us; our being who we are is what calms us. The Bible urges:

> *...Let every man be quick to listen but slow to use his tongue, and slow to lose his temper. For man's temper is never the means of achieving God's true goodness* (James 1:19-20 PNT).

The old proverb rings true that more flies are caught with honey than with vinegar.

Anger is a man's answer to fear, and fear is designed to control. Fear is not just an emotion, it is also a spirit, and spirits control us, not we them (see 2 Tim 1:7). If we operate in anger, it will control us.

> *Don't you realize that you become the slave of whatever you choose to obey? You can be a slave to sin, which leads to death, or you can choose to obey God, which leads to righteous living* (Romans 6:16 NLT).

God never uses anger or fear to control; He draws us with His love and goodness.

> *Are you, perhaps, misinterpreting God's generosity and patient mercy towards you as weakness on His part? Don't you realize that God's kindness is meant to lead you to repentance?* (Romans 2:4 PNT)

Fear and anger are satan's methods to manipulate us.

I (Ken) once was in a situation where I came under a controlling spirit. I completely buckled to someone's unreasonable demands and took blame for something I hadn't done. Jeanne recognized the problem and after the people left, confronted me with my sin. Because I had used domination and intimidation at work (forms of the Jezebel or control spirit), I could also be manipulated by it. She basically said to me:

> *Did you think that because He's such a nice God, He'd let you off the hook? Better think this one through from the beginning. God is kind, but He's not soft. In kindness He takes us firmly by the hand and leads us into a radical life-change* (Romans 2:4 MSG).

We must not change simply to please people, nor should we assume blame just because someone's upset. It is the goodness of God that leads people to repentance and to change, not our anger or our fears. When we are not controlling of our life on the inside, then we will attempt to control everything on the outside. We reason that if there are no outside disturbances then there will be no inside distress. If there is no storm in us, then we can ride out any storm that comes against us. Getting angry at the storm will not make it go away. Jesus, as the Prince of Peace, could impose His peace over the storm. Our peace will also prevent the storm from affecting us.

Anxiety

Anxiety or feelings of dread or an evil foreboding are blatant signs of toxic thinking. The Bible says, *"Do not be anxious about anything, but in every situation, by prayer and petition, with thanksgiving, present your requests to God"* (Phil. 4:6 NIV). Our fear of the future can only be calmed if we have assurances about that future. Jesus used peace when He encountered frightening circumstances; we often use anger to mask our fears. Jesus partook of flesh and blood:

> *That through death He might render powerless him who had the power of death, that is, the devil, and might free those who through fear of death were subject to slavery all their lives* (Hebrews 2:14-15 NASB).

The world is constantly fighting against the inevitable, putting on a brave, angry face saying:

Do not go gentle into that good night,

Old age should burn and rave at close of day;

Rage, rage against the dying of the light.[5]

Peace comes not from raging and fighting but from resting and receiving. The promises of God, if we trust Him, will give us that peace and relieve our fears. God promised that *"your strength will equal your days"* (Deut. 33:25 NIV). We are all going to die, but we don't have to die decrepit and broken. If we believe, we can enter the next life serenely and full of strength. We may not know the future, but our stress is removed when we know who holds the future.

> *Then turning to His disciples, Jesus said, "That is why I tell you not to worry about everyday life—whether you have enough food to eat or enough clothes to wear. For life is more than food, and your body more than clothing. Look at the ravens. They don't plant or harvest or store food in barns, for God feeds them. And you are far more valuable to Him than any birds! Can all your worries add a single moment to your life? And if worry can't accomplish a little thing like that, what's the use of worrying over bigger things? Look at the lilies and how they grow. They don't work or make*

their clothing, yet Solomon in all his glory was not dressed as beautifully as they are. And if God cares so wonderfully for flowers that are here today and thrown into the fire tomorrow, He will certainly care for you. Why do you have so little faith? And don't be concerned about what to eat and what to drink. Don't worry about such things. These things dominate the thoughts of unbelievers all over the world, but your Father already knows your needs. Seek the Kingdom of God above all else, and He will give you everything you need" (Luke 12:22-31 NLT).

God has always supplied for us during seasons of lack when we prayed and asked Him. He loves and cares for all His children. Ask Him for what you need; you will not be disappointed.

Frustration

Frustration, which is anger turned inward, also indicates a reservoir of toxic memories of unfulfilled expectations. Actually, frustration and anger are secondary emotions.[6] They are expressions of other wounds and offenses. There are many ways of expressing fear or anger. Some people are "spewers" who may blow up on anyone who is around or may be more manipulative and vindictive in their expression. Others are "leakers" who let it out in slowly in subversive actions or bit by bit in verbal snipes. Others are "stuffers" who repress and suppress their feelings. Some deny that they are angry; others are blind to it but internalized anger often leads to internal combustion.[7]

We will stuff our anger because it is not acceptable, in our minds, to be angry. Anger is bad, and if I am angry I am bad. That logic says it's better to stuff and deny than deal with my sin of anger. But God never says anger is bad. In fact, God gets angry (see Num. 22:22). He tells us, *"When angry, do not sin; do not ever let your wrath (your exasperation, your fury or indignation) last until the sun goes down"* (Eph. 4:26 AMP).

Anger is just an emotion, not a sin; the way we deal with anger can make it become a sin or a sickness. By burying it we are poisoning our bodies and our souls. We will shut down emotionally, afraid to express anything lest the anger leak out. We will let people walk on us just to avoid displeasing them and causing conflict.

Constant sickness such as ulcers, headaches, digestive problems, muscle tension, and high blood pressure all accompany buried anger.[8] We need to see our frustration as an indicator that something is out of order and needs to be addressed. Since maintenance of our health is an attribute of our spirit, constant sickness would indicate that our spirit is slumbering or not fully awake in this realm.[9] You need to choose life so that you may live (see Deut. 30:19).

When we choose to confront the people or situations that frustrate us, we must decide if the emotions they evoke are good for us or not. We need to forgive, forget (not bury), and rewrite the bad memories that are stirred up with the good that God is bringing through those memories. Faith receives the good now and waits patiently for the answer. Patience is the answer for frustration; longsuffering is the answer for anger. Both are aspects of God's power manifested through the Spirit (see Col. 1:11).

Ask God to strengthen you in these areas as you go through the situations that will develop you. *"For ye have need of patience, that, after ye have done the will of God, ye might receive the promise"* (Heb. 10:36). When I (Jeanne) first came to the Lord, I remember forgiving many people who had hurt me in the past. I not only had to forgive them, I had to forgive myself for the mistakes I had made and for the times I had hurt others.

Fears and Phobias

When we refuse to or can't identify what we are feeling, fear of the unknown and resulting phobias will dominate our thinking. Fears and phobias are buried negative thoughts that lie in the metacognitive regions of the brain, just beyond the reach of the conscious mind. Even though they cannot be expressed, these memories will leak toxic, negative molecules of emotions into the brain. The conscious mind interprets these negative emotions as an indication that something is wrong, something which needs to be feared. The mind will then search for situations in the past when these similar negative feelings arose.

If we encounter a spider, while under the stress of these negative emotions our minds will identify the spider as the source of the feelings, reinforcing the fear of spiders. Now even when a spider is not present, the fear of encountering one becomes exaggerated and out of proportion with the threat. The mind likes to be logical, and if no threat is present but the toxic feelings persist, it will create an enemy which it then logically fears. The most common phobias are the fear of heights, flying, public speaking, the dark, spiders, snakes, rejection, small confined spaces, failure, and open spaces.[10]

Jesus tells us many times not to fear. God is never caught off guard. He is not playing catch-up with the world. He knows everything that is going to happen and has prepared ahead for our choices. Jesus said:

> *Are not five sparrows sold for two farthings, and not one of them is forgotten before God? But even the very hairs of your head are all numbered. Fear not therefore: ye are of more value than many sparrows* (Luke 12:6-7).

Fears dissipate when we recognize that nothing can touch us except it pass through the loving hand of God first.

Before I (Jeanne) knew the Lord, I was extremely fearful of almost everything. As I read the Word and began understanding His love and protection for me, I began to let go and let Him have control. The root of control is always fear. I got over the fear of flying by flying to strange countries and the fear of public speaking by speaking before crowds of people. Looking back at what God has done, I can see that I am not the same person I was. Most people meeting me would never believe that I was too fearful to go out into my yard if the neighbor was out. Root out the basis of your fear, give it to God, and banish it from your mind. Remember, the fear is not real; it is False Evidence Appearing Real and only has the power you give it.

God limited the power satan had over Job even though Job had put himself in satan's hand by fearing what would happen to his children.

Job sent and sanctified them, and rose up early in the morning, and offered burnt offerings according to the number of them all: for Job said, It may be that my sons have sinned, and cursed God in their hearts. Thus did Job continually (Job 1:5).

Job had a fear that his children would sin and come under judgment. He wasn't offering sacrifices in faith, but through fear. *"The Lord said to Satan, 'Behold, all that he has is in your power; only do not lay a hand on his person'"* (Job 1:12 NKJV). God did not put Job under satan's power; Job did through voicing and acting on his fears. In a small way, Job understood that, for he later declared, *"The thing which I greatly feared is come upon me, and that which I was afraid of is come unto me"* (Job 3:25).

As said before, when we are out of control inside (are afraid), we will attempt to control the outside. Control is the fruit of fear. We can tell when we have toxic memories by how much we try to control the people and situations that surround us. The logic is that if I am in control of all that affects me, the things that I fear will be thwarted. The truth is that if we do not yield control to God, our fears will empower the things that we fear to come into being.

God created His world with words. *"By faith we understand that the worlds were prepared by the word of God, so that what is seen was not made out of things which are visible"* (Heb. 11:3 NASB). We are designed to create the same way. That is why we must not vent our fears but rather face them and strip them of their powers over us.

I (Ken) remember a humorous situation at a safety meeting on a job site. The superintendent was vehemently reaming everyone out, threatening them over some safety violations. The atmosphere was very tense until one man had enough and stood up to declare, "Fear! It's a thing of the past; I have a pension." Even the superintendent started to laugh and the power of the threats evaporated. When fears lose their power, we step into freedom.

Sickness

Constant sickness is another sign of toxic memories putting stress on our bodies.

The term "stress" was introduced by Canadian scientist Hans Selier (1936), who described stress as a reaction to neuropsychological strain that occurs in extraordinary situations and is intended to mobilize the body's defense mechanism. A moderate level of neuropsychological strain results in emotional or creative excitement. However, excessive or long-lasting stress (chronic stress) leads to a decrease of cerebral activity. It results in decompensation of energy consumption and the functioning of internal organs. In this regard, there are favorable conditions for the development of neurosis and hypertension.[11]

This long-term stress comes from the body's continuing reaction to a situation that once required action but has long since lost its urgency. It is a striving in the physical realm to fix a problem that only exists in the mental realm. Stress is the opposite of rest. It is striving to protect ourselves from a nonexistent enemy. The lie is that the situation still requires action or thought or worry. If the truth will make you free, then a lie will bind you (see John 8:32 NASB). Worry is a lie that binds us.

Jesus urges us to ask, seek, and knock when we feel we need something and we will receive (see Matt. 7:7-8). For our Father in Heaven gives what is good to those who ask Him (see Matt. 7:11). The natural way, when we want something, is to stress and strive to get it. Jesus challenged His disciples:

> Enter through the narrow gate; for the gate is wide and the way is broad that leads to destruction, and there are many who enter through it. For the gate is small and the way is narrow that leads to life, and there are few who find it (Matthew 7:13-14 NASB).

The narrow way of resting and receiving leads to life. The broad way of stressing and worry leads to destruction, both physically and mentally.

Part of the original curse bound Adam to produce his food through the sweat of his brow (see Gen 3:19). Sweat is part of the curse; rest is part of the blessing. The priests were told, *"They shall have linen bonnets upon their heads, and shall have linen breeches upon their loins; they shall not gird themselves with anything that causeth sweat"* (Ezek. 44:18). A survival book I read had this statement on the back flap: "You sweat, you die."[12] God is calling us to sweat-less victory, because He already sweated great drops of blood in the garden of Gethsemane so that we wouldn't have to (see Luke 22:44). If you continue to worry and try to make things work, you make Christ *"of no effect unto you"* as you stay under the curse with the resulting stress on your body (see Gal. 5:4). Rest is trusting in God.

Self-doubt

Self-doubt is a big indicator of toxic memories. Those voices that condemn and belittle come from seeds that were planted long ago by someone who should have been supportive and encouraging. Hurt people, hurt people. The only way to break the cycle of woundedness is to get healed. Take those toxic memories and forgive, forget, and rewrite. As children, we would brush off attacks with, "Sticks and stones can break my bones, but words can never hurt me." Unfortunately, denial is not an effective defense when it comes to hurtful words and the perceptions they create.

Children will risk many things when they know that they are loved. When I used to take my kids to a store, they had no trouble running off in every direction; they had no fear because I was there. However, if they felt abandoned or lost they cried out, wondering where I was. Knowing you are loved by God removes all the stress out of life; knowing you are loved by your spouse takes all the stress out of marriage.

If this has been you, pray this prayer with me.

> *Lord, I receive Your forgiveness for operating in a spirit of fear and not trusting You. I now cast this spirit out of my life and declare that I don't need you anymore because Jesus loves me and I am free.*

Most of us stress about making a mistake and going down the wrong path. These thoughts will immobilize us from making a decision, creating a "paralysis by analysis"—always second-guessing ourselves. I (Ken) was taught that if I made a mistake or caused an accident I was bad. When I broke something, the accusation was, "You bad boy, look what you did," or, "What were you thinking; are you stupid?" I eventually got to the point of lying about things so that I would not get blamed. A mistake became a bigger sin than a lie. In that mindset, I could not be wrong or I was bad.

I had to be perfect. If I were counseling someone with this mindset, I would say that they had "performance orientation"—the need to do everything right. This creates a tremendous amount of stress as no one can do everything perfectly. I was delivered from this toxic thinking when I heard Bob Jones say that anything worth doing was worth doing poorly. He meant that those things we want to do well, we must first do poorly. As a baby, when I began to talk, I talked poorly; when I began to walk, I walked poorly. Success is not the absence of failure; it is the overcoming of failure.

Immigrants learning a new language progress according to their willingness to sound stupid. Research shows that adults can actually learn languages faster than children, but children usually become more proficient at talking than their parents.[13] The children, who just want to communicate and fit in, will orally master a language in less than six months. The father, if he is in the work force and must communicate in the new language, will take about two years. The mother, if she is in the home and occasionally communicating outside the home, will usually take 10 or more years to speak proficiently. She is trying to do it right, the others are just doing it. Self-doubt, which is an expression of a poor self-image, will inhibit or paralyze our progress and growth. Heal the self-image; empower the restoration process.

Pray with me:

> Lord, I receive Your forgiveness for believing the lie that I have to do it perfectly. You did it perfectly, and my perfection is in You and not my performance.

EXPOSE STRONGHOLDS TO THE LIGHT

Prior to a battle, reconnaissance teams are dispatched to probe, locate the enemy, and assess their weakest points. Satan does that to us, but if we encounter his advance patrol, say in a dream or through an attack of fear or sickness, we then know where he is going to attack. Satan will always overplay his hand. Wherever we find ourselves encountering the enemy and giving in to his devises, we know that that area has not come under the Father's rule.

The Bible emphatically states, *"Whosoever* [or whatever] *is born of God doth not commit sin; for His seed remains in him: and he cannot sin, because he is born of God"* (1 John 3:9). Earlier John said, *"If we say that we have no sin, we deceive ourselves, and the truth is not in us"* (1 John 1:8). I am born of God, but I definitely sin; therefore I had a problem connecting these verses. I queried God on what the truth was. He said that the problem lies in the traditional doctrine that wherever the Holy Spirit resides, satan cannot. This is true, but the confusion comes in where the Spirit dwells.

Jesus explained to me that we are not like a big balloon, with just one compartment, but are made up of many rooms—many realms of the soul. In some of these realms we have seated Jesus on the throne and He has put His seed in there. In other areas we have not come into agreement with Jesus or His Word and are still occupying that throne ourselves, which in essence gives the devil access into those spheres.[14]

This has nothing to do with salvation; if we have repented, *"...the blood of Jesus His Son cleanses us from all sin"* (1 John 1:7 NKJV). The blood, shed once, covers all our sin for all time. The cross, which deals with our nature, must be applied daily (see Luke 9:23). So we have some realms in our souls that are under the lordship of Jesus and other areas that are controlled by fleshly or demonic structures and need to be converted to come into agreement with the Holy Spirit. This dichotomy of our soul becomes clear when we speak.

From the same mouth come both blessing and cursing. My breth-
ren, these things ought not to be this way. Does a fountain send
out from the same opening both fresh and bitter water? Can a fig
tree, my brethren, produce olives, or a vine produce figs? Nor can
salt water produce fresh (James 3:10-12 NASB).

Obviously, we have multiple springs spewing both good and evil out of
one mouth.

During the battle for Stalingrad in World War II, the fighting did not
occur house to house; it was fought room to room. The Russians were in
the kitchen while the Germans were in the living room. It is similar with
us; Jesus only occupies the rooms to which we have given Him access. In
those rooms He puts His seed, and there we do not sin. The unsanctified
rooms or structures are made up of thought patterns that are not from a
heavenly source and are earthly, natural, and demonic.

If you have bitter jealousy and selfish ambition in your heart,
do not be arrogant and so lie against the truth. This wisdom is
not that which comes down from above, but is earthly, natural,
demonic (James 3:14-15 NASB).

Because our thought patterns and memories are largely in place by the
age of three,[15] long before we encountered God's wisdom, many of these
demonic structures form the basis of our thinking. Research indicates that
it is doubtful that traumatic events prior to age two will become part of
our conscious autobiographical memory system, even though these events
may continue to influence behavior in the years to come.[16] If they are not
in the conscious yet are affecting behavior, then they are buried in the
subconscious. They may be beyond our recall, but they are not beyond our
reach. With God's help we can pull them up to our conscious level and
rewrite them in a healthy fashion.

We can tell where the Holy Spirit has control by the thoughts we think
and the wisdom we speak. The Bible says, *"But the wisdom from above is*
first pure, then peaceable, gentle, reasonable, full of mercy and good fruits,

unwavering, without hypocrisy" (James 3:17 NASB). If the fruit is bad, the root is bad: *"...evil things from the treasury of an evil heart. What you say flows from what is in your heart"* (Luke 6:45 NLT).

We reemphasize that God is not playing catch-up. Jesus is *"the Lamb slain from the foundation of the world"* (Rev. 13:8). As His life and death were laid out before the world was even formed, so our lives are also known to God.

> *Since his days are determined, the number of his months is with You; You have appointed his limits, so that he cannot pass* (Job 14:5 NKJV).

God has planned for every decision we make, every turn we take, and every attack we will endure. Even our mistakes and defeats are factored in so that we will reach our destiny:

> *According as He hath chosen us in Him before the foundation of the world, that we should be holy and without blame before Him in love: having predestinated us unto the adoption of children by Jesus Christ to Himself, according to the good pleasure of His will* (Ephesians 1:4-5).

God is never disillusioned with us; He never had any illusions about us. He *"...is able to keep you from falling, and to present you faultless before the presence of His glory with exceeding joy"* (Jude 24). If God is not upset with us, *"Let us therefore come boldly to the throne of grace, that we may obtain mercy and find grace to help in time of need"* (Heb. 4:16 NKJV). We do not need to slink off to hide in shame and guilt when we blow it. It is a lie that God is mad at us when we sin, for He is a loving Father. He already got mad at Jesus when He was hung on the cross, for He was *"...made a curse for us: for it is written, Cursed is every one that hangeth on a tree"* (Gal. 3:13). He took our punishment so that we can walk in His favor.

A lie may not be true, but it can still kill you. You can drown in a river that you were told was shallow; you can lose an investment that you were told was safe; you can die from a poisonous plant that you were told was benign. That is why we need to bring all those areas in our minds that contain lies from the enemy and get them converted or renewed so we can discern the truth. All those areas contain toxic, poisonous memories that if allowed to come to fruit will destroy us.

Bringing these areas to the light will expose the lie. Tests at school were to determine how much we understood of the subject we were studying, not to expose how stupid we were. I (Ken) still hate to expose my ignorance by uncovering my mistakes. I hate appearing stupid. By refusing to admit to making mistakes, I have cut myself off from seeing the truth and have blocked the way to getting to that truth. Edmund Burke stated, "Those who don't know history are destined to repeat it." If we will not honestly look at our own history, we too will repeat it.

As discussed in earlier chapters, the glial cells are designed to remove our toxic history (memories) in just a few days if we will expose them to the light and repent of believing the lies they contain. Much of this is done while we sleep. Solomon received wisdom (freedom from lies) in a dream. God said to him:

> "I will give you a wise and discerning heart, so that there will never have been anyone like you, nor will there ever be. Moreover, I will give you what you have not asked for—both wealth and honor—so that in your lifetime you will have no equal among kings. And if you walk in obedience to Me and keep my decrees and commands as David your father did, I will give you a long life." Then Solomon awoke—and he realized it had been **a dream** (1 Kings 3:12-15 NIV).

Ninety percent of all our memories are buried in our subconscious at the metacognitive level just beyond the reach of the conscious mind. Our dreams and intuitive thinking give us fleeting glimpses of what is beneath, but we need to draw those elusive images into our conscious mind to be able to truly examine our mindsets. Jesus said:

> But the Comforter, which is the Holy Ghost, whom the Father will send in my name, He shall teach you all things, and bring all things to your remembrance, whatsoever I have said unto you (John 14:26).

God will cause us to be able to remember and will give us the wisdom we need when we are ready to deal with it, just as He did with Solomon. If we are not ready, He will keep us blinded that He might show us mercy. If we see and yet are rebellious, we are in danger of judgment; if we are blind and are unbelieving, God can show us mercy.

> For I do not desire, brethren, that you should be ignorant of this mystery, lest you should be wise in your own opinion, that **blindness** in part has **happened to Israel** until the fullness of the Gentiles has come in. ...For God has committed them all to disobedience, **that He might have mercy** on all. Oh, the depth of the riches both of the wisdom and knowledge of God! How unsearchable are His judgments and His ways past finding out! (Romans 11:25,32-33 NKJV)

LEARNING TO REST

Much of our stressful thinking in relationships comes through our inability to forgive and forget. People often say, "I'll forgive, but I won't forget." That attitude seems a wise attitude to prevent getting hurt, but is not the way God responds and it opens us up to demonic influences, as we just discussed. If we don't align our thoughts with His, we will be aligned with a lie and we will bring death to ourselves. Jesus said, *"I am the way, the truth, and the life..."* (John 14:6); everything outside of Him is the wrong path, a lie, and brings death.

If we want to have a good life, we need to conform our thoughts to God's thoughts. There are multitudes of studies that quantitatively show that forgiveness is good for our health, both mental and physical.[17]

> To forgive, one must consider the other person, which stimulates empathy. To judge whether a decision is fair, though, does not necessarily bring in the human element and promote prosocial emotions.[18]

It is not about right and wrong, fair or unfair; it is about life and death—our life and our death.

Peter—who was a bull in a china shop when it came to relationships, needing more forgiveness than most—was having a hard time forgiving. He wanted to know:

> *"Lord, how often shall my brother sin against me, and I forgive him? Up to seven times?" Jesus said to him, "I do not say to you, up to seven times, but up to seventy times seven"* (Matthew 18:21-22 NKJV).

During a sixteen-hour day, that number works out to forgiving someone every two minutes. Jesus wants forgiveness to be a continuous attitude, as it is with Him. When we can't forgive, we need to look at our hearts and discover why not; our relationship with Jesus and our health demands it. Just as the Bible commands us to forgive, we are also told:

> *Be anxious for nothing, but in everything by prayer and supplication, with thanksgiving, let your requests be made known to God; and the peace of God, which surpasses all understanding, will guard your hearts and minds through Christ Jesus* (Philippians 4:6-7 NKJV).

Worry or rumination contributes to depressive symptoms, negative self-evaluations, pessimism, and alienation.[18] God's answer to worry is:

*Therefore humble yourselves under the mighty hand of God, that
He may exalt you in due time, casting all your care upon Him, for
He cares for you* (1 Peter 5:6-7 NKJV).

We have to humble ourselves to resist going back to old patterns
of thinking.

*It would have been better for them not to have known the way of
righteousness, than to have known it and then to turn their backs on
the sacred command that was passed on to them. Of them the proverbs are true: "A dog returns to its vomit," and, "A sow that is washed
returns to her wallowing in the mud"* (2 Peter 2:21-22 NIV).

We must be intentional in our decision to change our thinking, not
allowing our mind to passively stress over our circumstances—past, present, and future. Jesus never asks us to try and do anything; He commands
us. We have the choice to obey or disobey, believe or doubt, but where He
commands, He empowers. We can do anything that He says, but we must
change how we think to contain the power He wants to give us. Jesus said:

*Nor do they put new wine into old wineskins, or else the wine-
skins break, the wine is spilled, and the wineskins are ruined. But
they put new wine into new wineskins, and both are preserved*
(Matthew 9:17 NKJV).

He wants to preserve us and the Spirit He puts in us, but we must be
willing to let go of the idolatry of our own ideas and emotions or we will
lose everything.

God wants to rescue us, not stress us. He wants to carry our burdens,
but unless we put them down He can't take them. Jesus told His disciples
that they were going to pay a price for bringing the Kingdom of God to
the world. He said that, *"...Men will arrest you and persecute you, handing
you over to synagogue or prison, or bringing you before kings and governors,
for My name's sake"* (Luke 21:12 PNT). He had just told them of all the
troubles that they would face, and then He gave them a strategy.

*This will be your chance to witness for me. So **make up your minds not to think out your defence beforehand**. I will give you such eloquence and wisdom that none of your opponents will be able to resist or contradict it. But you will be betrayed, even by parents and brothers and kinsfolk and friends. And there will be **some of you who will be killed and you will be hated everywhere** for my name's sake. **Yet, not a hair of your head will perish**. Hold on, and you will win your souls!* (Luke 21:13-19 PNT)

Don't plan your defense! If I was going to die tomorrow depending on what I said in my defense, I think I would be planning my escape, not just my defense. But God said, "I have a better plan—trust Me, for I will look after you." We are all going to die; nobody gets out of here alive. The apostle Paul declared, *"...I am not ashamed: for I know whom I have believed, and am persuaded that He is able to keep that which I have committed unto Him against that day"* (2 Tim. 1:12). He was not depending on what he believed; he was depending on whom he believed and knew that He was able to keep him. Our worry, planning, and stress will not deliver us; our God will.

KEYS

- Don't rehearse toxic memories.

- Build memories and declare from God's perspective.

- Don't supress—remove toxic memories.

- A short temper indicates stress.

- Anxiety and worry indicates toxic memories.

- Anger turned inward will make you sick.

- Putting God's seed in realms of our soul will remove the power of sin.

- Bring toxic memories to the light to remove the lie.

Chapter 9

TROUBLE: THE DOOR TO OUR DESTINY

*If you change the way you look at things, the
things you look at change.* —WAYNE DYER

*Like success, failure is many things to many people. With
Positive Mental Attitude, failure is a learning experience, a
rung on the ladder, a plateau at which to get your thoughts
in order and prepare to try again.* —W. CLEMENT STONE

*I believe much trouble…would be saved if we
opened our hearts more.* —CHIEF JOSEPH

BITTER POOLS

When Israel left Egypt they didn't leave all their troubles behind them
as they had anticipated. Even freedom had its own challenges and stresses.
They had been a slave population in the most powerful nation on earth,
but now they were on their own. Israel had grown from a family to a
nation without experiencing the battles that they normally would have,
had they not been sequestered behind Egypt's huge military machine. The
only troubles they knew were the troubles they had just escaped. Therefore:

*God did not lead them along the main road that runs through
Philistine territory, even though that was the shortest route to the
Promised Land. God said, "If the people are faced with a battle,*

they might change their minds and return to Egypt" (Exodus 13:17 NLT).

Normally it would take eleven days to travel from Mount Sinai to the Promised Land, but it was forty years after the Israelites left Egypt when they finally arrived at the Jordan river across from Jericho (see Deut. 1:2-3). Why did it take so long? Because that first generation never moved past grumbling and complaining about every obstacle they faced. God said, *"Because all these men...have put Me to the test now these ten times...they certainly shall not see the land of which I swore to their fathers..."* (Num. 14:22-23 NKJV). Of those ten tests, nine resulted in them grumbling and complaining about what was happening, exposing their lack of trust and inability to glorify God.

The troubles they encountered were not real difficulties but opportunities designed by God to bring a revelation of Himself as the answer to those troubles. God is the most intentional individual in the universe. Nothing is done as an afterthought, by accident, or as a reaction. He knows the beginning from the end and wants us to trust His plans as being good for us. Most of all, He wants us to be intimate with Him so that we can be part of what He is doing. God started this revelation process immediately after Israel shook off the physical shackles of slavery.

> *Israel...went three days in the wilderness, and found no water. And when they came to Marah, they could not drink of the waters of Marah, for they were bitter: therefore the name of it was called Marah* (Exodus 15:22-23).

> *So* [Moses] *cried out to the Lord, and the Lord showed him a tree. When he cast it into the waters, the waters were made sweet. ...There He tested them, and said, "If you diligently heed the voice of the Lord your God and do what is right in His sight, give ear to His commandments and keep all His statutes, I will put none of the diseases on you which I have brought on the Egyptians. For **I am the Lord who heals** you"* (Exodus 15:25-26 NKJV).

God healed the bitter pools of Marah to reveal Himself as the healer. Israel was called to trust the words that God said, *"...To your descendants I have given this land, from the river of Egypt to the great river, the River Euphrates"* (Gen. 15:18 NKJV). God said they could own it. Their job was to believe it; His job was to do it. To do their part they had to see God as bigger than the box they had built in their minds to contain Him. Revelation was required to do that; trouble was designed to bring that revelation.

The purpose of the bitter pools we encounter is to expose our hearts and reveal what we truly believe. Those pools can be bitter due to disappointments in marriage, in business, in finances, or in ministry. The bitter pools can be discouragement with our physical health, our mental health, or the loss of our dreams and hopes. At the time, none of these seem positive or beneficial, but God is the answer.

When Job had lost all his children, his health, and his finances, he went into a total funk, wondering how this could happen to him. His comforters claimed that it must be Job's fault, as bad things only happen to bad people. Job snapped back that that was impossible for he was more or less perfect. Job finally got the revelation of God as the redeemer, the One who could restore all things. When Job realized his wrong thinking, he cried, *"I have heard of You by the hearing of the ear, but now my eye sees You. Therefore I abhor myself, and repent in dust and ashes"* (Job 42:5-6 NKJV). Without the trouble we seldom get a revelation of the truth or voluntarily change our minds and repent.

The prodigal son had to endure a famine and run out of money and friends before:

> *He came to his senses and cried aloud, "Why, dozens of my father's hired men have got more food than they can eat and here I am dying of hunger! I will get up and go back to my father..."* (Luke 15:17-18 PNT).

He intended to go back as one of the hired men, but the father had his own plans and revealed himself as forgiving, loving, and longing for relationship.

His father said to the servants, "...We must celebrate with a feast,
for this son of mine was dead and has now returned to life. He
was lost, but now he is found" (Luke 15:22-24 NLT).

Whenever you are disappointed, God wants to reappoint you. When
trouble comes, God says, *"Call to Me, and I will answer you, and show you*
great and mighty things, which you do not know" (Jer. 33:3 NKJV). Don't
waste your sorrows; they cost you a lot. The tuition to the best school is
never cheap, but it is only a waste if we learn nothing.

JEHOVAH RAPHA

We learn to access the things of God by faith, not by sight. Satan often
tries to immobilize us by showing us his plans and power. After the ten
spies viewed the Promised Land and saw the pending trouble, they brought
back an evil report. The spies saw the giants in the land, and because they
were still trusting in their own abilities, or lack thereof, they said that the
land and the inhabitance would devour the people (see Num. 13:32).

But Joshua the son of Nun and Caleb the son of Jephunneh...
spoke to all the congregation of the children of Israel, saying: "The
land we passed through to spy out is an exceedingly good land. If
the Lord delights in us, then He will bring us into this land and
give it to us.... Only do not rebel against the Lord, nor fear the
*people of the land, for **they are our bread**; their protection has*
departed from them, and the Lord is with us. Do not fear them"
(Numbers 14:6-9 NKJV).

What did they mean by saying the giants were their *bread* or *supply*?
They looked like they were going to be the impediment to Israel getting
their supply. The answer is found when we compare other scriptures. Jesus
said to the Syrophoenician lady that He shouldn't heal her daughter for
that was like throwing the children's bread to the dogs (see Mark 7:27).
He called *healing* the children's bread. The Hebrew root for *healing* is

râphâ, which means "to mend or heal."[1] The root for *giant* or *Rephaim* is also *râphâ*, meaning "to invigorate" (see Deut. 3:11). Moses referred to the giants as *Rephaim*, though various other nations called them the Anakim and the Emin (see Deut. 2:11).

One of the names of God is *Jehovah Râphâ*, the Lord our Healer. Caleb recognized that the giants in the land would not be a hindrance but rather a supply for them. They would be the supply and the invigorating influence to exercise their faith and take the land. The spies saw the problem; Joshua and Caleb had a different spirit or a different mindset and thus saw the trouble as the supply (see Num. 14:24). The giants were not going to consume Israel; Israel was destined to eat them.

HOPE

Caleb could get excited because he foresaw the victory in the end. We need to have that same spirit and learn to rejoice in the middle of our trials, not just when we get delivered. On one mine construction job, I (Ken) was demoted from superintendent to general foreman due to political wrangling higher up in the company. At the time, this demotion appeared as a defeat and definitely caused me trouble for a few days. It looked like I was going to be removed completely from the project, as the new superintendent was bringing his own general foreman. Jeanne and I prayed, and we got a peace that everything would be okay.

The project supplier and the mine owners intervened and insisted that I remain as general foreman. I had been on a salary as superintendent, but now as general foreman I was shifted to an hourly wage package. The job also shifted from working five days a week to working seven days a week. The end result: my demotion made me $25,000 more than I would have had I not been demoted. God designs trouble to be our supply, so trust in Him not in the situation.

Faith takes the word of the Lord as a *now* word, an already accomplished word, and acts with joy accordingly. Satan is trying to use fear and worry to wear out the saints by speaking opposite to what God has said (see Dan. 7:25). When trouble comes, if we can't bring to remembrance the nature of God, every obstacle will seem like a defeat. Our son Shannon got robbed of the money he had saved to go on a six-month mission trip with YWAM (Youth with a Mission). We prayed and God told us to pay for the trip. Two days later Ken lost his job. This was double trouble for us, but an opportunity for God.

Months earlier, Ken had spoken to a company that wanted him to work for them. The date they had set for Ken's decision was the Monday after he lost his job. Ken gathered his tools and began his new job in a seamless transition and proceeded to make double what he would have had he stayed in his old position. We need to see things as God does so that our troubles are not stressors but doors of supply. Trouble is our bread whereby we can glorify God.

Jeremiah lived in a time when Israel was coming under judgment and their enemies were running over them. He was interceding but nothing was changing. In Lamentations, Jeremiah goes through a list of woes. He cried out:

> *I am the man that hath seen affliction by the rod of his wrath.*
>
> *He hath led me, and brought me into darkness, but not into light.*
>
> *Surely against me is he turned; he turneth his hand against me all the day.*
>
> *My flesh and my skin hath he made old; he hath broken my bones.*
>
> *He hath builded against me, and compassed me with gall and travail.*
>
> *He hath set me in dark places, as they that be dead of old.*
>
> *He hath hedged me about, that I cannot get out: he hath made my chain heavy.*
>
> *Also when I cry and shout, he shutteth out my prayer.*
>
> *He hath inclosed my ways with hewn stone, he hath made my paths crooked.*

He was unto me as a bear lying in wait, and as a lion in secret places.

He hath turned aside my ways, and pulled me in pieces: he hath made me desolate.

He hath bent his bow, and set me as a mark for the arrow.

He hath caused the arrows of his quiver to enter into my reins.

I was a derision to all my people; and their song all the day.

He hath filled me with bitterness, he hath made me drunken with wormwood.

He hath also broken my teeth with gravel stones, he hath covered me with ashes.

And thou hast removed my soul far off from peace: I forgat prosperity.

And I said, My strength and my hope is perished from the Lord:

Remembering mine affliction and my misery, the wormwood and the gall (Lamentations 3:1-19).

Wow! What a litany of woe! Jeremiah was totally overwhelmed with the disasters and anguish that were going on in his life, but suddenly the mood changed. He said:

This I recall to my mind, therefore have I hope. It is of the Lord's mercies that we are not consumed, because His compassions fail not. They are new every morning: great is Thy faithfulness. The Lord is my portion, saith my soul; therefore will I hope in him (Lamentations 3:21-24).

He recalled his troubles and knew that because things had bottomed out, now with God there was hope. Hope and faith always work hand in hand to create what has been promised.

Just as the spies thought the giants were the hindrance to their goals, we usually see opposition as a bad thing. Yet the Bible declares that God will, "*...make the valley of Achor [troubling] to be for her a door of hope and* *expectation"* (Hos. 2:15 AMP). It is right in the middle of trouble that God opens a door of hope. We need to see it and go through it to get out of our troubles. God brought Israel to the edge of the Red Sea, seemingly trapping them "between the devil and the deep blue sea." He said:

> *I will harden Pharaoh's heart, that he shall follow after them; and I will be honoured upon Pharaoh, and upon all his host; that the Egyptians may know that I am the Lord* (Exodus 14:4).

God brought the trouble to defeat the enemy, not to cause Israel heartache. God wanted every enemy that Israel would encounter to remember what happened to Pharaoh and his armies. Rahab, the harlot, told the two spies how Jericho felt when they were faced with the prospect of opposing Israel's God. She said:

> *For we have heard how the Lord dried up the water of the Red sea for you, when ye came out of Egypt; and what ye did unto the two kings of the Amorites, that were on the other side Jordan, Sihon and Og, whom ye utterly destroyed. And as soon as we had heard these things,* **our hearts did melt, neither did there remain any more courage in any man, because of you**: *for the Lord your God, He is God in heaven above, and in earth beneath* (Joshua 2:10-11).

God wants the enemy to fear you, so He sets up situations that we would never choose to display His power. He makes us *"prisoners of hope"* so that He can restore double our former prosperity (see Zech. 9:12). If we understood that every loss would be restored double, we would say, "Bring it on; make my day," and laugh at any opposition. God does.

> *The kings of the earth rise up and the rulers band together against the Lord and against his anointed, saying, "Let us break their chains and throw off their shackles." The One enthroned in heaven laughs; the Lord scoffs at them* (Psalms 2:2-4 NIV).

If we want to be like God, we need to think and act like God. We may not like the situations that we get into, but trusting God shows our faith and allows Him to work out His will, both in us and in the earth. Jesus honored God by committing His life into His Father's hands, *"...for the joy that was set before Him endured the cross, despising the shame, and is set down at the right hand of the throne of God"* (Heb. 12:2). He was aware of the battle that was before Him, but He could endure the pain for the joy that was coming.

We made it a habit that every time Ken lost a job, I would insist that we go out for dinner to an elegant restaurant so we could celebrate. We were no longer dependent on the job supplying our needs; we were dependent on God supplying. We were celebrating what He was going to do, not bemoaning what we had lost. In all the years He supplied, there was never a lack or a failure. Better to be in His hands than depending on our own devices. Trust Him; it will give you peace of mind.

GOOD OUT OF EVIL

Joseph endured the consequences of his brothers' treacherous act of selling him for a slave because they were envious of him. Joseph had to endure great suffering because of the actions of his brothers. The Bible says:

> *...He was laid in chains of iron and his soul **entered into the iron**, until his word [to his cruel brothers] came true, until the word of the Lord tried and tested him* (Psalms 105:18-19 AMP).

That iron of imprisonment went right into his soul; he got depressed and hopeless. It was only later that he saw God's hand in the whole thing and realized that it was God who:

> *...Called for a famine upon the land [of Egypt]; He cut off every source of bread. **He sent a man** before them, **even Joseph**, who was sold as a servant* (Psalms 105:16-17 AMP).

Later Joseph could say:

You meant evil against me; but God meant it for good, in order to bring it about as it is this day, to save many people alive (Genesis 50:20 NKJV).

We have too small an opinion of God. We really don't believe that He is in control. If God is all-powerful and all-loving:

We know that God causes everything to work together for the good of those who love God and are called according to His purpose for them (Romans 8:28 NLT).

Jesus said:

...In the world you have tribulation and trials and distress and frustration; but be of good cheer [take courage; be confident, certain, undaunted]! For I have overcome the world. [I have deprived it of power to harm you and have conquered it for you.] (John 16:33 AMP).

Paul said to the early Christians, *"You...accepted joyfully the seizure of your property, knowing that you have for yourselves a better possession and a lasting one"* (Heb. 10:34 NASB). I once asked God, "How can anyone be joyful about being robbed of everything?" He said, "You can if you believe that you will get double back for everything that is stolen." Moses said, "...*The thief, if caught, must pay back double*" (Exod. 22:7 NIV). If we believe that God will restore all that has been stolen, then temporary setbacks do not become stressful situations.

Years ago I (Ken) borrowed to get into an investment that caused us to lose over a hundred thousand dollars. Jeanne had warned me that the company would overextend themselves and get into financial trouble, but I ignored her warning. It was my stupidity and greed that blinded me from seeing the obvious or listening to the Lord's warning through my wife. As predicted, the trouble happened and our money was stolen. I thought all was lost until God started to talk to us about Himself as a redeeming God. I was so legalistic and works-orientated that I didn't understand why God would fix things if it was my fault in the first place. God used an illustration to explain how He redeems.

Suppose I had put some money in my mailbox for someone to pick up. That would be a foolish thing to do, but unless a thief saw it the money would be safe. My stupidity would not change the fact that the money only disappeared because a thief stole it. It was the same with the investment; my greed and stupidity did not remove the fact that the theft was illegal. God said that because satan was the prime thief, I needed to call him on the theft and demand our money back (see John 10:10). I did and within one year all the money was restored, though not through the original investment. I had to overcome my own toxic memories, which had led me to believe that a father doesn't supply. We overcame those thoughts through a God's word that He was a God of restoration.

God told me, "Don't go down the toilet in an attempt to retrieve what has gone down the toilet. Let it go. Look for what was stolen to come from a fresh source." Graham Cooke once said that God loves to take a problem and make it a feature. God often doesn't remove a problem or situation; He incorporates it and uses it for His glory. We used that principle when we renovated our kitchen. There was a small, ugly cupboard with no door that incorporated the oven vent. We put a door over the opening and Jeanne classed it up, creating a grape mosaic for the door. Now that problem is the feature of our kitchen. God wants to take all our problems and make them features or testimonies of His goodness. Our job is to take His word and see things differently.

We recently heard a story about a Salvation Army captain who worked with the prostitutes in Vancouver. She had such success that the Army sent her to Australia to help them resolve similar situations. Australia legalized prostitution eighteen years ago, and was only now realizing that it might be increasing human trafficking. The captain from Canada and the Australian Army team were praying for a strategy when they received a phone call from a 72-year-old grandmother. She was having a concern about the brothel that was located in her neighborhood and wanted to talk to someone. The captain and the granny made an appointment for tea and she told her story.

She said that the telephone number for the brothel was so close to their own that she and her husband were constantly answering calls from men looking for the brothel. They were considering changing their number when God arrested her one morning in prayer. He said, "I don't want you to change your number; I want you to change the situation." She had no idea of what to do, so she phoned the Salvation Army.

The captain didn't know either but was prompted to ask the question, "What would you do if another of your neighbors was having a problem?"

The granny thought for a moment and then replied, "I would bake some cupcakes for them."

So the next day as the two of them walked up toward the brothel with a plate of cupcakes, the grandmother stopped and said, "I must do this alone; I am the neighbor."

The captain agreed and went back to the car and prayed up a storm as grandma went up to the door herself. She rang the bell, and when the manager of the brothel opened the door she held out the plate. Never having been on the doorstep of a brothel, she blurted out, "Hi, I made cupcakes for you." The manager, having never had a grandma come to the door of the brothel with cupcakes, invited her in. Before she emerged, she had met all the girls and gotten all their names, their cell numbers, and their birthdates. She even commandeered an invitation to return the next week. It wasn't long before granny was every girl's confidante.

In the end, when the Australian government's commission was looking for input, they called in granny because she alone knew the real situations that all these girls faced. She was able to influence a nation and strike a blow against a demonic stronghold because she used cupcakes to change a problem. What problem are you facing? What is in your hand? God can take your "moan-y" and make it a testimony. Don't be afraid of the problem; change your attitude because the problem is already subject to you. We don't have to be afraid because we are loved. *There is no fear in love; but perfect love casteth out fear: because fear hath torment..."* (1 John 4:18). If you are afraid, you don't understand the love that God has for you.

Since our victory is already won:

> *Do not be anxious about anything, but in every situation, by prayer and petition, with thanksgiving, present your requests to God* (Philippians 4:6 NIV).

> *Do everything without grumbling or arguing, so that you may become blameless and pure, "children of God without fault in a warped and crooked generation"* (Philippians 2:14-15 NIV).

God is changing our attitudes so that He can give us a victory.

ATTITUDE DETERMINES ALTITUDE

God is only limited by our attitude, not by our ability. The children of Israel *"turned back and tempted God, and limited the Holy One of Israel"* (Ps. 78:41). The root for the word *limit* is *tâvâh* in the Hebrew, which means to scratch or set a mark.[2] In other words, Israel scratched or drew a line in the sand saying, "This far and no further." We must always check our attitude so we don't block our own deliverance because God is not into overriding our will. Even Jesus's will was to avoid the cross, but He submitted saying, *"...My Father, if it is possible, let this cup pass away from Me; nevertheless, not what I will [not what I desire], but as You will and desire"* (Matt. 26:39 AMP). If we are to trust God we must believe that He is our friend, not a harsh taskmaster.

Trouble defines our commitment, and many get offended when things don't work out as they planned. John the Baptist had the privilege of announcing the Kingdom and introducing Jesus to Israel, but his ministry was short-lived. In fact, it only lasted five months and then he found himself in jail. That wasn't what he had expected and it shook his faith. He was offended by what happened and sent some of his disciples to Jesus to make sure he had heard right about Him. He told John's messengers:

> ...*Go and shew John again those things which ye do hear and see: the blind receive their sight, and the lame walk, the lepers are cleansed, and the deaf hear, the dead are raised up, and the poor have the gospel preached to them. And blessed is he, whosoever shall not be* **offended** *in me* (Matthew 11:4-6).

John had an expectation of his place in the Kingdom because he had been faithful to do his part, but his idea was not God's plan. We don't know the beginning from the end, but God does. Trouble teaches us to trust God even when everything goes wrong because He is faithful. Jesus was not upset with John's offense; He loved John and said of him, "...*among those that are born of women there is not a greater prophet than John the Baptist*" (Luke 7:28). That is high praise when we consider the company of prophets Jesus is comparing John to. John did the right thing when offended—he asked God for the truth. The truth will banish the offenses from our minds and give us peace.

The main reason we get offended is because we are not deeply grounded in God's love. Jesus said of some people:

> ...*Those who, when they hear the Word, at once receive and accept and welcome it with joy; and they have no real root in themselves, and so they endure for a little while; then when trouble or persecution arises on account of the Word, they immediately are* **offended** *(become displeased, indignant, resentful) and they stumble and fall away* (Mark 4:16-17 AMP).

Still waters run deep; when we are all excited and pumped, chances are that we have no depth to our commitment or character in that area. I (Ken) found that the more excited I was about a project or scheme, the more likely it was my flesh. If we get disappointed, we were trusting in the wrong thing because God never disappoints.

The Scripture says, No man who believes in Him [who adheres to, relies on, and trusts in Him] will [ever] be put to shame or be disappointed (Romans 10:11 AMP).

Bob Mumford used to say, "God fixes a fix to fix us, but if we fix the fix before we're fixed, He fixes another fix to fix us." It isn't our situation that God is so interested in; it's us He is interested in. God goes out of His way to pick a fight with the devil so we can win a victory (see Exod. 14:4).

*This doesn't mean, of course, that we have only a hope of future joys—we can be full of joy here and now **even in our trials and troubles***. *Taken in the right spirit these very things will give us **patient endurance**; this in turn will develop a **mature character**, and a character of this sort produces **a steady hope**, a hope **that will never disappoint** us...* (Romans 5:3-4 PNT).

The apostle Peter lays out a formula for our attitude that always works. He said, *"If when you do what is right and suffer for it you patiently endure it, this finds favor with God"* (1 Pet. 2:20 NASB). Doing what is right is our responsibility; being treated properly is our right. The formula then is: Responsibility – Rights + Patience = Favor with God. I would rather have favor than have my rights, because I know what I deserve and it certainly isn't favor.

We have applied this principle many times in our lives. We have often spent hours counseling people for free, lasting months or even a year. We take the responsibility of helping them in the Lord, but many are unappreciative of the time and effort spent on them. We will even help people in the natural things like fixing the plumbing, home repairs, or doing taxes. But we don't demand our right to be appreciated. Many promise to take us out for dinner or do something special for us, but it seldom happens. In fact, many people will shun you after you have heard their darkest secrets because they think you will judge them. By joyfully giving and not worrying about any return, we have been able to walk in great favor with the Lord. Jesus tells us, *"Give as freely as you have received!"* (Matt. 10:8 NLT).

We always say that we don't want compensation for what we do because God pays way more than anyone can afford. That requires an attitude shift if we are going to trust God for our compensation.

PERFECTION

Though the Lord gives you the bread of adversity and the water of affliction, yet your Teacher will not hide Himself any more, but your eyes will constantly behold your Teacher (Isaiah 30:20 AMP).

Trouble is not an indication that we have been abandoned by God. When Jesus was sleeping through a storm and their boat was in danger of sinking, the disciples panicked and cried, *"Master, do You not care that we are perishing?"* (Mark 4:38 AMP). We think trouble comes to "teach us a lesson," as if it were a harsh punishment. God is not teaching us a lesson because He is mad at us; He is teaching us about Himself as our Deliverer. We have had many trials and troubles over the years, but at the same time we have walked in great favor. One is not exclusive of the other, but rather they accompany each other. If we believe this:

*My brethren, count it all joy when ye fall into diverse temptations; knowing this, that the trying of your faith worketh patience. But let patience have her perfect work, that ye may be **perfect and entire, wanting nothing*** (James 1:2-4).

As we share with Jesus in our trouble, we will become like Him. Jesus, *"Though He was God's Son, He learned trusting-obedience by what He suffered, just as we do"* (Heb. 5:8 MSG).

*It was right and proper that in bringing many sons to glory, God… should make the Leader of their salvation a perfect leader through the fact that **He suffered**. For the One who makes men holy and the men who are made holy share a common humanity* (Hebrews 2:10-11 PNT).

As He shared our humanity, we share His glory. We have had many troubles come our way, but God has used them all.

> *Fear not [there is nothing to fear], for I am with you; do not look around you in terror and be dismayed, for I am your God. I will strengthen and **harden you to difficulties**, yes, I will help you...* (Isaiah 41:10 AMP).

One of the hardest situations we have faced was when our son was diagnosed with schizophrenia. That trouble pushed us to God for an answer. Out of that trial God revealed Himself as the Deliverer, producing our book *From Curses to Blessings*. Thousands of people worldwide have received deliverance and freedom because of that toxic situation.

AUTHORITY

Paul based his authority not on his power, his miracles, the letters written, revelation received, or his experience. He *based his authority on the things which he suffered*. When challenged and compared to others he said:

> *I've worked much harder, been jailed more often, beaten up more times than I can count, and at death's door time after time. I've been flogged five times with the Jews' thirty-nine lashes, beaten by Roman rods three times, pummeled with rocks once. I've been shipwrecked three times, and immersed in the open sea for a night and a day. In hard traveling year in and year out, I've had to ford rivers, fend off robbers, struggle with friends, struggle with foes. I've been at risk in the city, at risk in the country, endangered by desert sun and sea storm, and betrayed by those I thought were my brothers. I've known drudgery and hard labor, many a long and lonely night without sleep, many a missed meal, blasted by the cold, naked to the weather. And that's not the half of it, when you throw in the daily pressures and anxieties of all the churches* (2 Corinthians 11:23-28 MSG).

Most of us wouldn't choose to suffer and experience problems, but God knows we will never achieve the destiny that He has for us until we defeat some enemies. God led the children of Israel out of their slavery circumstances, but not out of their slavery mentality. He had already devastated Egypt so severely that the Egyptians were afraid of Israel and *"...they gave the Israelites whatever they asked for. So they stripped the Egyptians of their wealth! (Exod. 12:36 NLT).* They were now free, rich, and healed (see Ps. 105:37). They were headed for the Promised Land, but God led them in a circuitous route. That fooled Pharaoh and made him think, *"The Israelites are confused. They are trapped in the wilderness!"* God said, *"I will harden Pharaoh's heart, and he will chase after you..."* (Exod. 14:3-4 NLT).

If I were Israel, having just shaken off 400 years of slavery and plundering Egypt, the last thing I would want is to have Pharaoh's army coming after me in a rage. But God is not afraid of a little conflict. Rather, when *"the nations rage and the people plot a vain thing...He who sits in the heavens shall laugh; the Lord shall hold them in derision"* (Ps. 2:1-4 NKJV). If God is laughing about all the "huffing and puffing," we need to stop grumbling, get on God's bandwagon, and enjoy the ride. God told Moses:

> *"...I have planned this in order to display My glory through Pharaoh and his whole army. After this the Egyptians will know that I am the Lord!"* So the Israelites camped there as they were told (Exodus 14:4 NLT).

However:

> *As Pharaoh approached, the people of Israel looked up and panicked when they saw the Egyptians overtaking them. They cried out to the Lord, and they said to Moses, "Why did you bring us out here to die in the wilderness? Weren't there enough graves for us in Egypt? What have you done to us? Why did you make us leave Egypt? Didn't we tell you this would happen while we were still in Egypt? We said, 'Leave us alone! Let us be slaves to the*

Egyptians. It's better to be a slave in Egypt than a corpse in the wilderness!'" (Exodus 14:10-12 NLT).

As we can see, the slave attitude still dominated their thinking, not the glory of God. Israel was more interested in their comfort than God's glory.

Most of us are okay with God as our Redeemer, getting us out of trouble, but our reactions to Him putting us in harm's way indicate that we are not so thrilled about making Him Lord and giving Him free reign to run our lives. God is purposeful in everything He does; if He is going to get glory, it is going to spill over on us. God is gently working on us to believe, *"If we suffer, we shall also reign with Him…"* (2 Tim. 2:12). We need to shed our worldly thinking and slave mentality and embrace the Father as the answer to our troubles.

> *Then the Lord said to Moses, "Why are you crying out to me? Tell the people to get moving! Pick up your staff and raise your hand over the sea. Divide the water so the Israelites can walk through the middle of the sea on dry ground. And I will harden the hearts of the Egyptians, and they will charge in after the Israelites. My great glory will be displayed through Pharaoh and his troops, his chariots, and his charioteers. When My glory is displayed through them, all Egypt will see My glory and know that I am the Lord!"* (Exodus 14:15-18 NLT)

Sometimes we cry to the Lord for deliverance when we need to speak to our situation and create our deliverance. God could have parted the sea without Moses; He could have destroyed Pharaoh's army without Moses; but He chose to use Moses so that He could share His victory with Moses.

> *When the Israelites saw the mighty hand of the Lord displayed against the Egyptians, the people feared the Lord and put their trust in Him and in Moses His servant* (Exodus 14:31 NIV).

If we want to walk in authority, we can't kick and scream when things go wrong. God has already put in your hand everything you need to defeat the enemy and get the victory; it is our toxic memories that tell us otherwise.

Years ago, we were touring in the country when we got bogged down to the axles on a muddy road. The car was so deeply stuck that we had to abandon it and walk back to the place we were camping. In those days, we had no extra money for a tow truck, yet I needed the car for work. We prayed and God spoke a word about an east wind. In Alberta, an east wind always brings moisture, which we didn't need, but this time it just blew hard and dry. The next day we got a ride back to the road where the car was stuck. The wind had dried up the mud and with my pushing, Jeanne was able to drive it out. Trouble is designed to display God's power and increase our faith and authority. Our authority, if exercised in faith, will take us places that the enemy can't follow.

> *[Urged on] by faith the people crossed the Red Sea as [though] on dry land, but when the Egyptians tried to do the same thing they were swallowed up [by the sea]* (Hebrews 11:29 AMP).

We think trouble is the thing that blocks our progress, but God has placed it in our path to guarantee our success.

> *Blessed are those who are persecuted because of righteousness, for theirs is the kingdom of heaven. Blessed are you when people insult you, persecute you and falsely say all kinds of evil against you because of me. Rejoice and be glad, because great is your reward in heaven, for in the same way they persecuted the prophets who were before you* (Matthew 5:10-12 NIV).

Jesus said, *"All authority has been given to Me in heaven and on earth"* (Matt. 28:18 NASB). All authority means *all authority*. If authority was air and Jesus had all the air in a room, how much air is left for someone else? None! Jesus controls all the authority in the universe and gives it to whom He wills. Satan stole Adam's portion, but Jesus bought it back and is returning it to us, His Body (see Col. 1:24).

TEACHING WAR

The old adage says that what doesn't kill us makes us stronger. I had a football coach who believed that, so he made the practices much harder than the games. He understood Vince Lombardi, coach of the Super Bowl-winning Green Bay Packers, who said, "Fatigue makes cowards of us all." So he said, "I'm going to work you so hard that a game will seem like a picnic. You are going to be more afraid of me than any opponent." Fear is a demonic structure, but the principle of making the enemy nothing is sound.

God's method is to love us so much that there is no room for fear, for *"perfect love casteth out fear"* (1 John 4:18). So God commanded Joshua, *"… Be strong, vigorous, and very courageous. Be not afraid, neither be dismayed, for the Lord your God is with you wherever you go"* (Josh. 1:9 AMP). God never asks or encourages us to do anything; He commands us. And when He commands, He supplies. When Israel wouldn't obey and drive out the nations in Canaan, God also stopped driving them out. He left them *"to teach warfare to generations of Israelites who had no experience in battle"* (Judg. 3:2 NLT). God has also left enemies for us to learn how to fight.

> *For we are not wrestling with flesh and blood [contending only with physical opponents], but against the despotisms, against the powers, against [the master spirits who are] the world rulers of this present darkness, against the spirit forces of wickedness in the heavenly (supernatural) sphere* (Ephesians 6:12 AMP).

Our battlefield is in our mind, because that is the original realm in which satan overcame Eve and he still battles us there today. Satan uses lies and subtle suggestions which question God's integrity, goodness, and love for us. Our battle is to refuse the lies and dismantle the strongholds in us that agree with those lies.

God is for us, not against us. He is not mad at us; He already got mad at Jesus and poured out His wrath on Him on the cross. Jesus suffered for our sins so that we don't have to. Knowing this then we can endure like the Christians of the early church.

Others were tortured, not accepting deliverance, that they might obtain a better resurrection. Still others had trial of mockings and scourgings, yes, and of chains and imprisonment. They were stoned, they were sawn in two, were tempted, were slain with the sword. They wandered about in sheepskins and goatskins, being destitute, afflicted, tormented (Hebrews 11:35-37 NKJV).

*Take, my brethren, the prophets, who have spoken in the name of the Lord, for an **example of suffering** affliction, and of patience. Behold, **we count them happy which endure**. Ye have heard of the patience of Job, and have seen the end of the Lord; that the Lord is very pitiful, and of tender mercy* (James 5:10-11).

There are always casualties in wars, but if we are wounded we will be healed; if we are killed, we will be resurrected. That is the *"power of an endless life"* (Heb. 7:16 NKJV). With this endless life all our troubles are not things to shun, but are opportunities to love and do exploits because nothing can hurt us.

GLORY

Beloved, do not think it strange concerning the fiery trial which is to try you, as though some strange thing happened to you; but rejoice to the extent that you partake of Christ's sufferings, that when His glory is revealed, you may also be glad with exceeding joy. If you are reproached for the name of Christ, blessed are you, for the Spirit of glory and of God rests upon you (1 Peter 4:12-14 NKJV).

God loves to share His glory, especially when we share His suffering. Jesus declared concerning His disciples, *"I have given to them the glory and honor which You have given Me, that they may be one [even] as We are one"* (John 17:22 AMP).

*But we have this treasure in earthen vessels, that the excellency of the power may be of God, and not of us. We are **troubled** on* *every side, yet not distressed; we are **perplexed**, but not in despair; **persecuted**, but not forsaken; **cast down**, but not destroyed; always bearing about in the body the dying of the Lord Jesus, that the life also of Jesus might be made manifest in our body. For we which live are always **delivered unto death for Jesus' sake**, that the life also of Jesus might be made manifest in our mortal flesh* (2 Corinthians 4:7-11).

No matter what comes our way, we are not going to be defeated. With that attitude, we can have trouble, get perplexed, be persecuted, or be cast down and not get stressed or lose our peace. Jesus's resurrected, overcoming life will shine through us and the world will see it. Trouble presents us an opportunity to get delivered from our toxic memories. All we have to do to minister life to others is to die to ourselves—die to our fears, our guilt, and our persecutions. *"Death is working in us, but life in you"* (2 Cor. 4:12 NKJV).

> *This is how we've come to understand and experience love: Christ sacrificed His life for us. This is why we ought to live sacrificially for our fellow believers, and not just be out for ourselves* (1 John 3:16 MSG).

Jesus reiterated the truth when He said:

> *Listen carefully: Unless a grain of wheat is buried in the ground, dead to the world, it is never any more than a grain of wheat. But if it is buried, it sprouts and reproduces itself many times over. In the same way, anyone who holds on to life just as it is destroys that life. But if you let it go, reckless in your love, you'll have it forever, real and eternal* (John 12:24-25 MSG).

Toxic memories are strengthened by continually looking at them. The best way to break their hold on our mind is to get our mind off them by serving others. I am reminded of the saying, "I was upset that I had no shoes until I met a man with no feet." There is always someone who is worse off than us and who needs our help. Many times we have changed our plans when people phone with "emergencies" in their lives. We have been willing to change our plans and die to what we wanted to do to assist them.

One day we had two families in crisis come to our house at the same time. We put one in the family room and the other in the living room. One family even brought their kids and we had to get a babysitter, feed everyone lunch and supper, and counsel them. The last family left at 9 P.M. We gave them our whole day and saved these two marriages. Later, one of the men complained about how we had ministered to him and spoke against us. There was no thanks or pay, just complaints and accusations. We could not even defend ourselves against the accusation because of the confidentiality of not exposing the situation. No one knows the truth except God. *"What then shall we say to [all] this? If God is for us, who [can be] against us? [Who can be our foe, if God is on our side?]"* (Rom. 8:31 AMP).

GRACE IS SUFFICIENT

When things go wrong we think we are having a bad day, and when things go well it is a good day. If we embrace conflict and trials, even the bad days are good. In the movie *We Were Soldiers*, sergeant major Basil L. Plumley was the ramrod of the 1st Battalion, 7th Cavalry Regiment fighting in Vietnam in the Battle of Ia Drang. During training, when a soldier cheerfully greeted him with, "Good morning, sergeant major," Plumley snarled back, "Who made you the [expletive deleted] weather man?" Later, when the battle of Ia Drang was at its heaviest, the sergeant major, unperturbed, calmly turned to the same shell-shocked soldier and declared, "Now this is a good day." With the right attitude, any day can be a good day.

The truth is there are no good days or bad days; they are all days of grace. Some days are days of grace to enjoy; some are days of grace to endure. Therefore:

> *...Let us run with endurance the race God has set before us. We do this by keeping our eyes on Jesus, the champion who initiates and*

*perfects our faith. Because of the **joy awaiting** Him, He **endured** the cross, **disregarding its shame*** (Hebrews 12:1-2 NLT).

Jesus could endure because He kept His eyes on the prize. We may not have the strength of character or conduct to endure, but God does and He is carrying us.

The apostle Paul was having so much revelation that pride began to rise in him. Like everything we get from God, revelation is a function of grace; we don't get it because we are so smart or because we are so holy; we get it because God chose to give it to us. Paul said, *"...In order to keep me from becoming conceited, I was given a thorn in my flesh, a messenger of Satan, to torment me"* (2 Cor. 12:7 NIV). This was not a sickness; God does not make His children sick. God is good all the time. We would jail a man who gave his children poison to teach them a lesson. Accusing God of such a despicable action is not only an affront to Him but displays how twisted some of our toxic doctrines are. Paul said of his thorn in the flesh:

> *I was given the gift of a handicap to keep me in constant touch with my limitations. Satan's angel did his best to get me down; what he in fact did was push me to my knees. No danger then of walking around high and mighty! At first I didn't think of it as a gift, and begged God to remove it. Three times I did that...* (2 Corinthians 12:7-8 MSG).

> *But He said to me, "My grace is sufficient for you, for my power is made perfect in weakness." Therefore I will boast all the more gladly about my weaknesses, so that Christ's power may rest on me. That is why, for Christ's sake, I delight in weaknesses, in insults, in hardships, in persecutions, in difficulties. For when I am weak, then I am strong* (2 Corinthians 12:9-10 NIV).

God was not punishing or hurting Paul; He was allowing satan to attack, likely with all his demonically-inspired opposition. Jesus had to deal with the same thing and so do we. Opposition is designed to keep us close to the Father as it did for Paul.

Paul was not upset with what was conspiring against him, for he said:

> Who shall separate us from the love of Christ? Shall tribulation, or distress, or persecution, or famine, or nakedness, or peril, or sword? As it is written: "For Your sake we are killed all day long; we are accounted as sheep for the slaughter." Yet in all these things we are more than conquerors through Him who loved us. For I am persuaded that neither death nor life, nor angels nor principalities nor powers, nor things present nor things to come, nor height nor depth, nor any other created thing, shall be able to separate us from the love of God which is in Christ Jesus our Lord (Romans 8:35-39 NKJV).

Often when God asks me (Jeanne) to do something, I feel very inadequate with nothing to give. Then I recall the Scripture: "I can do all things through Christ which strengtheneth me" (Phil. 4:13). Afterward I am amazed at how well the event turned out because God became my strength.

HOW TO CHANGE

We are changed and our situations change when we see things differently. Job got a revelation of God and then was able to intercede for his "friends." "When Job prayed for his friends, the Lord restored his fortunes. In fact, the Lord gave him twice as much as before!" (Job 42:10 NLT). Our suffering comes because we are in a war, not because we are in sin; our victory comes because we look to the Lord and enter into His peace. That will require us to change some of our thoughts and actions.

I (Jeanne) often have taken this story personally and prayed for friends who asked for help when we were going through far worse circumstances than they were. I realized at an early age that if I met someone else's needs, then God would meet mine. The day I was asked to preach for the first time, I got a phone call from a man asking me to pray for him as he too had to speak at a church. He had ministered often but felt the need for additional prayer. I didn't tell him that I was also speaking but was apprehensive; I just agreed to pray for him and trusted God for myself. God came through with salvations, healings, and people getting filled with the Spirit. Because I looked after the needs of another, God looked after mine.

The psalmist Asaph declared God's viewpoint, saying, *"Whoever offers praise glorifies Me; and to him who orders his conduct aright I will show the salvation of God"* (Ps. 50:23 NKJV). *Conduct* could be translated *conversation* or *speech*.[3] God responds to our faith; the way we talk mirrors that faith and the way we are thinking. If we can praise in the middle of disaster, we are demonstrating our faith and trust in God. If we murmur and complain we are expressing our lack of faith in God's omnipotent power and His love for us.

Our friend Chang Su Yoo recently went to a Korean Christian businessmen's conference in Shanghai, China as the guest of the main speaker. Chang Su is an investment banker, but he and his partners had just closed down the operations in Seoul, where he worked, and he was wondering what his business card should say. He was still a director of the branch in Hong Kong and thought that he might list that on the business card, but God had a different plan. God told Chang Su to simply handwrite his name and telephone number and nothing else—no title, no connections, no businesses listed.

When Chang Su arrived in Shanghai, he realized that he had been the first foreign banker to enter China when it opened up to foreigners in 1992. God was talking to him of the significant role he would be playing in the future. However, at the conference, among all the most powerful and influential businessmen, he was nothing. He said he got the weirdest looks as the men attempted to assess him and his "business" card with no business listed. They were even more confused finding out that he had only been a Christian for ten years. He appeared to have no significant business or Christian connections, yet was invited by the main speaker to this Christian businessmen's conference. Unable to put Chang Su in a slot, they chose to ignore him.

"It is the glory of God to conceal a thing: but the honour of kings is to search out a matter" (Prov. 25:2). Though God had concealed Chang Su, He had not forgotten him. Through a series of bizarre circumstances, Chang Su has become involved in developing a mining concession in an Asian country that has a potential value of over two billion dollars. His obedience to God's word prevented him from making connections at the conference; his obedience also made it possible for God to make connections for him. If we order our conversation aright, God will order up our salvation (see Ps. 50:23). If we believe that and live it, all the stress of trying to get ahead evaporates.

Anyone who wants to live all-out for Christ is in for a lot of trouble; there's no getting around it (see 2 Tim. 3:12).

> *That no one [of you] should be disturbed and beguiled and led astray by these afflictions and difficulties [to which I have referred]. For you yourselves know that this is [unavoidable in our position, and must be recognized as] our appointed lot. For even when we were with you, [you know] we warned you plainly beforehand that we were to be pressed with difficulties and made to suffer affliction, just as to your own knowledge it has [since] happened* (1 Thessalonians 3:3-4 AMP).

We may attract trouble from the enemy, but we don't have to come under that trouble.

> *[He] made us sit together in the heavenly places in Christ Jesus* (Ephesians 2:6 NKJV).

> *Far above all principality and power and might and dominion, and every name that is named, not only in this age but also in that which is to come* (Ephesians 1:21).

The grain of sand that falls into an oyster is an annoyance that the oyster covers with mother of pearl to reduce the irritation. That irritation produces something beautiful, but the oyster would prefer to remove the sand completely. Sometimes it is possible to completely remove the influence of the enemy, but if not then God will use the stumbling block and make it a stepping stone for us. God is not about managing a problem or limiting its influence; He is about transformation and deliverance.

God does not want us to enter a monastery to limit the influence of the world; He wants us to enter Him (abide in Him) so that He can take the attacks of the enemy in His own body (see Matt. 8:17). We are not a religious form of Alcoholics Anonymous so that we declare, "Hi, I am Ken. I'm a sinner." I was a sinner, but now *"...Christ made us right with God; He made us pure and holy, and He freed us from sin"* (1 Cor. 1:30 NLT). God is not about behavior modification; He is about heart transformation. Trouble makes us look at our responses to that trouble and thus our heart and head attitudes.

The only way our hearts are changed is by beholding Jesus. If we look at our circumstances, we will be discouraged. If we look at ourselves, our actions, and our thoughts, we will be condemned. If we look at the Bible as a book of rules and principles, we will be hopeless with our inability to perform. But if we look at Jesus, who is in us, we will have hope.

> *All of us, as with unveiled face, [because we]* **continued to behold** *[in the Word of God]* **as in a mirror the glory of the Lord,** *are constantly being transfigured into His very own image in ever increasing splendor and from one degree of glory to another...* (2 Corinthians 3:18 AMP).

If we are beholding the glory in a mirror, we are seeing it shine out of us. *"The refining pot is for silver and the furnace for gold, but the Lord tests hearts"* (Prov. 17:3 NASB). Trouble is the heat that God uses to bring the dross in us to the surface. As the dross comes to the surface, the refiner scrapes it off. Because silver is used as backings on mirrors, the refiner looks in the silver to see if he can see his face. If the silver is pure, the reflection will be clear; if not, he heats it some more. When more dross floats to the surface, he scrapes that off and looks again. He will only be satisfied when he can see his reflection clearly. We are the silver, God is the Refiner, trouble is the heat. *"We all, with open face beholding as in a glass the glory of the Lord, are changed into the same image from glory to glory"* (2 Cor. 3:18). Embrace the trouble, for God loves to see the face of His Son in us.

> ***You're here to be light***, *bringing out the God-colors in the world. God is not a secret to be kept. We're going public with this, as public as a city on a hill. If I make you light-bearers, you don't think I'm going to hide you under a bucket, do you?* ***I'm putting you on a light stand***. *Now that I've put you there on a hilltop, on a light stand—shine! Keep open house; be generous with your lives. By opening up to others,* ***you'll prompt people to open up with God***, *this generous Father in heaven* (Matthew 5:14-16 MSG).

A light always shines brighter in the darkness, so don't despair of the darkness—use it to magnify God's glory.

KEYS

- Use your problems to reveal God as the answer.

- Our problems (giants) are God's supply.

- Our troubles contain within them our door of hope.

- God is able to convert evil into good for us.

- Our attitude will dictate what God can do with our troubles.

- God is in control, no matter how out-of-control trouble may look.

- Knowing God allows us to exhibit joy in adversity.

- Trouble is a sign of our authority, not our sin.

- Trouble is designed to teach us how to defeat the enemy.

- If we suffer with Jesus, we will reign with Him.

- Trouble teaches us that God's grace is sufficient.

- Trouble motivates us to change.

- Refuse the troubles; focus on God. See the potential, not the problem.

Chapter 10

SEE JESUS; SEE THE NEW YOU

When you're in the muck you can only see muck. If you somehow manage to float above it, you still see the muck but you see it from a different perspective. And you see other things too. —DAVID CRONENBERG

It's not what you look at that matters, it's what you see. —HENRY DAVID THOREAU

Faith is taking the first step even when you don't see the whole staircase. —MARTIN LUTHER KING, JR.

Copper-colored snakes were everywhere, slithering and striking at anything that moved. The people beat them off with sticks and poles, but they were so fast and poisonous that when they bit the people, many Israelites died (see Num. 21:6). What were they to do? Where had this plague come from? The answer was obvious—they had grumbled and complained.

> *And the people spoke against God and against Moses, Why have you brought us out of Egypt to die in the wilderness? For there is no bread, neither is there any water, and we loathe this light (contemptible, unsubstantial) manna* (Numbers 21:5 AMP).

Now their words proved prophetic as many were dying from the bites.

> *So the people came to Moses and said, "We have sinned, because we have spoken against the Lord and you; intercede with the Lord, that He may **remove the serpents** from us." ...Then the Lord*

said to Moses, "Make a fiery serpent, and set it on a standard;
*and it shall come about, that everyone who is bitten, **when he***
***looks** at it, **he will live**." And Moses made a bronze serpent and*
set it on the standard; and it came about, that if a serpent bit any
*man, when **he looked** to the bronze serpent, **he lived*** (Numbers
21:7-9 NASB).

LOOK AND LIVE

Jesus reiterated this story, telling the Jewish leader Nicodemus:

As Moses lifted up the serpent in the wilderness, even so must the
*Son of Man be lifted up; so that **whoever believes** will in Him*
have eternal life (John 3:14-15 NASB).

This is the first mention of eternal life in the Bible; therefore we need
to examine how Jesus introduced the subject to be able to step into the
fullness of that life. Israel hated the manna, calling it contemptible and
unsubstantial. *"They ate the bread of the mighty angels,"* and yet had contempt for it (Ps. 78:25 MSG).

Israel should have known better than to speak like that. The encounter
with the snakes occurred near the end of Israel's wilderness wanderings,
just before they entered the Promised Land. Their speech revealed that
despite all the miracles God had done for them, one toxic memory per-
sisted. It originally surfaced before Israel crossed the Red Sea, when they
complained, *"Why did you bring us out here to die in the wilderness?"* (Exod.
14:11 NLT). From then on, every difficult situation they encountered
brought up that same accusation and the same fears. This fearful complaining opened the doors for the plague of serpents.

The serpents had always been in the wilderness, but God erected an
invisible wall of protection that prevented the snakes from attacking Israel.
Their toxic expectation about dying in the wilderness and their vocal
despising of their provision eventually broke down their hedge. Israel was
never thankful for that protection, nor could they even acknowledge that

God had looked after them. They had been given shade by day, heat at night, divine guidance, divine protection, divine health, and divine food and water for almost forty years. Their clothes never even wore out, and every morning the day's provision arrived from Heaven, but that one toxic thought blocked them from acknowledging God's provision and opened the door for the snake attacks.

During the attacks, Israel begged Moses, *"...Pray unto the Lord, that He take away the serpents from us"* (Num. 21:7). That is always the world's way of dealing with problems—remove them. It is a type of avoidance: *"touch not; taste not; handle not"* (Col. 2:21). But avoidance or removal of the problem wouldn't help those who had already been bitten, and it won't help those of us who have already been bitten and have within us the toxins of bad experiences. God had a radically different approach to dealing with the attacks of the devil's snakes.

> *Moses made a serpent of bronze and put it on a pole, and if a serpent had bitten any man, **when he looked** to the serpent of bronze [attentively, expectantly, with a steady and absorbing gaze], **he lived*** (Numbers 21:9 AMP).

Our natural tendency after being bit is to look at the snake bite, but that is the enemy's tactic, keeping us absorbed with the wound rather than the cure. However, Moses instructed the Israelites to *"look attentively, expectantly, with a steady and absorbing gaze"* at the bronze serpent. This clearly is more than just a casual glance. The look that could save was fixed on God, filled with faith, and trusting in Him to keep His promise and save them.

Interestingly, the word *bite* is the Hebrew word *nâshak*, meaning "to strike," but it also means "to oppress with interest on a loan."[1] Many of us have been bitten with bad investments, car loans, credit card loans, an excessive mortgage, an unpayable line of credit, or a personal loan that oppressed us with interest payments we could not afford. Stress over finances is the number one cause of marriage breakups,[2] because couples fixate on the problem instead of looking to God for the solution.

When interest rates skyrocketed in the eighties, we felt led to get out from under the burden of our house mortgage. Instead of looking at the huge debt, we went to the Lord to get a strategy for our finances. Each year God gave us a specific amount to pay that seemed impossible at the time but would miraculously materialize when our anniversary date arrived. We learned to be specific in our prayers concerning the exact amount of money we would need. Within four years, our mortgage was wiped out and we were debt free. Don't look at the snake bite that is overwhelming you; look to the Lord and He will bring life to a dead situation.

I (Ken) remember when our son Mike got sent home at a critical point of a job when our company was assisting in lowering a dragline boom. He phoned and said the other company didn't want us back for several days until the boom was ready to go back up. As we had a dozen men working for us, this was going to cost us thousands of dollars that we had not budgeted for. I remember getting mad and being upset that we got sent home.

The next day, I got a phone call asking us to come back to the mine site as they were experiencing problems. Mike and the crew had been sent home with the boom only inches away from being set down on the cribbing that would support it while the repairs were being done. The other company's supervision was green and unaware that once the boom was down, the pressure would come off the lowering cables and the massive sheaves that held them would spin if not restrained.

The result—we spent an extra week reeving new lines, as the old ones were ruined when the sheaves spun. The thousands of dollars that we lost (whine and complain) became tens of thousands of dollars that we gained (praise the Lord). Real faith is trusting God when everything goes wrong, before it goes right. Situations don't change and deliver us; God delivers us and situations change. Since then our company motto is "Chaos is Cash."

The gospel message of the cross is that God delivers us from sin, sickness, and financial disasters. We can remove the effect of the poison of the snake bite by *"fixing our eyes on Jesus, the author and perfecter of faith, who for the joy set before Him endured the cross..."* (Heb. 12:2 NASB). The true revelation of the cross is that Jesus did not just die for us; He died as us. Therefore we do not live for Him, we live as Him (see Rom. 6:8). If we are going to live as Him, we need to see who He is in order to see who we are, *"because as He is, so are we in this world"* (1 John 4:17). To de-stress, we must stop looking at ourselves, our bad situations, our wounds, or our lack. *"We do this by keeping our eyes on Jesus, the champion who initiates and perfects our faith..."* (Heb. 12:2 NLT). Look and live!

THE DIVINE EXCHANGE

Our stress usually comes when we try to change ourselves or a situation to please people. Our job is not to change things; our job is to exchange with Jesus everything He is for everything we were, so that we might relax in being like Him. When Jesus hung on the cross, He hung there as us. Jesus cried, *"My God, my God, why have You forsaken Me?"* (Matt. 27:46 NKJV). That was the only time that He called God, "God." All other times He called Him "Father." This time it was you and I who hung there, and He called out as us—fearful, abandoned, wondering what was happening. Because we hung there with Him, all the requirements and the punishment of the law, for us, were fulfilled. When we accept this divine exchange, all the memories of the past lose their power to affect our future.

God made Jesus to be sin for us, *"...who knew no sin; that we might be made the righteousness of God in Him"* (2 Cor. 5:21). We are not just sinners saved by grace; we are the righteousness of God in Jesus and we can live in peace. Every religion tells us we have to pay for our sins; Jesus tells us He paid so we are free if we accept the payment.

Jesus exchanged His life and health for our sickness. *"He Himself took [in order to carry away] our weaknesses and infirmities and bore away our diseases"* (Matt. 8:17 AMP).

Jesus, *"...though He was rich, yet for your sakes He became poor, that ye through His poverty might be rich"* (2 Cor. 8:9). Jesus was not poor; He became poor just as He became sin. Appropriating His riches frees us from our striving for wealth or what the world considers gain—the gold, the girls, and the glory. We had a friend who was very wealthy and had many "toys." He spent all his time trying to keep those toys running so that everybody else could have fun. The toys weren't worth all the agony.

Jesus took all the shame we deserved and gave us all the glory He possessed. He, who had all the glory of Heaven *"endured the cross, despising the shame"* (Heb. 12:2). He hung there naked, exposed, and unable to cover Himself, for all to gawk and laugh at Him. He hung there so we wouldn't have to. Jesus covered our sin so that we would not be exposed because He values us.

Jesus exchanged our mistakes and sin for His perfection. Our faith in His exchange has made us perfect even though we don't act perfect. The bronze serpent represented Jesus on that pole and prophetically declared that sin and sickness have been judged on the cross. Since sin and sickness have been judged, we are free. We can exchange our old lives for His new one. We don't have to be perfect when we know we are loved. *"I have been crucified with Christ and I no longer live, but Christ lives in me"* (Gal. 2:20 NIV).

PROBLEMS OR SINS

When we talk about the toxic areas in our life, we often say, "I have a problem with _____." But if we have a problem, we will have a problem all our life; if we have a sin, we can get rid of it today. All we need to do is repent and receive God's forgiveness. Repent in the Greek is *metanōia*.[3] It means to think differently or to reconsider. Repentance is not weeping and wailing and gnashing of teeth; it is simply changing your mind. We need to change our mind if we are to break out of destructive habits. When we are driving and discover that we are going the wrong direction, we need to alter our course to get to our destination. Be willing to change your mind to believe that God has a great destiny for you.

Habits are choices that we continually make over a period of time. These habits become so ingrained in our behavior and in our thinking that eventually they become strongholds in our minds. Strongholds are literal structures of neural synapses that are like ruts connected in our brain. These toxic pathways are often initiated by negative words that have been spoken over us by critical parents, teachers, siblings, coaches, spouses, or bosses. Whenever we encounter a situation that is similar to our stronghold, we end up going down the same rutted path of habitual thinking from which we are unable to extract ourselves.

We may attempt to justify our actions, saying such things as, "That's just who I am," or, "I couldn't help myself," or, "I don't know what came over me," or, "I don't know what I was thinking; I just reacted." We respond this way when our neural pathways go into auto-pilot, spitting out conditioned responses such as rejection, blame, hiding, fear, self-pity, etc. We need to receive forgiveness, not blame. The easiest way to forgive yourself is to first receive God's forgiveness by accepting Jesus's payment of His life for our mistakes.

Prayer

> *Lord, I repent of accepting a spirit of criticism and in Jesus's name I command these spirits out of my life. I also reject all thoughts and the criticism against myself connected to self-pity, rejection, and fear and declare that I am powerful, not pitiful; that I am accepted, and I am not afraid.*

We need to get our eyes off of self and see through God's eyes. He is not seeing us; He is seeing Jesus in us. Because He sees us as Jesus, He is not critical about out problems but excited since He knows our destiny. God has determined that we are worth loving.

In the movie *Apocalypto*, the main character, Jaguar Paw, is running for his life from some Mayans intent on killing him for revenge. Jaguar Paw feels intimidated and powerless to do anything but run away until he enters the forest of his clan. At that point, he senses his family's destiny and declares that he and his descendants will hunt here forever. Recognizing the prophetic impact of his own words, he lifts his fist and shouts, "And I am not afraid!" From that point on, though he still must flee for his life, he is running not in fear but with purpose, strategically plotting out his victory. We must also change our minds to see our destiny and change our situations.

Declare

> *I am completely forgiven, wonderfully loved, and God is in control; therefore I am not afraid. If God is for me, who can ever be against me? Since He did not spare even His own Son but gave Him up for me, won't He also give me everything else?* (See Romans 8:31-32.)

God valued us so much that He gave the most valuable thing in the universe, His Son, for us. If we are valued that much, we need to adjust our thinking to know that He will give us whatever we need to accomplish the destiny that Jesus sacrificed to provide for us.

The apostle Peter knew that he was not afraid to go to prison and even die with Jesus (see Luke 22:33). He was incredulous when Jesus said that he would deny Him. Peter thought that Jesus was coming to power right away, because that was the "best idea." When things went wrong and Jesus was taken captive, Peter couldn't see this as part of God's plan and buckled to his emotions and fears as he stepped out of faith. He didn't recognize that not everything in him was in agreement with God's plan. He didn't know that within him were areas that could alternately function in the spirit and in the flesh.

We also have many such areas in ourselves that are not yet purified. These unsanctified areas, still dominated by the flesh, need to be converted to enable that area to think like Jesus. I (Ken) once told God, "If You want me to act like You, I will need to think like You; if I am going to think like You, I will need to see things the way You do." My limited perspective had locked me into my low thinking and thus my low living. God has a higher plane for us to operate from. But how do we get healed and get a better perspective on life? How do we see things the way Jesus did? Begin cultivating a positive outlook versus a negative one. See what God is doing not what the devil is doing.

GOD ON THE JOB

We don't know what is good for us and what is bad. Laura Clarke was crossing the street in the West Village in New York, when she saw Gwyneth Paltrow stopped at the intersection in her SUV. Clarke walked over to Paltrow's vehicle, and the two of them exchanged greetings. As a result of the slight delay, Clarke missed her train to work—on the 77th floor of Building 2 of the World Trade Center.

Clarke was both upset over missing her train and excited to tell her co-workers who she had just seen. She took the next train instead, and arrived just in time to see the first plane hit. "If I had made that train I would have been at my desk on the 77th floor of 2 World Trade Center," Clarke said.[4] God is always working to turn situations for our good.

Jesus said that the works He did, we would do also (see John 14:12). We are just like Jesus except for one thing. Jesus has a Body; we have a body. Jesus has a soul; we have a soul. Jesus is the Spirit of God; we have the Spirit of God (see Rom. 8:9). However, Jesus was conceived by the Spirit of God, and that Spirit led Him and formed His foundational thinking from the time of His conception. On the other hand, we were not introduced to God until maybe age five, or ten, or twenty, or forty. The only difference between us and Jesus is that He has only godly memories and thought patterns, and we are encumbered with toxic memories and thought patterns. Thus when Jesus encountered a stressful situation, He could draw on the truth of God's wisdom and His experience with God's deliverance to de-stress the situation.

Our personal spirit directs our thinking until our minds develop enough cognition or perception to take over. Since our personal spirits were not renewed until we encountered Jesus, our foundational thoughts were based on worldly wisdom. James says, *"This [superficial] wisdom is not such as comes down from above, but is earthly, unspiritual (animal), even devilish (demoniacal)* (James 3:15 AMP). As we were not connected to Jesus, who is the truth, then we were tied into lies. These lies are still embedded in our thought processes (the foundational way we think) via the brain's neural pathways. So when we encounter a stressful situation, we pull up all the fears and worries that afflicted us in the past and now expect more of the same.

I (Jeanne) ministered to a lady who could not trust God to protect her or her family. After much prayer, God revealed to us that she had made a judgment against God at age six. She had seen a movie in which a satanic group killed a Christian family by burning them to death in their motor home. She created a stronghold at this point, believing that satan was stronger than God and that God could not protect her family against an attack by the devil. She began to use worry and fear as her protectors—if she was afraid and worried enough she could avoid the attacks. This one fear became many fears, making her lose weight and have stomach problems as she worried about almost everything. As soon as she repented, broke off the judgment, and practiced not worrying or fearing, things began to change. As she trusted God for protection, she was released from all kinds of fears and her health returned. *"The spirit of a man will sustain his infirmity; but a wounded spirit who can bear?"* (Prov. 18:14).

Unlike Jesus, most of our foundational thinking is not godly. Our memories also are not godly and thus toxic to our bodies and our minds. If our memories can be healed then our minds will not draw from unhealthy patterns to make decisions. The restoration of proper thinking that God is working out in us is for our health, prosperity, and wholeness in our relationships and communion with Him. We can't walk in step with God until we have the mind of Christ, but as we are renewed in the spirit of our minds, we are getting delivered from our toxic memories (see 1 Cor. 2:16; Eph. 4:23).

Your mind strings many of these toxic memories together to form strongholds of thinking. We all have dozens, if not hundreds, of mindsets that we develop to cope with life. Unfortunately, most of them are ungodly and cause us grief as we use them. Through a series of rejections, I (Ken) developed a stronghold to protect me from further rejection. I used offense as my defense; I would offend people and drive them away before they came close enough to hurt me. I would also attempt to use work as a way of compensating for my lack of self-worth. If I could outwork everyone, I would be accepted. These structures work—that's why we use them—but they will cause us problems in the end. On the other hand, *"The blessing of the Lord—it makes [truly] rich, and He adds no sorrow with it..."* (Prov. 10:22 AMP).

TRUTHS THAT OVERCOME TOXIC LIES

1. *When I'm wrong, I'm not bad.*

One of the biggest lies embedded in our minds is, "If I do something wrong, I am bad." That thought makes my worth dependent on my ability to perform. Satan must have presumed that Jesus was under the same delusion, for when he tested Jesus he followed that line of reasoning. Satan tried to make Jesus perform.

> *During that time the devil came and said to Him, **"If you are** the Son of God, **tell these stones** to become loaves of bread"* (Matthew 4:3 NLT).

> *"...**If you are** the Son of God, **jump off!**** (Matthew 4:6 NLT)

> *Next the devil...showed Him all the kingdoms of the world and their glory. "I will give it all to you," he said, "**if you will kneel** down and worship me"* (Matthew 4:9 NLT).

Satan didn't understand that Jesus didn't have to perform to be or to get; He had already heard God's commendation. Days earlier, before Jesus had done anything, God had declared, *"...This is my dearly loved Son, who brings Me great joy"* (Matt. 3:17 NLT). He was loved for who He was, not for what He did. Because Christ lives in you, you are loved the same way—just for who you are (see Col. 1:27).

We are designed in such a way that our minds respond to what we believe more than what we see. The anorexic believes that she is fat even if the mirror shows she is skinny. A girl may believe she is ugly even if she is beautiful. If you hear you are stupid often enough, even straight As won't make you feel smart. Each of us has our own paradigm based on the way we interact with and interpret the world around us. Our memories lock us into experiencing the emotions of every event that we have ever encountered, thereby clouding our perception.

As a union ironworker, I (Ken) have often been hired out of the hall to work on jobs as a general foreman or foreman with companies I don't know. They chose me either from reputation or on the recommendation of the dispatcher at the union hall. They expected me to be able to do the job because of my experience. I expected to have a hard time performing my job based on my experience—not my experience ironworking or supervising, but my experience of doubting myself. I have 40-plus years of ironworking experience, but I have 60-plus years of self-doubt and fear.

I went to each job nervous and afraid, thinking I didn't know what I was doing and fearing everybody would see my incompetence, to my shame. It usually took two to three days before I could shake my inferiority and recognize that I actually knew more than everyone else on the job site of how to do what I had been hired to do. Once I shed the negative emotions, I was excited to try even those things that I had never experienced. Lies about my personal value overruled my confidence at ironwork, earned through years of expertise. Wordsworth said it best: "The child is father of the Man."[5] The seeds sown in the child will be reaped in the adult. Victory over these negative thoughts comes when we ask Jesus to reap what we have been sowing and refuse to believe the lies any longer.

The amygdala—the library where all the emotions are stored—unfortunately doesn't pass on the facts of each memory for our perusal; it only brings up the emotions connected with our decisions. The truth no longer matters; our feelings become the truth. Thus the old saying, "Don't confuse me with the facts; my mind is already made up." God has provided revelation for us to go back and examine our past decision, to see if the emotions connected to them have life. If they don't have life they will produce death and we must refuse to think them. It is at this point that we must decide whether we want to forgive, forget, and rewrite those memories or cling to our feelings.

We have ministered to couples where adultery had broken down their ability to trust and love again. With some of the couples, forgiveness flowed and the love was rekindled. Others could not get past the betrayal and hurt; it was just too painful. Your feelings are just a reaction to chemicals flowing through your body. They are powerful, but not permanent unless you keep stimulating the flow by regurgitating the events that initiated them. Stop the thoughts and the chemicals stop. Stop the chemicals and the painful emotions stop.

God has created the capacity for us to choose our thoughts. It's not that we can't stop thinking, it's that we won't. When I say I will forgive you, it means I *will to* forgive you. If I can will to forgive, I can also will not to forgive. Forgiveness is a choice, not a feeling. The feelings will flow out of what we will to do and to believe. Most of us have never disciplined our mind to think about only what we want it to think about. As mentioned earlier, the undisciplined mind is like an undisciplined dog—it goes where it wants, dragging the owner along; it barks at everything, will pee on anything, and is an embarrassment to accompany. Train the dog or the mind and it can be your best friend and companion.

It's not about being right or wrong; it's about life or death. The chemical packets that transmit the emotional component of our memories will either be life-giving or destructive to our bodies and our minds. If we allow destructive memories to dominate our thinking, we will get sick. God instructed us:

> ...*Whatsoever things are true, whatsoever things are honest, what-soever things are just, whatsoever things are pure, whatsoever things are lovely, whatsoever things are of good report; if there*

*be any virtue, and if there be any praise, **think on these things*** (Philippians 4:8).

This is not a Pollyanna attitude; this is a life-giving attitude. It is right believing, not right living (performing) that brings life. God called us to be believers, not achievers.

2. Rules aren't necessary to control me.

The big lie is that doing things right will make us right with God; the truth is that Jesus made us right with God. We have extrapolated that lie and deducted that if we follow our self-imposed laws we will defeat our destructive behavior. The opposite is true for *"the strength of sin is the law,"* any law (1 Cor. 15:56). We don't have to follow the Ten Commandments to be under law. We continually create our own laws that we equally can't follow. This is the crux of the problem—our conscience accuses us when we break our laws, but our mind tells us that if we do well the accusations will cease. The trouble is we can't stop hurting people or violating our own conscience, so we feel guilty and stressed out all the time. Our subconscious buries the memories of our failures so that we aren't confronted with our shortcomings on a daily basis, but that ploy only increases the long-term stress on our bodies.

I (Jeanne) usually try to get a lot done in a day but am often interrupted with phone calls from people with problems. Often, on those days when I don't accomplish what I had planned, I feel guilty because I didn't achieve my goals. I have come to realize that helping people is just as important as getting tasks done. I now know that taking breaks and getting rest is healthy and pleases God as much as the work I do. Jesus said that the ability to be flexible and adaptable was the key to being able to contain His power. If we want to do something for God but are not flexible, God's power will put such pressure on us that we will literally get sick (see Luke 5:36-38).

The apostle Paul also battled the rules issue. He said:

I want to do good, but in practice I do evil...In my mind I am God's willing servant, but in my own nature I am bound fast, as

I say, to the law of sin and death. It is an agonizing situation, and who on earth can set me free from the clutches of my sinful nature? I thank God there is a way out through Jesus Christ our Lord (Romans 7:21-25 PNT).

Our way out is to see Jesus, taking on the sinful nature of the bronze snake, as being judged on the cross. If Jesus took the judgment against us in His own body, our bodies don't have to pay the high price.

Since Jesus died as me, I am now free of the guilt of my transgressions of the law and I am now under grace. The Bible says, *"For sin shall not have dominion over you, for you are not under law, but under grace"* (Rom. 6:14 NKJV). If you put yourself under a law, *sin shall have dominion over you.* Conversely, if sin has dominion over you, you must have put yourself under some law that calls for your performance. Pressure to perform, put on by ourselves or other people, will put you under law, which will eventually cause you to sin. That is why we need to maintain healthy boundaries with people and forgive them when they try to cross those boundaries. Our health, both mental and physical, depends on us trusting the unmerited favor of Jesus and avoiding getting stuck under some artificial rule.

3. Jesus is more powerful than toxic memories.

We cannot change our flesh, but we can change our minds by healing our toxic memories and receiving the seed of God's Word. The way to get victory and remove guilt is to replace the guilty parts of our nature with God's nature. The Bible says, *"Whoever has been born of God does not sin, for His seed remains in him; and he cannot sin…"* (1 John 3:9 NKJV). Every area of our soul that has God's seed in it cannot sin because of the seed, which is God's nature. Having the seed in an area is equivalent to being converted or made alive in that area. We become God-like in that area because God is in that area; the light is in that area. Where there is light there is no darkness; and where there is no darkness there is no sin.

Where we break our laws and offend our conscience, God's seed has not come and we need to be converted. Paul said, *"So then with the mind*

I myself serve the law of God; but with the flesh the law of sin" (Rom. 7:25). When we change our minds by including the redemptive touch of God in a situation, the memories we have will no longer be toxic. We can then say with Joseph, *"You meant evil against me; but God meant it for good…"* (Gen. 50:20 NKJV). When we can forgive and forget, we will be able to truly love the people who hurt us.

4. *Righteousness has nothing to do with doing things right.*

This statement may not compute in our mind. It contradicts one of the biggest lies that we have believed—that righteousness comes when we stop doing wrong things. Sin is what Adam brought on the human race; righteousness is what Jesus brought. *"For as by one man's [Adam's] disobedience many were made sinners, so by the obedience of one [Christ] shall many be made righteous"* (Rom. 5:19). As we shed our thinking that we have to do things right, we can remove the toxic thoughts that are associated with doing things wrong. Jesus did it right and yet came to take our guilt for what we did wrong. That guilt is stored in our memories; as we remove the memories, the guilt will also dissipate.

Guilt stemming from a toxic memory is the most destructive of human emotions. It is basically self-directed anger—seeing yourself as a bad person for having done something wrong. Guilt can destroy us from the inside, making us feel inferior, lack confidence, and become insecure. Guilty people often try perfectionism as a way to mitigate their guilt. They may also develop stress-related diseases.[6]

The Father is not looking at either our good deeds or our bad deeds; He is looking at Jesus's righteous deeds. Many toxic memories are connected to our thoughts about trying to please our fathers or our father figure—God. Because Jesus pleased the Father, if we are in Jesus we are pleasing to the Father. Believing that thought will heal many wounds from our past failures when we were displeasing to our fathers.

My (Jeanne's) father was a hard, critical man. He would rant about the economy, politics, doctors, lawyers, or leaders with equal disdain. It was very hard to please him. Getting good grades was never good enough; you could always have done better. My father did not kiss and hug or praise me as a daughter. He loved me but couldn't reinforce these values in me. As a result I never felt good enough or that I measured up. When I met Jesus, God began a process of working on my thinking to know how much I was loved and how proud He was of me.

The truth is that you are a worthwhile human being (not a human doing), as God created you in His image. He loves you so much that He sent Jesus, His Son, to die for you. You give Him pleasure and we are His glorious inheritance in the saints (see Eph. 1:18).

We need to retrain our minds to believe that Jesus's righteousness is our righteousness; His favor is our favor; His obedience is our obedience. We are to take every negative thought about our obedience and bring it into captivity to the obedience of Christ (see 2 Cor. 10:5). We are to see His obedience as the answer. We normally do not believe that we are righteous because we have been taught that unrighteous deeds make us unrighteous. We need to revise our thinking. Our disobedience didn't make us displeasing to God and our obedience won't make us more pleasing. Jesus's actions are what God is looking at, and He is pleasing to God. We need deliverance from our toxic memories that prevent us from allowing the Holy Spirit to convict us of our righteousness in Christ (see John 16:10).

5. We can do it wrong and still please God.

Religion is as poor a substitute for relationship as duty is for passion. Religion is about behavior modification; Jesus is about heart transformation. We can change our actions and still not change our hearts. We are transformed through changing our thinking, not changing our actions. *"Let God transform you into a new person by changing the way you think. Then you will learn to know God's will for you..."* (Rom. 12:2 NLT). The law is like a mirror to show you every imperfection that you have. We look in the mirror and see a spot on our face, but we don't use the mirror to clean our face; it is only designed to expose, not repair.

Neither can the laws we try to obey renew us; they can only condemn us. *"God did not send His Son into the world to condemn the world, but that the world through Him might be saved"* (John 3:17 NKJV). Looking at Jesus and what He did on the cross allows the love of God to penetrate and change us and remove the toxicity of condemnation. I (Jeanne) was so fearful that I could hardly come out of my house. Now I travel all over the world and speak to large audiences. Getting to know God's love and protection for me enabled me to be fearless when I know I am in His will. I (Ken) was so independent that I could not relate properly as a husband or even empathize when anyone was hurting. Seeing Jesus's love and care for everyone He encountered broke down my walls and allowed me to let Him do the same through me.

Just as a mirror makes us conscious of every imperfection in our face, *"...[the real function of] the Law is to make men recognize and be conscious of sin"* (Rom. 3:20 AMP). Even being right doesn't make us right. We can be 100 percent correct in an argument with our spouse but bring death to the relationship. It is not about right and wrong; it's about life and death. King David built a tabernacle in the wrong place, out of the wrong material, allowed the wrong people to enter, had the wrong order of service, and completely omitted the veil before the Ark, but it had life because the focus was on the Lord, who is the author of life. It was all wrong, according to the pattern, but it had life and God loved it. David's tabernacle made everyone who entered conscious of the Lord and His goodness.

Moses's tabernacle was architecturally perfect; the service was perfect, the sacrifices were perfect, but it was centered on death, not life (see Exod. 25:9). God is life and decided, *"I will come back, and will rebuild the house of David...I will rebuild its [very] ruins, and I will set it up again"* (Acts 15:16 AMP). God wasn't worried about what David did wrong; He was interested in his heart. David committed many sins and made many mistakes, but God's verdict was, *"I have found David son of Jesse, a man after my own heart"* (Act 13:22 NLT). *"People judge by outward appearance, but the Lord looks at the heart"* (1 Sam. 16:7 NLT). When we allow God to transform our heart, life grows and toxic thinking against ourselves cannot grow.

6. *Receiving forgiveness increases our love.*

Jesus went for dinner at Simon the Pharisee's house:

> *And behold, a woman of the town who was an **especially wicked*** *
> ***sinner**...brought an alabaster flask of ointment* (perfume). *...She*
> *began to wet His feet with [her] tears...and anointed them with*
> *the ointment. Now when the Pharisee who had invited Him saw*
> *it, he said to himself, If this Man were a prophet, He would surely*
> *know who and what sort of woman this is who is touching Him...*
> (Luke 7:37-39 AMP).

Pharisees look for our sin; Jesus looks for our potential. Jesus knew the accusation that was in Simon's heart and proposed to him a parable to correct his wrong thinking.

> *And Jesus, replying, said to him, Simon, I have something to*
> *say to you. And he answered, Teacher, say it. A certain lender*
> *of money [at interest] had two debtors: one owed him five*
> *hundred denarii, and the other fifty. When they had no means*
> *of paying, he freely forgave them both. Now which of them will*
> *love him more? Simon answered, The one, I take it, for whom*
> *he forgave and cancelled more. And Jesus said to him, You have*
> *decided correctly.*

> *Then turning toward the woman, He said to Simon, Do you see*
> *this woman? When I came into your house, **you gave Me no*** *
> ***water** for My feet, but she has wet My feet with her tears and*
> *wiped them with her hair. **You gave Me no kiss**, but she from*
> *the moment I came in has not ceased [intermittently] to kiss My*
> *feet tenderly and caressingly. **You did not anoint My head** with*
> *[cheap, ordinary] oil, but she has anointed My feet with [costly,*
> *rare] perfume. Therefore I tell you, her sins, many [as they are],*
> *are forgiven her—because she has loved much. But **he who is*** *
> ***forgiven little loves little*** (Luke 7:40-47 AMP).

Our ability to love God depends on our recognizing how much we have been forgiven. *"This is real love—not that we loved God, but that He loved us…"* (1 John 4:10 NLT). The law is about us loving God and others; grace is about us being loved. We have never loved God with all our heart, soul, mind, and strength or our neighbor as ourselves. That is God's prerogative; He loved us with all His heart, soul, mind, and strength and His neighbors as Himself. The way to increase our love for God is to receive His love and forgiveness and reject the guilt for what we do wrong. We need a total shift in our mindsets to trust that what someone else does right can pay for what I do wrong.

A man (call him Roy) told us his story of how he changed when he recognized God's love for him. Roy was a big, rough man with a wife who had just given her heart to the Lord. Roy was jealous and blamed the pastor for bringing his wife to Jesus. Every time he ran into the pastor, Roy would rough him up and threaten him. Even though his wife remained sweet and loyal to him, Roy hated the fact that she had fallen in love with Jesus. When his wife wanted to go to prayer meeting, Roy would not let her have the truck and actually drove along beside her, berating her and bumping her with the vehicle as she walked several miles to the church.

The whole church was praying for Roy, but he just became more obstinate. Later that week, he caught the pastor in a grocery store and pushed him into the shelves telling him to back off or he would kill him. Even though Roy was becoming angrier, he also was becoming depressed. Finally, after his wife had gone to a mid-week prayer meeting, Roy took his rifle, drove into the woods, and put the gun under his chin, determined to commit suicide. When he pulled the trigger, the gun misfired and jammed.

At that moment Roy broke! The love of God overwhelmed him and he started to cry. Roy jumped back in the pickup and headed for the church. With tears still streaming down his cheeks, Roy jumped out of the truck and rushed into the church. Not thinking, Roy had grabbed his rifle when he got out of the truck and was now crying and yelling, waving the rifle as he ran toward the front of the church. Not being privy to Roy's sudden change of heart, the pastor breathed out his last prayer, committing his soul to God. To his shock Roy grabbed him, begging for forgiveness and asking how to get give his heart to Jesus. That was many years ago. "Roy" has since traveled the world prophetically speaking the love of God. He knew he had been forgiven much and now could love much.

My own son, who was going through a bad stretch, had the thought go through his head that he was a throw-away as he sat in church listening to Roy speak. As I was driving Roy to lunch, he saw my son trudging through the church parking lot and asked me to stop. He rolled the window down, and not knowing who he was, waved my son over. In his own soft way he said, "Son, God told me to tell you that you are not a throw-away. He loves you!" With that simple word, we drove away. Later, my son told me the whole story as he started his journey back to the Father. God loves us and will seek us out even if our mind is set against Him and we are going the wrong way.

God's love doesn't depend on our performance. The apostle Paul even had the faith to say, *"If I do what I don't want to do, I am not really the one doing wrong; it is sin living in me that does it"* (Rom. 7:20 NLT). In other words, "It's not me, it's the other guy!" That seems like such a cop-out, but it is the Word of God. Paul was refusing to take the blame for his deeds that Jesus had already paid for. Paul reckoned he was *"...dead indeed unto sin, but alive unto God through Jesus Christ"* (Rom. 6:11). God is trying to get us to see ourselves that way, saying, *"Ye are dead, and your life is hid with Christ in God"* (Col. 3:3). If we know we are forgiven, we do not have to receive guilt; we are not throw-aways, rather we are wondrously loved children of God.

7. Guilt does not disqualify us.

Guilt's whole purpose is to disqualify us in our minds so we won't be able to act like Jesus. His best weapon is the Law, which is the ministry of death and condemnation (see 2 Cor. 3:7,9 NKJV). If he can't get people to accuse us, he will get our conscience to accuse us. However, God loves to counter guilt's tactics by using His grace to qualify us.

Jeanne and I are ordinary people, living extraordinary lives. As ambassadors for Jesus we have shared His love in a hospital, on the radio and television, with a consulting firm, and with generals of a foreign nation. We have been privileged to speak in churches in many nations as well. Neither of us has pastoral or Bible school training, but we have been chosen to represent a loving God to a wounded world. Don't let the guilt of your past dictate your future; use your past to be a testimony of the grace of God.

> *God has chosen what the world calls foolish to shame the wise; He has chosen what the world calls weak to shame the strong. He has chosen things of little strength and small repute, yes and even things which have no real existence to explode the pretensions of the things that are—that no man may boast in the presence of God. Yet from this same God* **you have received your standing in Jesus Christ**... (1 Corinthians 1:27-30 PNT).

The genealogy of Jesus is a point in fact. There are just five women mentioned in Jesus's ancestral line—Tamar, Rahab, Ruth, Bathsheba, and Mary, even though there were 42 generations of men listed (see Matt. 1:1-17). God was qualifying or highlighting these women because their pasts and people's opinions disqualified them all:

- Tamar's son Perez was the result of her incestuous affair with Judah.

- Rahab was a harlot.

- Ruth was a Moabitess, alienated from Israel's covenants (see Deut 23:3).

- Bathsheba was an adulteress with David.

- Mary was under suspicion of fornication, as Joseph was not the biological father of Jesus.

The Law would disqualify all of us, but God is in the business of re-qualifying us. Therefore, we can banish all those toxic, negative

words spoken over us about being worthless, useless, lazy, hopeless, stupid, and amounting to nothing. *"Let no one defraud you by acting as an
umpire and declaring you unworthy and disqualifying you for the prize..."*
(Col. 2:18 AMP). We don't have to qualify; Jesus already qualified for
us. Receiving His qualification allows us to heal our memories from
all accusations.

Before Peter betrayed Him, Jesus prophesied that Peter would change the
way he thought and then would strengthen his brothers (see Luke 22:32).
Jesus was not disillusioned with Peter when he failed; He never had any
illusions about Peter. So when Jesus confronted Peter after the resurrection,
He was re-qualifying him for his task, not judging or reprimanding him.
When Jesus asked Peter if he loved Him, He used the word *agapé*, which
is God's love; Peter responded with *philéo*, which is brotherly love or kindness. The conversation went something like this:

Jesus: "Do you *love* Me?"

Peter: "I like You."

Jesus: "Feed my lambs. Do you *love* Me?"

Peter: "I like you."

Jesus: "Take care of My sheep. Do you *like* Me?"

Peter: "You know."

Jesus: "Feed My sheep." (See John 21:15-17.)

Jesus lowered His demands of Peter from *love* to *like*, but never lowered
His plans for Peter's destiny. He restored Peter because He loved him, not
because Peter was useful. We must know in our hearts that we are completely forgiven, wonderfully loved, and under His covering if we are to
fulfill our calling and be delivered from our shameful, toxic thinking.

Declaration

> *God has a purpose for you. Your failures and guilt won't keep
> you from that destiny. God has declared that you are of great
> value because Jesus loved you by dying for you.*

8. *Receiving love will bring intimacy.*

By any standard that we would use, Peter disqualified himself by deny-ing Jesus. Peter often acted out of a fleshly mindset and needed constant correction. By his flamboyant actions, Peter was always trying to get in Jesus's good books and qualify himself for promotion. But despite his self-confidence, Peter never felt close to Jesus. He was always bragging on his love for Jesus, but there was another disciple who was confident of Jesus's love for him.

John was called the disciple whom Jesus loved (see John 20:2). Five times in Scripture this phrase is used. Interestingly, all five are in the book of John (see John 13:23; 19:26; 20:2; 21:7,20). It wasn't that Jesus loved John more; it was that John knew more that he was loved. Knowing that banished all his negative thoughts, gave him confidence, and allowed him to be intimate with the Lord.

I (Ken) translated my toxic belief—that I was only valued for what I do—into my walk with God. I only felt peace when I had worked and sacrificed for God. I told Jeanne when we were first married that I would have to go off to Africa as a missionary if God called me. In reality it was not God calling but my toxic, independent martyr complex that was driv-ing me. If our thoughts and plans are from God they will have life and peace on them; if they are forged from our guilt, they will bring strife, con-fusion, and every evil work (see James 3:16). God never calls us to abandon our wife and family; He calls us to be partners with them. As I grew in the love of God, I grew in the love of my wife. Now we are partners in all that we do, even if we are doing it separately.

Peter, despite his efforts, didn't feel confident enough to get close to Jesus. At the last supper, when Jesus revealed that one of the twelve was going to betray him, Peter was reluctant to ask Jesus who it was. *"Now there was leaning on Jesus' bosom one of His disciples, whom Jesus loved. Simon Peter therefore motioned to him to ask who it was of whom He spoke"* (John 13:23-24 NKJV). Peter was two feet away but didn't feel intimate enough to ask on his own; he had to ask John to ask Jesus who it was. Peter's attempts to love Jesus never made him feel close, while John's acceptance of Jesus's love allowed him the confidence to lay back and rest on Jesus.

We all have memories of not feeling loved or being rejected by those we loved. Those toxic memories can be replaced with positive ones as we accept how much God loves us.

Reflect

Take a deep breath; banish all thoughts of rejection; allow God to love you now; accept your worth as a child of the King. With those healing thoughts, you will know that you are worth loving.

9. Where we are weak He is strong.

God is not relying on our strengths; He is supplying for our weaknesses. In all our weak places, Jesus wants to be our strength, and part of His strength is His prayers for us. Jesus told Peter, *"Satan has demanded permission to sift you like wheat; but I have prayed for you, that your faith may not fail..."* (Luke 22:31-32 NASB). Jesus didn't stop the attack; He didn't limit the temptation; He didn't even promise that the attack wouldn't work. He simply prayed that Peter's faith would not fail even if Peter failed. Failure is often vital for success, not a hindrance to success. Failure moves our trust off of ourselves and onto Jesus.

Abraham Lincoln never gave up, no matter what "failures" he encountered. Here is a brief glance at Lincoln's life until he became President of the United States:

- 1816: His family was forced out of their home. He had to work to support them.
- 1818: His mother died.
- 1831: He failed in business.
- 1832: He ran for state legislature and lost.
- 1832: He also lost his job that same year; he wanted to go to law school but couldn't get in.

- 1833: Borrowed some money from a friend to begin a business and by the end of the year he was bankrupt with a debt it took him the next 17 years to pay off.

- 1834: Ran for state legislature again and won this time.

- 1835: He was engaged to be married, but his sweetheart died.

- 1836: Had a total nervous breakdown and was in bed for six months.

- 1838: Sought to become speaker of the state legislature and was defeated.

- 1840: Sought to become an elector and was defeated.

- 1843: Ran for Congress and lost.

- 1846: Ran for Congress again and won this time.

- 1848: Ran for re-election to Congress and lost.

- 1849: Sought the job of land officer in his home state and was rejected.

- 1854: Ran for Senate of the United States and lost.

- 1856: Sought the vice-presidential nomination at his party's national convention and got less than 100 votes.

- 1858: Ran for U.S. Senate again and lost again.

- 1860: He was elected president of the United States.[6]

Lincoln said, "Success is going from failure to failure without losing your enthusiasm." With that attitude, Lincoln overcame his failures and refused to be governed by any toxic memories. You may have failed, but you are not a failure. The formula for success usually has an element of failure in it. When our success doesn't depend on our accomplishments, we are free to rely on our true source of strength—God's love and approval.

10. Humility is not a sign of weakness.

To walk in humility we need a revelation that as Christians we are citizens of Heaven (see Phil. 3:20 PNT). Heaven knows it, hell knows it, but we often forget it. Because we are citizens of Heaven, we, like Christ, derive our priesthood *"from the power of indestructible life"* (Heb. 7:16 PNT). Jesus declared to Nicodemus that whoever believes in God will not perish but have eternal life (see John 3:16).

Through the power of this eternal, indestructible life we all can do exploits. If a group of soldiers were stuck in a foxhole, pinned down by a machine gun, the one who knew he could not die would not be afraid to charge out and destroy the enemy. Like a superhero in the movies, he could fearlessly leap over the top and attack; if he got wounded, the wounds would miraculously heal; if he got killed, he would come back to life. Nothing could stop him from saving his friends and destroying the machine gun nest. Knowing who you are expels every toxic thought about your worth and allows you to do great exploits.

The world needs heroes, but heroes don't just do brave things and ride off into the sunset. True heroes are willing to do menial tasks like taking out the garbage, wiping the baby's bum, and telling the kids bedtime stories when they are exhausted. Jesus, *knowing who He was and where He had come from,* chose to humbly wash the disciples' feet (see John 13:5).

Knowing who we are also allows us to act with humility. Not knowing who we are locks us into pride and arrogance and makes us act like a king, demanding that others serve us. Many of our toxic memories come from situations where pride manifested in us. Knowing who we are allows us to resist that tendency toward pride in us and gives us compassion when pride rises in others.

SEE JESUS, SEE OURSELVES

The Holy Spirit came to reveal Jesus as the beloved Son of the Father. If we can see Jesus in that exalted position, we can see ourselves there as well, *"because as He is, so are we in this world"* (1 John 4:17). As He is now, so are we now. In Heaven Jesus is loved by the Father; so are we on earth. In Heaven Jesus has authority; so have we on earth. In Heaven Jesus is righteous; so are we on earth.

We need to look at Him and not at ourselves to see who we are and what our inheritance is. If we do that, we can humbly take the role of the servant while still reigning in power. We need to change our minds about how God relates to us and how He deals with our sin. We need to remember that God sees us as He sees Jesus and that we are wonderfully loved and truly forgiven. Knowing these truths and acknowledging that God is in total control will deliver us from the roots of all of our toxic memories.

KEYS

- The key to healing is to look at our sickness or disease as judged on the cross.

- Jesus didn't just die for us, He died as us. Look and live.

- The world uses avoidance; the Kingdom relies on healing and deliverance.

- Jesus exchanged all that He is for all that we are.

- Our words have power, and we need to use them productively.

- Repentance is about changing our minds.

- The root of our toxic thinking is buried in the lies we believe; if we change our minds, we will change our actions.

- Righteousness is not about our actions, it's about Jesus's actions.

- The Law is perfect, but it can't make you perfect.

- The Father sees Jesus when He sees us.

🔑 God is always qualifying us, even when we feel disqualified.

🔑 Where we are weak, He is strong.

🔑 We must strive to enter His rest.

🔑 Knowing who we are and where we come from allows us to humbly serve others.

Chapter 11

THE TRUTH

*A little kingdom I possess, where thoughts and
feelings dwell; and very hard the task I find of
governing it well.* —LOUISA MAY ALCOTT

*If you have not chosen the Kingdom of God first,
it will in the end make no difference what you
have chosen instead.* —WILLIAM LAW

*Faith is to believe what you do not see; the reward of this
faith is to see what you believe.* —SAINT AUGUSTINE

REVEAL AND HEAL

God doesn't want us to cover up and bury our wounds or unhealthy thoughts just so that they don't irritate us, like an oyster does with a piece of sand. God doesn't want us to manage our problems or our thoughts; He wants to remove them from us, heal us, and rewire our thinking. God tells us:

> *Do not be conformed to this world (this age), [fashioned after and adapted to its external, superficial customs], but be **transformed (changed) by the [entire] renewal of your mind** [by its new ideals and its new attitude], so that you may prove [for yourselves] what is the good and acceptable and perfect will of God...* (Romans 12:2 AMP).

Once buried, the unconscious region of the mind will actually induce physical pain in the body for the specific purpose of diverting the conscious mind's attention away from recognizing that buried emotional pain. This process is called tension myositis syndrome (TMS), and it happens when the brain send signals to cause reduced blood flow to a certain body part. The affected area experiences mild oxygen deprivation, pain, and other symptoms, depending on where in the body it happens.[1] If the symptoms are treated, the subconscious will direct its diversionary pain to another area of the body. The flesh becomes like the computer HAL in *2001: A Space Odyssey*. It will rather lie to us than reveal the truth hidden inside and will kill us to relieve the stress that action causes.

Psychosomatic disorders like this will spread through the population like an epidemic, much like bacteriological diseases. Interestingly, these disorders tend to reach epidemic proportions when they are in fashion and well-known in the society. People who have emotional pain in their sub-conscious will often unconsciously develop common disorders like back pain, hay fever, carpal tunnel syndrome, or eczema.[2] That is why just burying a wound is so dangerous.

These repressed emotions, without conscious perception or outlet, will remain within us for a lifetime. Life-long repression stimulates the nervous system at a low level; persistent stimulation over the course of years leads to constant high blood pressure and heart disease. The emotions we bury are often more powerful and painful than the emotions we recognize. They are more dangerous than the emotions we feel because we have no way of ridding ourselves of those things we have repressed and are unaware of.[3] We need deliverance from these toxic memories as they are the source of most of the toxic chemicals that attack our bodies. Only God can reveal to us the hidden things in our heart so that we can release them and be healed. When the Lord comes, He *"will both bring to light the hidden things of darkness and reveal the counsels of the hearts..."* (1 Cor. 4:5 NKJV).

Though Jesus was resurrected with open wounds, they were not bleed-ing or injurious to Him; they were glorified just as the rest of His body was glorified (see 1 Cor. 15:42-43). Under the Old Covenant, *unhealed wounds disqualified* the priests from ministering (see Lev. 21:17-21). Under the New

Covenant, Jesus's *resurrected wounds empowered* Him to minister healing for *"by His wounds you are healed"* (1 Pet. 2:24 NLT). Our wounds, if they are unhealed, will make us sick. Those same wounds, if they are healed, will empower us to bring healing to ourselves and others.

Knowing that Jesus had a resurrected, physical body gives us the faith to believe that *"…just as God raised Christ Jesus from the dead, He will give life to your mortal bodies by this same Spirit living within you"* (Rom. 8:11 NLT). Altering our lifestyle has some benefit, but ultimately our health depends on our belief—that the Spirit who gave life to Jesus's body will give life to our body. Not at the resurrection, but now, while it is still a mortal body.

MIXTURE

Wavering in our beliefs causes confusion in our bodies as well as our minds. To be healthy, our bodies must be united with our spirits and our minds. If we are not congruent in all our parts, there will be tension and stress created. This tension comes from being double-minded and is easily recognized by our inability to make decisions and our second guessing. This is also evident in our prayer life and our inability to trust. When we pray, we need faith.

> *But he must ask in sincere faith without secret doubts…. The man who trusts God, but with **inward reservations**, is like a wave of the sea, **carried forward by the wind one moment and driven back the next**. That sort of man cannot hope to receive anything from God, and the life of a man of divided loyalty will reveal **instability at every turn** (James 1:5-8 PNT).*

Confusion results from a mixture of thoughts but *"God is not the author of confusion, but of peace"* (1 Cor. 14:33). He loves purity and thus hates mixture. Jesus asked the Pharisees:

> *Who would patch old clothing with new cloth? For the new patch would shrink and rip away from the old cloth, leaving an even*

*bigger tear than before. And no one puts new wine into old wine-skins. For **the old skins would burst from the pressure, spilling the wine and ruining the skins**. New wine is stored in new wineskins so that both are preserved* (Matthew 9:16-17 NLT).

We can't put ideas that have life on them into our traditional mind-sets or we will blow our minds. We have to remove the old thoughts and memories and replace them with new thoughts and memories; otherwise, in the ensuing stress we will lose both our minds and our memories.

Jesus told the last church in Revelation:

I know your [record of] works and what you are doing; you are neither cold nor hot. Would that you were cold or hot! So, because you are lukewarm and neither cold nor hot, I will spew you out of My mouth! (Revelation 3:15-16 AMP)

It has often been taught that *hot*, being hot after God, means loving Him fervently. *Cold* is fighting God, living a self-centered, selfish life. But that definition doesn't make sense. It is physically impossible to get from cold to hot without passing through lukewarm. If we follow that line of reasoning, then the person who is living a selfish life is more pleasing to God than a person who's beginning to look for God and starting to hate what they are doing. God does not hate an immature expression of love but is excited with growth, as growth is an indicator of life. Rather, hot and cold here refer to our relationship with God.

When we are hot for someone, we want to be intimate with them. When we are cold, we give them the cold shoulder and will only tolerate a casual relationship. Cold is representative of the law—duty, not joy; service, not love; distance, not intimacy. When the Law was given on Mount Sinai, the people were told, *"Beware that you do not go up on the mountain or touch the border of it; whoever touches the mountain shall surely be put to death"* (Exod. 19:12 NASB). Under grace, God called us to *"draw near with confidence to the throne of grace, so that we may receive mercy and find grace to help in time of need"* (Heb. 4:16 NASB). Law creates distance; grace draws us into intimacy.

The lukewarmness that God hates is the mixture of legalism (cold) and grace (hot). Trying to mix both produces a lukewarm, vacillating, adulterous relationship. God made provision for the Law and for grace, but not for a mixture of the two.

> The **law was our schoolmaster** to bring us unto Christ, that we might be justified by faith. But **after that faith is come, we are no longer under a schoolmaster**. For ye are all the children of God by faith in Christ Jesus (Galatians 3:24-26).

Once we come to Christ we must divorce ourselves from the law of trying to do it right. Think of the Law as the bridge taking us from the land of sin to the land of life in Christ. If after coming to Christ we were to go back on the bridge, the only place it could lead us is back to the dominion of sin. We must choose either marriage to doing it right or marriage to Jesus (see Rom. 7:4). Legalism and the resulting guilt is one of the main sources of the toxic memories that afflict us. Just as an adulterous affair brings stress and confusion, vacillating between freedom and legalism compounds our guilt and self-loathing.

HOW WE CHANGE

Self-effort and self-improvement cannot change us for the law (doing it right) never made anything perfect (see Heb. 7:19).

- Giving will not remove covetousness.
- Not committing adultery will not cause me to love my wife.
- Not yelling and fighting will not remove anger.
- Acting more humble will not remove pride.
- Not stealing will not remove greed.
- Not fornicating will not remove lust.

Such rules are mere human teachings about things that deteriorate as we use them. These rules may seem wise because they require strong devotion, pious self-denial, and severe bodily discipline. But **they provide no help in conquering a person's evil desires** (Colossians 2:22-23 NLT).

Our behavior is the fruit of the roots in us. Pruning fruit does not lessen the trees ability to produce fruit, it actually increases it by strengthening the root.

The flow of who we are is like a river. You can't stop a river by simply damming it. The flow may stop for a while, but if that river has not dried up, it will find a new channel to flow through or it will break the dam because of the pressure buildup. In either case the damage will be great. Our actions are like that river. Simply refusing them an outlet will create pressure (stress) in us. We must stop the river at the source—our thoughts. Changing our actions will not change our minds, but changing our minds will change our actions.

- Realizing that all I have belongs to God will allow me to cheerfully give where He wants.

- Musing on my wife's good qualities will make me adore her more.

- Esteeming others as greater than myself will stop me from demanding my own way.

- Knowing that I am loved and forgiven will allow me to happily humble myself.

- Valuing other people will prevent me from stealing from them.

- Recognizing that my body is the temple of the Holy Spirit will make me treat it as holy.

Lay the axe to the root and the bad fruit will fall off. The root is what is in our heart.

Those things which proceed out of the mouth come forth from the heart; and they defile the man. For out of the heart proceed evil thoughts, murders, adulteries, fornications, thefts, false witness, blasphemies (Matthew 15:18-19).

We need to think about what we are thinking about and cut off what we don't want with words. Our actions will align with what we say. What we declare in the spirit will overcome the promptings of what we feel. As we rewrite our memories, we will develop neural pathways that will allow an expression to positive emotions.

Rewriting (developing new neural pathways) is not just substitution of one thought for another; rewriting requires seeing God in the picture. Jesus could transcend the limits of the physical world because He saw into the spiritual realm. We can rise above and go beyond the limits of our thoughts when we see Jesus in every situation. Our stress comes when we are fighting things over which we have no control. If we recognize that Jesus has been given all authority in Heaven and on earth, then through Him we also have that authority (see Matt. 28:18). The more we see that God is in control, the more we will be able to recognize His presence, even in the places where we thought we were alone.

Recently we had to change a clause in the Memorandum of Association for our charitable corporation. Unfortunately this required us to get a court order to authorize the new direction we wanted to take the charity. I (Ken) was at a loss of how to proceed. I checked the Internet, made phone calls, and even went to talk to a clerk at the local courthouse to no avail. We quickly scheduled a meeting of our board to pass a special resolution authorizing the changes. Finally one of my contacts yielded an email with some instructions.

I rushed to the court room the next day at 8:00 A.M., and after several misdirections and waiting in various lines, I was connected to a former court clerk who knew all the ins and outs of courtroom procedure. Even though none of the assistants had ever seen my particular problem, they were able to do the paperwork and get me before a judge at 10:00 A.M. They warned me that the judge would be adverse to a non-lawyer representing a corporation, but if I was lucky he might allow it.

As I sat in the courtroom, I could feel the stress in my chest. I had gotten further than I had hoped, but now I needed more favor to finish this quest that I was on. Sure enough the judge was not happy with my presence and told me so. He also said that I had things out of order and that my paperwork was missing a page. He said that I needed to file before he would sign, though the ladies had told me he needed to sign before I could file. I could see that this was not going to work when suddenly the judge shifted his demeanor and consented to sign if I included the missing page in my deposition.

I hurried back to find my helper only to discover that I needed to again sign my name to the bottom of the waiting list. There were four people in front of me, and the lady I had worked with had her door closed. If I didn't connect immediately, the court would be closed, the judge gone, and my case would be sitting in limbo. I said a quick prayer crying out for help. Suddenly two of the people in front of me in the line were simultaneously called up just as my clerk stepped out of her office. She called the next two names on the list but no one responded, so I rejoined her.

As my clerk went out to copy the missing page, one of the people who was in front of me on the list noticed her and asked if she was free, as he had been waiting for her. She had called but he had not heard, even though the waiting room was actually a library and he had been sitting only twenty feet from where she had called out. She said she was sorry, but she was dealing with me now. Apparently you snooze, you lose. An hour later, I left the courthouse with my court order signed and filed and found two minutes remaining on my parking meter.

When I got home I found an email informing me of the proper procedure for filing which included first going to registries and giving them 10 days to process the changes before going to court. I phoned the person in charge and explained that I apparently jumped queue and already had the court order. She couldn't believe what I had accomplished and told me to send it in. She said doing what I had done would likely knock a week off the registry time.

I had stepped into a situation that should have required a lawyer at a cost of over a thousand dollars, got a court order in three hours that should have taken two weeks, skipped the 10-day registry time, and got home for lunch. I counted five separate instances where God intervened, allowing me to pass through the legal labyrinth without me having a clue what I was doing. Jesus promised, *"…I will never desert you, nor will I ever forsake you"* (Heb. 13:5 NASB). The stress I felt being out of control would not have compared with the stress had He not been in control. "Thank You, Jesus."

> *You search the Scriptures because you think that in them you have eternal life; it is **these that testify about Me*** (John 5:39 NASB).

> *All of us, as with unveiled face… **behold [in the Word of God]** as in a mirror **the glory of the Lord**, are constantly being trans-figured into His very own image…* (2 Corinthians 3:18 AMP).

That is how we change the way we think and are transformed—seeing Jesus in the Scriptures and in our situations. The Bible has principles in it, it has rules, it has examples, but it is the Word of God and Jesus is that Word. The Bible reveals the beauty, authority, power, and character of God.

> *For God, who commanded the light to shine out of darkness, hath shined in our hearts, to give the light of the **knowledge of the glory of God in the face of Jesus Christ*** (2 Corinthians 4:6).

As we see Jesus in the Bible, we will see God, and our thoughts and perceptions will be changed into His thoughts and wisdom. Our toxic thoughts will be replaced by His word and His love for us.

AUTHORITY ON EARTH

Part of that change will be the way we see authority. *"The heavens are the heavens of the Lord, but the earth He has given to the sons of men"* (Ps. 115:16 NASB). We have authority on the earth; God has the power. Satan has no rights or power to operate here except we give it to him. He is only *"the god of this world"* because men blindly yielded their authority to him (2 Cor. 4:4 NASB). Satan lost his access to Heaven when he rebelled, but stealthily got it back by taking robbing Adam of his place (see Ezek. 28:13-17; Job 1:6-7). As soon as Jesus appointed the seventy disciples, they had authority over the enemy.

> *The seventy returned again with joy, saying, Lord, even the devils are subject unto us through thy name. And He said unto them, I beheld* **Satan as lightning fall from heaven.** *Behold, I give unto you power to tread on serpents and scorpions, and over all the power of the enemy: and nothing shall by any means hurt you* (Luke 10:17-19).

When the disciples took Jesus's authority as their authority, satan began to lose his access to Heaven. Jesus completed that victory when He rose from the dead. At that point an angel announced:

> *Now is come salvation, and strength, and the Kingdom of our God, and the power of His Christ: for the accuser of our brethren is cast down, which accused them before our God day and night* (Revelation 12:10).

Now satan's only place to bring an accusation is in our minds. If we refuse the accusations, he will have no access to give us toxic thoughts and we will have peace as we walk in Jesus's authority.

We spoke a word to someone as we were ministering in a foreign country, but it seemed to fall to the ground. The person was having marriage issues and never responded to the word we spoke. We were immediately attacked that the word we gave may have been inappropriate or even incorrect. Talking together that night, we decided to commit the word to God and entered into a peace. If we were wrong, we would admit it and repent. A year later we were told that the word we gave had a great impact on their marriage and brought them healing. Since there had been no initial response, we were admittedly surprised but delighted. Satan's accusation had not taken root because we had not received it.

Prayer

> *Lord, we repent for believing that the enemy still has authority over us and we declare that as Jesus has authority over the enemy in this world, so do we. Amen* (see 1 John 4:17).

We have also been given authority to perform miracles. Jesus said, *"The person who trusts Me will not only do what I'm doing but even greater things…"* (John 14:12 MSG). Miracles appear wondrous because we don't understand the laws that control them, which overrule the natural laws. Jesus could miraculously walk on water and walk through walls (see Matt. 14:25-29; John 20:19). God showed me that even these miracles operated on higher laws.

Solid objects are not solid; they appear solid because of the movement of the electrons. But over 99 percent of the space occupied by an atom is empty. That is why a small particle like an x-ray can pass through seemingly solid objects. After His resurrection, Jesus walked through the wall of the upper room where the disciples were meeting behind locked doors.

> *…Jesus Himself stood in the midst of them, and said to them, "Peace to you." But they were terrified and frightened, and* **supposed they had seen a spirit**. *And He said to them, "Why are you troubled? And why do doubts arise in your hearts? Behold My hands and My feet, that it is I Myself. Handle Me and see, for* **a spirit does not have flesh and bones** *as you see I have* (Luke 24:36-39 NKJV).

Jesus synced the molecules in the wall with His molecular structure and easily stepped through open spaces in the wall.

On the reverse end of the scale, Jesus demonstrated that by synchronizing the molecules of water opposite to His molecules, they became solid and able to support Him. Peter was also able, in faith, to walk on water. When he took his eyes off Jesus, he got out of sync with Him and thus out of sync with the water, and he sank. God has more ways to alter the structure of water than just through temperature. God is increasing our faith and authority to be able to do whatever He commands, and He uses His creation to work in harmony with us to achieve His goals. We need to throw out any thinking that says everything is conspiring against us to prevent us from reaching our goals. The truth is that God has ordained *"that all things work together for good to them that love God"* (Rom. 8:28).

FAITH

Faith is one of the most discussed and least understood aspects of life and therefore has led to much disappointment, confusion, and stress. Faith is only mentioned twice in the Old Testament, so understanding its fulfillment is related to Jesus appearing on the scene. Jesus came to manifest the Father to us and faith is an aspect of that relationship. The relationship of marriage will not last unless both partners in that relationship are happy. If one is upset, the intimacy is disrupted and peace is lost. Hopelessness sets in when we don't know what upset the other one.

That is why God made it clear that it is impossible to please God without faith (see Heb. 11:5). To operate in faith we must believe the best about God.

> *God is not a man, so He does not lie. He is not human, so He does not change His mind. Has He ever spoken and failed to act? Has He ever promised and not carried it through?* (Numbers 23:19 NLT)

It is faith in God's character, not faith in the outcome, that pleases God. Knowing that God is pleased with us will take away most of the stress in our lives.

We tend to think that great faith will produce answers immediately, yet Abraham, who is the father of faith, waited 25 years to get his answer. If we understand how faith works, many of our toxic thoughts about our relationship with God will be healed. Jesus pointed out two individuals who He said had great faith. One was a Roman centurion and the other was a Canaanite lady. They had one thing in common—they were both Gentiles who were not under the law. Trying to do it right to earn God's favor doesn't take faith because *"the law is not of faith"* (Gal. 3:12).

Both these individuals knew that they were not worthy to receive what they were asking for. At first, Jesus didn't even offer the Canaanite women healing for her daughter. Jesus even said that it wasn't right to take the children's bread (healing) and give it to ones the Jews considered dogs (see Matt. 15:26). Despite the insult, *"She came and, kneeling, worshiped Him and kept praying, Lord, help me!"* (Matt. 15:25 AMP).

She took that insult as an opportunity to humble herself, and removing herself from the equation, she replied, *"Yes, Lord; but even the dogs feed on the crumbs which fall from their masters' table"* (Matt. 15:27 NASB). She knew she didn't need the full manifestation of the miracle, *even a little crumb* from the master's table would do. True faith does not have confidence in the outcome; true faith has confidence in the Lord.

Being equally humble, the centurion didn't feel worthy to come to Jesus himself, so *"...he sent some Jewish elders asking Him to come and save the life of his slave"* (Luke 7:3 NASB). Jesus happily responded.

> *...When He was not far from the house, the centurion sent friends, saying to Him, "Lord, do not trouble Yourself further, for* **I am not worthy** *for You to come under my roof...**just say the word**, and my servant will be healed* (Luke 7:6-7 NASB).

> *Now when Jesus heard this, He marveled at him, and turned and said to the crowd that was following Him, "I say to you, not even in Israel have I found such* **great faith**" (Luke 7:9 NASB).

The centurion was *satisfied with the seed*—Jesus's words—and didn't require Jesus to come and perform a miracle. The miracle was not about his worth or his character, it was about the character of Jesus. Too long we have thought that God required us to add to what He was doing. We don't add; we simply receive.

In the time of Elisha, a Syrian captain called Naaman was a leper who also heard about the healing power of the God of Israel. He originally thought that to get a miracle, the prophet would do something great

> *...I thought that he would surely come out to me and stand and call on the name of the Lord his God, wave his hand over the spot and cure me of my leprosy* (2 Kings 5:11 NIV).

But Elisha didn't even come out to talk to him. He just sent his servant, who gave him a word to dip seven times in the Jordan River.

> *...So he turned and went off in a rage. Naaman's servants went to him and said, "My father, if the prophet had told you to* **do some great thing**, *would you not have done it? How much more, then, when he tells you,* '**Wash and be cleansed**. *So he went down and dipped himself in the Jordan seven times...and his flesh was restored and became clean like that of a young boy* (2 Kings 5:12-14 NIV).

Simple obedience had brought total healing of the leprosy.

Naaman thought to have a great miracle required great acts. God wanted to show him that little seeds of faith can grow into big miracles when we obediently plant them. We won't plant them when our toxic memories cause us to doubt God's ability or His willingness to help. Each one of these people had to overcome their own prejudices and doubts to properly respond. They were mentioned by Jesus as an example of *how faith works—taking a little seed* and *trusting* in the power of *God* to use that seed to produce what is needed. His own disciples once asked Jesus to increase their faith.

> *The apostles said to the Lord, Increase our faith.... And the Lord answered, If you had* **faith** *(trust and confidence in God) even [so small] like a grain of mustard seed, you could say to this*

mulberry tree, Be pulled up by the roots, and be planted in the sea, and it would obey you (Luke 17:5-6 AMP).

Jesus told His disciples that *all you need is the seed.* They too were looking for miracles to result from greater faith; Jesus pointed them to the seed to obtain greater faith. Then He spoke a parable to illustrate His point.

> *Which of you, having a slave plowing or tending sheep, will say to him when he has come in from the field, "Come immediately and sit down to eat"? But will he not say to him, "Prepare something for me to eat, and properly clothe yourself and serve me while I eat and drink; and afterward you may eat and drink"? He does not thank the slave because he did the things which were commanded, does he? So you too, when you do all the things which are commanded you, say, "**We are unworthy slaves**; we have done only that which we ought to have done"* (Luke 17:7-10 NASB).

Jesus is repeating that faith is not about us; it's about Him, in seed form. Jesus wanted His disciples to get their eyes off of themselves, just as this servant did. He realized that even though he seemed unworthy or worthless he was able to serve and please the master and still do whatever he was commanded. We have to say when it comes to faith: "It's not about me" and how I earn it. That is a toxic lie that blocks us from getting our breakthrough. Believing that only worthy people get their prayers answered causes us to assume that God is disappointed and angry at us because we don't measure up. None of us deserve to get anything from God, but it's not about us; it's about Jesus being worthy. Faith is not earned; we just receive it and release it.

Prayer

> *Lord, I repent of believing that I had to use faith to pry a miracle out of Your hands. I repent of believing that You won't answer my prayers because I have not been pleasing to You. I repent of believing that You won't answer my prayers because I*

am not righteous enough. I repent of believing that You didn't answer because I didn't see results. I declare now that You want to answer more than I want an answer and that You love me and see me as You see Jesus. I declare, as You declared, that before I call, You will answer; while I am still speaking, You will hear (see Isa. 65:24). *Lord, I put my faith in You and not in the manifestation of my prayers. You are good all the time and You said, "Call to Me, and I will answer you, and show you great and mighty things, which you do not know"* (Jer. 33:3 NKJV). *I trust You.*

SEED OF FAITH

Faith is not just something we believe; it is something we say. *"The righteousness of faith speaks..."* (Rom. 10:6 NKJV). Thoughts will die or be eliminated by the glial cells if they are not given a voice to reinforce them. When Jesus was instructing His disciples on how to get out of worry He said, *"Take no thought, saying, What shall we eat? or, What shall we drink? or, Wherewithal shall we be clothed?"* (Matt. 6:31). Speaking will sow either the seed of doubt or the seed of faith. By saying what God says to us, a seed is planted that is not dependent on circumstances; it is dependent on the life in the seed. Thus whoever believes *"will have whatever he says"* (Mark 11:23 NKJV).

The faith seed we are planting is actually Jesus in seed form. *"Faith is the substance of things hoped for, the evidence of things not seen"* (Heb. 11:1). The word *substance* comes from the Greek word *hupŏstasis*. That word is used earlier in Hebrews concerning Jesus, who was *"the brightness of His glory, and the express image of His person..."* (Heb 1:3). The word *person* is also *hupŏstasis*. **Therefore the substance of faith is the person of Jesus.** He is the seed that will produce the things we are hoping for.

Mary activated her faith when she received God, in seed form, into her womb. She spoke permission for God to implant His DNA into her womb. That seed of God grew into the baby Jesus. That baby, conceived by her faith, conquered sin, satan, hell, and death when He reached His destiny. The same happens to us; we pray, God speaks the answer, we believe, we receive the seed of Jesus into the situation, and the seed grows into the manifestation of what we believed for. Our job is to receive and to incubate the Word (Jesus) until it is birthed. Going back to that word from God prevented Mary from getting bitter and wounded from the accusations that surrounded Jesus's birth.

God told me (Ken) that I would write a book ten years before I ever put pen to paper. When the time was right, I received the outline for our first two books in a 45-minute download. Once when I lost a job and was worried, God told me not to worry as I would have another one soon. Before the night was out a job, which paid double the one I lost, tracked me down (see Deut 28:2). God is faithful to His word!

God told me (Jeanne) that I didn't have breast cancer even though the mammogram showed two lumps. I declared, "It's nothing," out loud in the examining room in agreement with God's word. The next mammogram came into agreement with the word and showed no evidence of any lumps.

The life is in the seed. We don't have to understand how God will do the work; we just have to exercise our faith (plant the seed) and mix it with the word spoken to our heart. Israel heard the word that they could possess the Promised Land, "...but the word which they heard did not profit them, not being mixed with faith in those who heard it" (Heb. 4:2 NKJV). Our unbelief is directly connected to our toxic memories. If we believe the lies buried in our memories, we will not believe the truth declared by our God. True faith is faith in the seed—Jesus, the Word of God—not faith in the outcome.

I (Ken) had gout in my big toes for twelve years. I prayed for many years but nothing seemed to happen. I repented, fasted, asked forgiveness, cast things out, rebuked, declared, believed, cursed, bound, unbound, spoke deliverance, and refused the lying symptoms but still had the gout. I finally quit trying and stopped praying about it altogether. I resigned myself to living with the pain, but the seed was still in my heart. As I forgot about the gout and concentrated on the Lord, that seed was growing, though I was unaware. My awareness of what was happening to the word of healing that had been planted was not vital to its ability to come to fruit.

I awoke one night with a start. I don't know if an angel nudged me or if one just entered the room, but something jarred me out of my sleep. As I looked around for the cause of my sudden wakefulness, I realized that my toes didn't hurt and that I could wiggle them freely! I was healed! I hadn't prayed for my toes for more than two years. Jesus manifested as the healing that I had prayed for and planted a dozen years before. He is the substance of what we are hoping for and if we will plant Him in faith into our situation, He will manifest as the answer. Trust in God removes all striving and worry concerning a problem. Faith is activating that trust by simply having a good opinion of God and His ability, not our effort or our ability.

UNVEILING JESUS OPENS THE DOOR TO THE KINGDOM

A while back, I came up to our car in a crowded parking lot and hit the unlock button on the key but the door didn't open. I tried it again and still no response. I thought that perhaps the electric locks had messed up so I tried the key in the door only to finally realize that I was trying to open the wrong door; it was not our car. It was the same model, same color but not our car. Ours was parked two stalls down. God has given us many keys, but we often try to use them to open the wrong door.

Jesus said, *"I am the door; if anyone enters through Me, he will be saved, and will go in and out and find pasture"* (John 10:9 NASB). This is not the door to Heaven, as people do not usually go in and out of Heaven; this is the door to the Kingdom. God opened that door when Jesus dismissed His spirit on the cross and *"...breathed His last. At that moment, the Temple curtain was ripped in two, top to bottom..."* (Matt. 27:50-51 MSG). God opened the door of access to Himself by tearing the curtain or veil that covered the Ark of His presence. Now, *"we have confidence to enter the Holy Place by the blood of Jesus, by a new and living way which He inaugurated for us through the veil, that is, His flesh* (Heb. 10:19-20 NASB). We need to be healed of our toxic memories that say we are not able to come into God's presence because we are unworthy. True, we are not worthy, but Jesus was and He opened the way for us.

The key to expanding God's presence in us is to unveil Jesus as Lord. Unveiling our sin only makes us sin-conscious and will not change or heal our memories. Unveiling Jesus makes us God-conscious and allows the Holy Spirit access into our head and into our heart.

> *So all of us who have had that veil removed can see and reflect the glory of the Lord. And the Lord—who is the Spirit—makes us more and more like Him as we are changed into His glorious image* (2 Corinthians 3:18 NLT).

Our toxic memories will accuse us, causing us to re-erect that veil and shut us out of God's presence. Changing what we think allows us to see the truth, and the truth will make you free (see John 3:32).

KEYS

- God loves His creation, both the physical and spiritual realms.

- Don't bury wounds; reveal them and let the Lord heal them.

- Our health depends on believing in Jesus's physical resurrection.

- God hates it when we mix performance with grace.

- The Law is designed to make our need of Jesus paramount.

- The Law is holy but can't make us holy.

- We have authority on earth; satan only has access to the authority we give him.

- Performance is not connected to faith.

- Great faith is not about us; it is about receiving the Word in seed form.

- The seed of faith is the person of Jesus planted in a situation.

- Faith needs to be declared to be empowered.

- The key to success is to unveil Jesus.

Chapter 12

GRATEFUL HEART, PEACEFUL REST

The most valuable possession you can own is an open heart. The most powerful weapon you can be is an instrument of peace. —CARLOS SANTANA

God has two dwellings; one in heaven, and the other in a meek and thankful heart. —IZAAK WALTON

Keep your eyes open to your mercies. The man who forgets to be thankful has fallen asleep in life. —ROBERT LOUIS STEVENSON

BEING GRATEFUL AND THANKFUL

"Oh, give thanks to the Lord, for He is good! For His mercy endures forever" (1 Chron. 16:34 NKJV). We want to thank God because He is good, not just because He does good. We want to thank Him because His mercy endures forever, not just because He was merciful. Gratefulness and thankfulness are to flow from a mindset and not just as responses to favorable situations. The Levites were appointed to look after all the duties in the house of the Lord. *"They are also to stand every morning to thank and praise the Lord, and likewise at evening"* (1 Chron. 23:30 AMP). They praised and thanked God in the morning, before anything happened, and in the evening, no matter what things happened.

It is interesting that the word for thanksgiving comes from the Hebrew root *yâdâh,* which means "an open hand extended."[1] This word is also used as one of the expressions of praise and is the word used for confession of sin (see Ps. 32:5). From this we can surmise that those who are not repentant are not grateful! We must change our mind (repent) to be grateful no matter what comes. We need to change our minds to believe that God is good all the time, no matter what comes. We need to repent to believe that God is merciful, no matter what happens.

If we look at what the devil is doing, we will continually be anxious and worried. If we are watching what God is doing, we will be filled with gratitude, peace, and thanks. Being thankful is a lifestyle, not an event. Most of our prayers are petitions, asking God to change some situation or circumstance. That is the problem—we are looking at the problem and not at the Lord. When the children of Israel were bitten by the snakes in the wilderness, they had to look away from their wounds to the bronze snake to get healed.

Problems become idols—they occupy our energy and attention if we let them define who we are. If we continue to view our problems as part of us, we will become like them. We will be paralyzed and unable to speak, see, hear, or move in concert with God (see Ps. 115:4-8). Lot's wife looked back, viewing the destruction of Sodom and Gomorrah, and was destroyed (see Gen. 19:26). What we fixate on, we become. Look at Jesus if you have been bitten. *"...If a serpent bit any man, when he looked to the bronze serpent, he lived"* (Num. 21:9 NASB).

I (Jeanne) was ministering to a lady friend whose husband was working in Brazil. While he was there, he began an affair with someone involved in witchcraft. When I placed my hands on my friend, I felt a jolt of electricity go through me and I saw in the spirit a large eel. Not knowing what that represented, I excused myself and went to our encyclopedia set (this was before the Internet). I found out that some of the eels in South America use large electric shocks to immobilize their victims.

Now the shock I got and the picture made sense. My friend was so fearful of what was happening in her life that she was paralyzed with fear. I knew that the lady in witchcraft had been praying against my friend, so I got her to repent of allowing fear to come into her life, bound the demonic prayers that had been prayed against her, and broke off the paralyzing fear. She was immediately released from the fear and was able to function in her life again. Satan is frantic for us to look at what he is doing so he can immobilize us.

Jesus ministered to ten lepers, then sent them to see the priest.

> ...*It came to pass, that, as they went, they were cleansed. And one of them, when he saw that he was healed, turned back, and with a loud voice glorified God, and **fell down on his face at His feet, giving Him thanks**: and he was a Samaritan* (Luke 17:14-16).

Jesus was shocked that only one returned to give thanks.

> *Were there not **ten cleansed**? but where are the nine? There are not found that returned to give glory to God, save this stranger. And He said unto him, Arise, go thy way: **thy faith hath made thee whole*** (Luke 17:17-19).

Ten were cleansed, but only one was made whole. The word *whole* is the Greek word *sōzō*, which means to save.[2] We don't just want our problems eliminated; we want a complete salvation—body, soul, and spirit. If our problems are fixed but we are not, we are doomed to recreate the same errors. Being thankful and looking at Jesus allows God to do a work in us, not just for us.

This didn't happen when one of Judah's kings fell ill.

> *In those days, Hezekiah became mortally ill; and he prayed to the Lord, and the Lord spoke to him and gave him a sign. But Hezekiah gave **no return for the benefit** he received, because **his heart was proud*** (2 Chronicles 32:24-25 NASB).

God healed him, did a miracle as a sign, and yet Hezekiah was not grateful. Later, Hezekiah revealed the state of his heart when he was rebuked by

Isaiah concerning the ambassadors from Babylon. Hezekiah showed them all the treasures of his kingdom, never suspecting that these emissaries were spies. Isaiah was in despair as he prophesied that in the future everything in the palace would be hauled off to Babylon.

> …*God says that there will be nothing left. Nothing. And not only your things but your sons. Some of your sons will be taken into exile, ending up as eunuchs in the palace of the king of Babylon. Hezekiah replied to Isaiah, "Good. If God says so, **it's good**." Within himself he was thinking, "But surely **nothing bad will happen in my lifetime**. I'll enjoy peace and stability as long as I live"* (Isaiah 39:6-8 MSG).

Hezekiah was healed, but he was not changed or thankful and certainly was not made whole. He was disconnected from his family; he didn't care that disaster was coming for them as long as it didn't happen to him. That attitude affected his children, especially his son Manasseh who was born during the extra fifteen years that Hezekiah lived (see Isa. 38:5; 2 Kings 21:9).

Manasseh means "forgetting," and Manasseh felt forgotten.[3] Hezekiah was a great king; only one other king tore down the high places and commemorated the Passover. Yet he was not grateful; *Hezekiah gave no return for the benefit he received.* Because he was not grateful, he could not repent or change his selfish nature toward his family. This produced anger and resentment in Manasseh, and poisoned by his toxic memories he became the cruelest and most rebellious king Judah produced. Though Hezekiah was one of the great kings of Judah, he could not pass it to the next generation because he could not change his mind. When God tested his heart, Hezekiah was found lacking; not only in compassion for his family but in gratefulness to his God.

That unthankful and ungrateful attitude infected Israel as soon as they came out of Egypt. When they complained about lack of food, God sent them manna. Israel found fault and complained about the manna,[4] which God called bread from Heaven and angels' food (see Exod. 16:4; Ps. 78:25).

"The Israelites named it manna (What is it?)..." (Exod. 16:31 MSG). For the next 40 years they ate the "whatever it was" but despised it. They *"ate the bread of the mighty"* but called it *"light (contemptible, unsubstantial) manna"* (Ps. 78:25; Num. 21:5 AMP). For 40 years, that ungrateful attitude infected them as they continually griped about their plight. They forgot that they had been slaves, that their children had been killed, and that they were beaten if they didn't produce enough. They blocked the bad memories and created a fantasy about their former life.

There have been many instances of physically abused women who have left their abusive husbands only to go back when the men convince them that they have changed. The women excuse and forget the bad times and build a picture of their perfect family in their minds. Friends and family counsel them not to go back, as they can accurately discern the lack of change. Tragically, some of these women have ended up murdered when their husband's rage went out of control. In these women's minds, the false perception of their husband's mental state outweighed the truth. We need to be delivered from false memories if we are to discern the truth.

> The rabble with them began to crave other food, and again the Israelites started wailing and said, "If only we had meat to eat! We remember the fish we ate in Egypt at no cost—also the cucumbers, melons, leeks, onions and garlic. But now we have lost our appetite; we never see anything but this manna! (Numbers 11:4-6 NIV)

They selectively remembered the good and forgot the bad. Ten times they tested God and treated Him with contempt by grumbling, complaining, and being ungrateful when things didn't go their way (see Num. 14:22-23).

Do we see the cup as half full or half empty? Thankfulness is a mindset; griping is a mindset. We've noticed that as people get older they stop trying to hide what they feel. They say what they want and don't care who hears. They drift into one of two streams; they either become bitter or better.

They become mean and cantankerous or they become sweet and grateful. We are all moving toward one of those goals. We should: *"Confess your faults one to another, and pray one for another, that ye may be healed* (James 5:16). If we keep it bottled up, we are just storing it up to be uncorked at an inconvenient time. Confess your toxic memories now so you can be thankful later.

Contentment is the plumb line we use to measure if we are grateful or not. Paul said:

> ...*I have learned **in whatever state I am, to be content**: I know how to be abased, and I know how to abound. Everywhere and in all things I have learned both to be full and to be hungry, both to abound and to suffer need. **I can do all things through Christ who strengthens me*** (Philippians 4:11-13).

Paul used the strength of Christ to empower him to be content no matter what his situation.

When we are not content with our situation, we open the door to envy—wanting someone else's position, situation, or possessions. The Pharisees pretended that they wanted Jesus crucified because He blasphemed by making Himself equal to God, but Pilate *"knew that it was because of envy that they had handed Him over to him"* (Matt. 27:18 AMP). Envy put Jesus on the cross, not just the Pharisee's envy but our envy—He died for us.

Our first house was just 800 square feet, but it was a palace to us. When it rained the basement flooded, but we were so grateful to have our own home that it didn't matter. I thank God for that problem, for I (Ken) got a solution to fix the problem from God. That was the beginning of many dreams and words that God was to give me. These words made me look like an expert even though I often knew nothing. Today we are in a much larger house with many amenities, but we were just as happy in our little house. We have maintained an attitude of gratefulness, and that has allowed God to give us much. If we gripe about what God has already given, why would you expect Him to give you more to gripe about?

Envy prompted satan's rebellion. He said, *"I will ascend above the heights of the clouds; I will make myself like the Most High"* (Isa. 14:14 AMP). Envy prompted Eve to sin, for the devil deceived her saying, *"In the day you eat of it your eyes will be opened, and you will be like God…"* (Gen. 3:5 NKJV). Even Cain murdering Abel was a result of envy (see Gen. 4:3-5).

> *If ye have bitter envying and strife in your hearts, glory not…. This wisdom…is earthly, sensual, devilish. For where envying and strife is, there is **confusion** and every evil work* (James 3:14-16).

Envy will bring confusion to our minds; contentment lets us see clearly as God sees.

Prayer

> *Lord, forgive me for being ungrateful and unthankful and opening the door for envy and jealousy to come into my life. I ask You to strengthen me through Jesus to repent and change my mind about my situation and to be content with the good life You have given me. I bless those who have more than me.*

GOD THE REWARDER

Israel forgot that for 40 years they never worked, their clothes and sandals didn't wear out, God supplied food and water, defeated their enemies, provided shade by day and heat by night. They had skewed vision, thinking everything in the past was better. Their denial was a type of repression, where the Israelites as a group pushed all the bad experiences and emotions into the subconscious.[5]

God could have healed them if they had trusted and obeyed Him, but they would not. God warned them:

> *Because you did not **serve the Lord** your God **with joy and a glad heart**, for the **abundance of all things**; therefore you **shall serve your enemies** whom the Lord will send against you, in*

*hunger, in thirst, in nakedness, and **in the lack of all things**...*
(Deuteronomy 28:47-48 NASB).

Their words continually propagated the lie they believed—that they were better off as slaves. A mindset of joy and gratitude effectively closes the door to the enemy's activity in our lives by keeping his thoughts out of our minds and off our lips.

Our son Michael entered a Mother's Day contest as a young boy and prayed that he would win. The prize was a large credit at our family's favorite restaurant. A week later, we got a phone call that he had won. Immediately, he bowed his head and thanked God. The whole family, grandparents included, went out for a wonderful supper on Mother's Day. The kids ordered everything they wanted, including desserts, and we still couldn't spend the entire prize. It was a tearful grace as we thanked God for blessing us.

God does not want slaves, He wants sons and daughters who will reign with Him (see 2 Tim. 2:12). A son *"who comes to God must believe that He is and that He is a rewarder of those who seek Him"* (Heb. 11:6 NASB). Jesus told His disciples:

> *I promise you...nobody leaves home or brothers or sisters or mother or father or children or property for My sake and the Gospel's without **getting back a hundred times over**, now in this present life, homes and brothers and sisters, mothers and children and land—though not without persecution—and in the next world eternal life* (Mark 10:29-30 PNT).

We must change what we believe. We don't work in order to receive an inheritance, we simply inherit. When God was correcting David over his adultery and murder, He said:

> *I gave you your master's house and your master's wives into your keeping, and gave you the house of Israel and Judah. And **if that had been too little**, I also would have **given you much more**!*

Why have you despised the commandment of the Lord, to do evil in His sight? (2 Samuel 12:8-9 NKJV)

David acted like a king in taking what he wanted. God wanted him to act like a son and ask his Father for what he needed.

David already had more than he needed. He gave the equivalent of over $200 billion in gold and $45 billion in silver to build the temple out of his own funds (see 1 Chron. 22:14). That didn't include all the iron, the bronze, the timber, and the cut stone, which was not weighed as there was too much. David was a multi-billionaire, but God told him *if that had been too little, I also would have given you much more.*

I am not suggesting that all Christians should be millionaires, but all should be fruitful whatever their station in life. God is not short of wealth and is not cheap with His children. We need to break out of whatever poverty mindset has locked us up and repent, to believe God is:

Him Who, by (in consequence of) the [action of His] power that is at work within us, is able to [carry out His purpose and] do super-abundantly, far over and above all that we [dare] ask or think [infinitely beyond our highest prayers, desires, thoughts, hopes, or dreams] (Ephesians 3:20 AMP).

The Kingdom already belongs to us; we don't have to strive to get it (see Luke 12:32).

An inability to sit and rest is an inability to trust God for what is coming. Always striving and never resting in God's supply was the primary cause of Israel being removed from the Promised Land. It wasn't their sin; it wasn't their unfaithfulness; it wasn't their lack of social justice; it was their unwillingness to rest on the Sabbath that sealed their fate. After coming out of slavery, God instructed them to give their land a Sabbath rest every seven years. For 490 years they didn't trust God enough to obey that command.

Seventy years of captivity was the equivalent of the missed Sabbaths that Israel had refused to take (490 divided by 7 equals 70). The covenant they made with God was to rest the land every seven years. Even though God supplied enough food for three years during the sixth year (see Lev. 25:20-22), Israel couldn't rest on the seventh because they didn't have a son's mindset of abundance. They were still stuck in the slave mindset of lack. God supplied a triple harvest on the sixth year, but they hated the thought of depending on God. They had more than enough, but to a slave when is enough, enough? Never!

> *Roll your works upon the Lord [commit and trust them wholly to Him; He will **cause your thoughts to become agreeable to His will**, and] so shall your plans be established and succeed* (Proverbs 16:3 AMP).

If we let God have control, His thoughts will become our thoughts and we will be free from worry. What are His thoughts? Thoughts of peace, not of evil, to give you an expected end (see Jer. 29:11). *"How precious are your thoughts about me, O God. They cannot be numbered!"* (Ps. 139:17 NLT). We need to learn to receive from God, allowing Him *"...through His mighty power at work within us, to accomplish infinitely more than we might ask or think"* (Eph. 3:20 NLT). We need a revelation of God as a Father of rest. Jesus said:

> *Come to Me, all of you who are weary and carry heavy burdens, and I will give you rest. Take My yoke upon you. Let Me teach you, because I am humble and gentle at heart, and you will find rest for your souls. For My yoke is easy to bear, and the burden I give you is light* (Matthew 11:28-30 NLTP).

The world has no rest because they have no Father looking after them. We have a Father who loves us. If we can be delivered from our toxic memories concerning fathers, then we can rest in the Father's love and not worry about His supply.

> *Do not set your heart on what you will eat or drink; **do not worry about it**. For the pagan world runs after all such things,*

*and **your Father knows that you need them**. But seek His Kingdom, and these things will be given to you as well* (Luke 12:29-31 NIV).

If we are resting in God, we know the Father is watching and we can venture to do new things. When Peter was walking on the water, he panicked. *"...When he looked down at the waves churning beneath his feet, he lost his nerve and started to sink. He cried, 'Master, save me!'"* (Matt. 14:30 MSG).

Peter panicked when he saw the wind and the waves, but the wind and the waves were just a distraction, they were not a danger. If there had been no wind and waves, Peter, in the natural, could not have walked on the water. Satan tries to get our eyes off of Jesus by bringing distractions. The distraction is not the problem; the sickness is not the problem; the financial problem is not the problem. The problem comes when we look at what satan is doing (creating wind and waves) and take our eyes off the Lord and what He is doing. We are not to think less of ourselves; we are to think of ourselves less.

*Let us strip off every weight that slows us down, especially the sin that so easily trips us up. And **let us run with endurance the race God has set before us**. We do this by **keeping our eyes on Jesus**, the champion **who initiates and perfects our faith*** (Hebrews 12:1-2 NLT).

Getting our eyes off of us and looking at Jesus will keep our mind in a right perspective.

Satan is out to destroy the world, but God has commissioned us to act as ambassadors for Christ (see 2 Cor. 5:20 NASB). *"...That the world through Him might be saved"* (John 3:17). If we are to be proper ambassadors, we must know the will of the King, we must think like the King, and we must speak like the King. We can do that because we already have the mind of Christ (see 1 Cor. 2:16). All that is left for us to do to enter our destiny is to be delivered from our toxic memories. God will do that for us as we forgive, forget, and rewrite those memories in the light of God's faithfulness and mercy.

> *Although the fig tree shall not blossom, neither shall fruit be in the vines; the labour of the olive shall fail, and the fields shall yield no meat; the flock shall be cut off from the fold, and there shall be no herd in the stalls:* **yet I will rejoice in the Lord, I will joy in the God of my salvation. The Lord God is my strength** (Habakkuk 3:17-19).

Although Habakkuk was facing a destructive army from which God said there would be no deliverance, he was able to rejoice because he trusted in the character of God rather than the situation.

Job said of God, *"Though He slay me, yet will I trust in Him…"* (Job 13:15). Paul said, *"In every thing give thanks: for this is the will of God in Christ Jesus concerning you"* (1 Thess. 5:18). Every hero of the faith came to the same conclusion: *"If we are faithless [do not believe and are untrue to Him], He remains true (faithful to His Word and His righteous character), for He cannot deny Himself"* (2 Tim. 2:13 AMP). Fix it in your mind—God is good, all the time.

KEYS

God has prepared a place of rest for us.

Abiding, not striving, will produce fruit.

Jesus has conquered the enemy and has given us the keys to release people.

We must keep our eyes on Jesus and off the enemy's distractions.

When God blesses, we must respond with thanksgiving.

- We must believe that God is a rewarder when we operate in faith.

- We are depending on God's character, not our nature or efforts.

- God is good—all the time.

CONCLUSION

THE SITUATION

A missionary was walking through the back streets of Hong Kong, checking out all the shops and street vendors' stalls, when he came upon a tattoo parlor. The window was filled with a variety of designs and sayings that were available inside. There were psychedelic patterns, Chinese scripts, as well as many pop art depictions. The missionary casually looked over the display and was just about to move on when one tattoo caught his eye. Curious, he entered the shop to talk to the proprietor.

An elderly, shriveled up Chinese gentleman squatting in the corner glanced up. With a surprised look on his face, he accosted the missionary with a cryptic question.

"You want tattoo?"

"No," the missionary laughed. "I have a question about one of the sayings you have in your window. One says 'Born to Lose.' Has anyone ever gotten that tattoo?"

"Oh, yes," came the reply, "many!"

"Why would anyone want to tattoo such a negative statement on their body?"

The old man rose up and approached the missionary. Reaching out his bony finger, he tapped the missionary on the head and pointedly said, "Tattooed here," and then touching his arm, "before tattooed here."

As a man thinks in his heart, so is he (see Prov. 23:7). Our thoughts become memories when we tattoo them in our mind. They permanently define who we are as they direct the flow of emotions and the recall of events that, though long buried in the past, can still impact our present and even our future. They are indelibly imprinted on our neural pathways with the intent of giving us information to draw on as we encounter life. If the information is healthy and accurate, we will joyfully make informed decisions. If the information is toxic and skewed, we will sadly stumble into the same destructive patterns that trapped us before.

Many of those memories were implanted before we were even conscious of their existence, and they will stay in the unconscious, undetectable except for the reactions that they cause. Some of the feelings they emit will be toxic and make us sick, fearful, or hopeless. Others will have life on them and make us healthy, confident, and hopeful. As the song goes:

> *You got to accentuate the positive,*
> *Eliminate the negative.*[1]

Our mind does not operate alone in storing and recalling memories. Even the ancients knew that the kidneys (reins)[2] were the seat of emotions; the heart was the organ of intelligence, and the brain was the organ of cognition. The whole body is not only involved in storing the thought processes, it is also affected by those thought processes. Because the subconscious mind hides the toxic memories from the conscious mind, it has been next to impossible to ferret out the dysfunctional thoughts.

THE HEALING

God has a solution! Forgive, forget, repent (rewrite by changing your mind). Many years ago, God gave me (Ken) a dream about the problem with my thinking. From a top view, I saw that I had a brain tumor that covered almost the entire surface of the brain. I thought, "Good, let's just cut it out and be done with it." The problem was, as my viewing angle shifted to the side, the tumor was not a solid mass but rather it was a fibrous tumor that had sent tentacles into almost every area of my brain. You could not cut it out; you needed to unravel each fiber from the neurons. This seemed like it would be a long, tedious job, but as some of the tentacles were unwrapped, others seemed to lose their grip. When the main roots were disentangled, the lesser ones released with them.

We have dealt with many toxic memories, both in our own lives and with those brave enough to let us probe around their brains. Here are some ways to detect and eliminate toxic memories.

Divine Revelation

God gives you a picture or helps you recall an event. If someone bumps into a stronghold, you'll know by your overreaction; ask God to reveal the root. If one event triggered the formation of the stronghold, seeing or reliving that event will often expose the erroneous thoughts that latched onto it which you falsely believed. If this is the keystone thought that holds up the entire stronghold, then when you forgive, forget, and rewrite this memory, the entire structure will collapse. All the logic associated with the lie will seem so ridiculous as to be ludicrous. Without the foundational lie, the rest of the thoughts become humorous instead of being poisonous. When you can laugh at what you thought and what locked you up, you know you have dismantled the stronghold.

When I (Ken) was praying about my inability to freely give, God showed me a picture of a chipmunk. This little rodent had filled his cheek pockets so full of nuts that his head was almost three times as wide as it was high. He looked ridiculous. God said that was me when I allowed greed to control me. I laughed that so small a thing could control me so completely. As I pondered my hoarding, I recalled my grandmother and a ball of string that she was saving. My grandparents were not poor or destitute, just cheap. I repented of letting their hoarding affect me and shooed that structure away. After that, I enjoyed giving people gifts and favors beyond their expectations. I was able to give with an open hand, not a clenched fist.

Familiar Thoughts

Some memories are traveled so often that they are like a four-lane highway. You want to change your thinking, but you keep traveling down that same road, bringing up the same pictures and thoughts. God recently showed me that part of bringing a thought captive means not letting it have free rein. When a horse wants to run, pulling back on the reins will slow it down and even stop it if we pull hard enough. Sometimes we don't exert our will very much when it comes to thinking. For most of us, *"You have not yet resisted to bloodshed, striving against sin,"* or a toxic memory (Heb. 12:4 NKJV).

During a ministry time, concerning someone's toxic thoughts, God gave me a picture of a highway running through a jungle. When the traffic on the road lessened, the jungle started to choke the highway. It became difficult to go down that road. In a matter of time, with no traffic the jungle became so dense that you could no longer go down that road at all. Our neural pathways are like that; they follow the rule, "use it or lose it." Why do we forget the two years of Spanish or French we took in high school? Because we stopped using it! That is a good philosophy to follow with toxic thoughts.

Some of us just need to "not go there" when it comes to certain thoughts about offenses, pornography, anger, bitterness, or self-pity. In such incidents, it is not one event that triggered the toxic memories, but a series of minor situations that we ruminated on. Starve the thought out and it will die as it has no life of its own. These thoughts feed on our constant attention. Refuse the thought, and after a while, like the jungle road, you will wonder how you ever went down that path and thought those petty thoughts.

To stop thinking about a hurtful situation, we must declare that toxic memory to be insignificant. I know most of us wouldn't care if Riga Dinamo (who?) traded their backup goalie or not. Why not? It's insignificant; it doesn't affect my life. When you hear that your former girlfriend is dating a famous football player, it won't affect you if it is insignificant. To break free from toxic memories, we need to assign insignificance to them and not let them rent any space in our head because they are insignificant.

Look to Jesus

Some wounds can be cured simply by looking at the sacrifice and love of Jesus. Those memories are like the snake bites in the wilderness. We may have gotten bitten, but if we will look at Jesus we will live and the effect of the bite will be healed. It would be nice if all our toxic memories would evaporate that easily, but the truth is many won't. With some memories we spent decades forming them. They make up a good portion of our personality and character. God doesn't just want us *"...to be unclothed but to be clothed...so that what is mortal may be swallowed up by life"* (2 Cor. 5:4 NIV). If the life of God is going to swallow up our toxic thoughts, then we have to clothe ourselves with His healing thoughts.

THE PREVENTION

If we don't control our thoughts, they will control us. So how do we stop new toxic memories from forming? The beginning of wisdom is the hatred of evil (see Prov. 8:13; 9:10). There is no temptation to do the things we hate. If we hate the evil, we will *"refuse the evil, and choose the good"* (Isa. 7:15). We don't watch television we don't like and we won't eat things that we hate. This is not about denying ourselves; this is about changing our thinking to align with God's thinking. We can't stop birds from flying over our heads, but we don't have to let them build nests in our hair.

Toxic thoughts will come, but memories are only built when we muse on them. God has created our spirits to discern life. If a thought has life—if it builds up, if it encourages, if it comforts—then accept it. If a thought only tears down—if it is discouraging, if it causes agitation in your spirit—then it is bringing death and needs to be rejected. If we are prisoners to our thoughts, we will be tormented by our memories.

We don't have to wait for death to be able to change. If death frees us from our toxic thinking, then death is our savior and not Jesus. We are able to do this here and now because Jesus died to set us free from our old nature. *"Let the Spirit renew your thoughts and attitudes. Put on your new nature, created to be like God—truly righteous and holy"* (Eph. 4:23-24 NLT). To stay free from toxic thoughts, the most important thing to remember is that you are completely forgiven, wonderfully loved, and totally secure in the hands of your glorious God.

> *Today salvation has come...for the Son of Man has come to seek and to save that which was lost* (Luke 19:9-10 NKJV).

THE STRESS SCALE

This table is taken from "The Social Readjustment Rating Scale," Thomas H. Holmes and Richard H. Rahe, *Journal of Psychosomatic Research*, Volume 11, Issue 2, August 1967, pages 213-218. Copyright © 1967 published by Elsevier Science Inc. All rights reserved. Permission to reproduce granted by the publisher.

THE STRESS SCALE

To score your stress levels, simply check the box in the right-hand column next to all the events that have happened to you in the last year.

This scale must not be used in any way to cause harm to an individual's professional career.

	LIFE EVENT	VALUE	CHECK IF THIS APPLIES
1	Death of spouse	100	
2	Divorce	73	
3	Marital separation	65	
4	Jail term	63	
5	Death of close family member	63	
6	Personal injury or illness	53	
7	Marriage	50	
8	Fired at work	47	

	LIFE EVENT	VALUE	CHECK IF THIS APPLIES
9	Marital reconciliation	45	
10	Retirement	45	
11	Change in health of family member	44	
12	Pregnancy	40	
13	Sex difficulties	39	
14	Gain of new family member	39	
15	Business readjustment	39	
16	Change in financial state	38	
17	Death of close friend	37	
18	Change to a different line of work	36	
19	Change in number of arguments with spouse	35	
20	A large mortgage or loan	31	
21	Foreclosure of mortgage or loan	30	
22	Change in responsibilities at work	29	
23	Son or daughter leaving home	29	
24	Trouble with in-laws	29	
25	Outstanding personal achievement	28	
26	Spouse begins or stops work	26	
27	Begin or end school/college	26	
28	Change in living conditions	25	
29	Revision of personal habits	24	
30	Trouble with boss	23	

	LIFE EVENT	VALUE	CHECK IF THIS APPLIES
31	Change in work hours or conditions	20	
32	Change in residence	20	
33	Change in school/college	20	
34	Change in recreation	19	
35	Change in church activities	19	
36	Change in social activities	18	
37	A moderate loan or mortgage	17	
38	Change in sleeping habits	16	
39	Change in number of family get-togethers	15	
40	Change in eating habits	15	
41	Vacation	13	
42	Christmas	12	
43	Minor violations of the law	11	
YOUR TOTAL			

Note: If you experienced the same event more than once, then to gain a more accurate total, add the score again for each extra occurrence of the event.

SCORE	INTERPRETATION
300+	You have a high or very high risk of becoming ill in the near future.
150-299	You have a moderate to high chance of becoming ill in the near future.
<150	You have only a low to moderate chance of becoming ill in the near future.

According to Dr. Don Colbert, a score of 300+ indicates an 80 percent chance of getting sick in the near future; 150-299 indicates a 50 percent chance of illness; <150 lowers this to 30 percent chance of illness.[1]

THE ZUNG SELF-RATING DEPRESSION SCALE

Patient's Initials

_____

Date of Assessment

_____

Please read each statement and decide how much of the time the statement describes how you have been feeling during the past several days.

MAKE CHECK MARK IN APPROPRIATE COLUMN	A LITTLE OF THE TIME	SOME OF THE TIME	GOOD PART OF THE TIME	MOST OF THE TIME
1. I feel down-hearted and blue				
2. Morning is when I feel the best				
3. I have crying spells or feel like it				
4. I have trouble sleeping at night				
5. I eat as much as I used to				
6. I still enjoy sex				
7. I notice that I am losing weight				
8. I have trouble with constipation				
9. My heart beats faster than usual				
10. I get tired for no reason				

MAKE CHECK MARK IN APPROPRIATE COLUMN	A LITTLE OF THE TIME	SOME OF THE TIME	GOOD PART OF THE TIME	MOST OF THE TIME
11. My mind is as clear as it used to be				
12. I find it easy to do the things I used to				
13. I am restless and can't keep still				
14. I feel hopeful about the future				
15. I am more irritable than usual				
16. I find it easy to make decisions				
17. I feel that I am useful and needed				
18. My life is pretty full				
19. I feel that others would be better off if I were dead				
20. I still enjoy the things I used to do				

KEY TO SCORING THE ZUNG SELF-RATING DEPRESSION SCALE

Consult this key for the value (1-4) that correlates with patients' responses to each statement. Add up the numbers for a total score. Most people with depression score between 50 and 69. The highest possible score is 80.[1]

MAKE CHECK MARK IN APPROPRIATE COLUMN	A LITTLE OF THE TIME	SOME OF THE TIME	GOOD PART OF THE TIME	MOST OF THE TIME
1. I feel down-hearted and blue	1	2	3	4
2. Morning is when I feel the best	4	3	2	1
3. I have crying spells or feel like it	1	2	3	4
4. I have trouble sleeping at night	1	2	3	4
5. I eat as much as I used to	4	3	2	1
6. I still enjoy sex	4	3	2	1
7. I notice that I am losing weight	1	2	3	4
8. I have trouble with constipation	1	2	3	4
9. My heart beats faster than usual	1	2	3	4
10. I get tired for no reason	1	2	3	4
11. My mind is as clear as it used to be	4	3	2	1
12. I find it easy to do the things I used to	4	3	2	1
13. I am restless and can't keep still	1	2	3	4
14. I feel hopeful about the future	4	3	2	1
15. I am more irritable than usual	1	2	3	4
16. I find it easy to make decisions	4	3	2	1
17. I feel that I am useful and needed	4	3	2	1

MAKE CHECK MARK IN APPROPRIATE COLUMN	A LITTLE OF THE TIME	SOME OF THE TIME	GOOD PART OF THE TIME	MOST OF THE TIME
18. My life is pretty full	4	3	2	1
19. I feel that others would be better off if I were dead	1	2	3	4
20. I still enjoy the things I used to do	4	3	2	1

NOVACO ANGER INVENTORY

The items on this scale describe situations that are related to anger arousal. For each of the items, please rate the degree to which the incident described would anger or provoke you by ticking the appropriate degree of annoyance. Try to imagine the incident actually happening to you, and then indicate the extent to which it would have made you angry. This scale is concerned with your general reactions. Please do your best to rate your responses in this general fashion.

NOVACO ANGER INVENTORY (SHORT FORM)

Rate the degree to which you would feel angry/annoyed in the following situations from 0-4.

SITUATION/REACTION SCORE	VERY LITTLE 0	LITTLE 1	MODERATE AMOUNT 2	MUCH 3	VERY MUCH 4
1. You unpack an appliance you have just bought, plug it in, and discover that it doesn't work.					
2. Being overcharged by a repair person who has you over a barrel.					
3. Being singled out for a correction, while the actions of others go unnoticed.					
4. Getting your car stuck in the mud or sand.					

SITUATION/REACTION SCORE	VERY LITTLE 0	LITTLE 1	MODERATE AMOUNT 2	MUCH 3	VERY MUCH 4
5. You are talking to someone and they don't answer you.					
6. Someone pretends to be something they are not.					
7. While you are struggling to carry four cups of coffee to your table at a cafeteria, someone bumps into you, spilling the coffee.					
8. You have hung up your clothes, but someone knocks them to the floor and fails to pick them up.					
9. You are hounded by a sales person from the moment you walk into the store.					
10. You have made arrangements to go somewhere with a person who backs off at the last minute and leaves you dangling.					
11. Being joked about or teased.					
12. Your car is stalled at a traffic light, and the person behind you keeps blowing his horn.					
13. You accidentally make the wrong kind of turn in a car park. As you get out of your car someone yells at you, "Where did you learn to drive?"					
14. Someone makes a mistake and blames it on you.					
15. You are trying to concentrate, but a person near you is tapping their foot.					
16. You lend someone an important book or tool, and they fail to return it.					

SITUATION/REACTION SCORE	VERY LITTLE 0	LITTLE 1	MODERATE AMOUNT 2	MUCH 3	VERY MUCH 4
17. You have had a busy day, and the person you live with starts to complain about how you forgot to do something you agreed to.					
18. You are trying to discuss something important with your mate or partner who isn't giving you a chance to express your feelings.					
19. You are in a discussion with someone who persists in arguing about a topic they know very little about.					
20. Someone sticks his or her nose into an argument between you and someone else.					
21. You need to get somewhere quickly, but the car in front of you is going 40 mph in a 60 mph zone, and you can't pass.					
22. Stepping on a lump of chewing gum.					
23. Being mocked by a small group of people as you pass them.					
24. In a hurry to get somewhere, you tear a good pair of trousers/skirt on a sharp object.					
25. You use your last coin to make a phone call, but you are disconnected before you finish dialing and the coin is lost.					

Total Score: _____

SCORING

0—you would feel very little or no annoyance

1—you would feel a little irritated

2—you would feel moderately upset

3—you would feel quite angry

4—you would feel very angry

Now that you have completed the Anger Inventory, you are in a position to calculate your IQ, your Irritability Quotient. Make sure that you have not skipped any items. Add up your score for each of the twenty-five incidents.

You can now interpret your total score according to the following scale:

0-45: The amount of anger and annoyance you generally experience is remarkably low. Only a few percent of the population will score this low on the test. You are one of the select few.

46-55: You are substantially more peaceful than the average person.

56-75: You respond to life's annoyances with an average amount of anger.

76-85: You frequently react in an angry way to life's many annoyances. You are substantially more irritable than the average person.

86-100: You are a true anger champion, and you are plagued by frequent, intense, furious reactions that do not quickly disappear. You probably harbor negative feelings long after the initial insult has passed. You may have the reputation of a firecracker or a hothead among people you know. You may experience frequent tension headaches and elevated blood pressure. Your anger may often get out of control and lead to impulsive hostile outbursts, which at times get you into trouble. Only a few percent of the adult population react as intensely as you do.

ENDNOTES

CHAPTER 1

1. Caroline M. Leaf, *Who Switched off My Brain?* (South Africa: Switch on Your Brain Organization, 2007), 3.
2. Ibid., 4.
3. Don Colbert, *Deadly Emotions: Understand the Mind-Body-Spirit Connection That Can Heal or Destroy You* (Nashville, TN: Thomas Nelson, 2003), Appx. A.
4. Rebecca Lin and Ming-Ling Hsieh, "Psychosomatic Disorders: Taiwan's New Health Killer," ChinaPost, June 13, 2011, accessed April 05, 2013, http://www .chinapost.com.tw/commentary/the-china-post/special-to-the-china -post/2011/06/13/306003/p1/Psychosomatic-disorders.htm.
5. Candace B. Pert, *Molecules of Emotion: Why You Feel the Way You Feel* (New York, NY: Scribner, 1997).
6. Robert E. Thayer, *The Biopsychology of Mood and Arousal* (New York, NY: Oxford University Press, 1989), 12.
7. Ken Harrington and Jeanne Harrington, *Shift! Moving from the Natural to the Supernatural* (Shippensburg, PA: Destiny Image Publishers, 2009), 279.
8. C. Miles and R. Jenkins, "Recency and Suffix Effects with Serial Recall of Odours," *Memory* 8 (2000): 195-206.
9. R.W. Moncrieff, *The Chemical Senses* (London: Leonard Hill, 1967).
10. S. Chu and J.J. Downes, "Odour-evoked Autobiographical Memories: Psychological Investigations of Proustian Phenomena," *ChemSenses* 25 (2000): 111-116.
11. Tim Jacob, "Smell (Olfaction): A Tutorial on the Sense of Smell," Cardiff School of Biosciences, Smell and Memory, accessed April 06, 2013, http://www.cardiff .ac.uk/biosi/staffinfo/jacob/teaching/sensory/olfact1.html.
12. Marcel Proust, *Swann's Way* (CreateSpace, 2013), 34.
13. Jacob, "Smell," The Limbic System.
14. Doyle, "Proust Effect," Science Teacher, November 6, 2008, accessed April 06, 2013, http://doyle-scienceteach.blogspot.com/2008/11/proust-effect.html.
15. Jacob, "Smell," Smell and Memory.
16. Charles Dickens, *A Christmas Carol* (London, UK, Chapman & Hall, 1843).
17. *Webster's New Twentieth Century Dictionary*, s.v. "Conscience."
18. Ibid., s.v. "Communion."
19. Spiros Zodhiates, *The Complete Word Study Dictionary: New Testament* (Chattanooga, TN: AMG Publishers, 1992), #2198, #5590.
20. John Sandford and Paula Sandford, *Healing the Wounded Spirit* (Tulsa, OK: Victory House, 1985), 117.

21. Ken Harrington and Jeanne Harrington, *From Curses to Blessings: Removing Generational Curses* (Shippensburg, PA: Destiny Image Publishers, 2011), 219-220.
22. Sandford, *Healing the Wounded Spirit,* 117.
23. *Webster's,* s.v. "Inspiration."
24. Mary Bellis, "George Washington Carver," About.com, God Gave Them to Me, accessed April 07, 2013, http://inventors.about.com/od/cstartinventors/a/GWC.htm.
25. "George Washington Carver Quotes," About.com, God, accessed April 07, 2013, http://quotations.about.com/cs/morepeople/a/george_w_carver.htm.
26. Sandford, *Healing the Wounded Spirit,* 112-113.
27. Amir Sufi, "Household Debt Is at Heart of Weak U.S. Economy: Business Class," Bloomberg, July 7, 2011, accessed April 07, 2013, http://www.bloomberg.com/news/2011-07-08/household-debt-is-at-heart-of-weak-u-s-economy-business-class.html.
28. Bob Adelmann, "On Halloween, Nat'l Debt Exceeds Gross Domestic Product," The New American, November 2, 2011, accessed April 07, 2013, http://www.thenewamerican.com/economy/commentary/item/4103-on-halloween-natl-debt-exceeds-gross-domestic-product.
29. Thomas Mitchell, "Las Vegas Review-Journal," Kicking the Can on Entitlement Reform, April 10, 2011, accessed April 07, 2013, http://www.lvrj.com/opinion/-today-it-s-not-a-problem-119558509.html?ref=509.
30. Derry Bresee, "The Trigger of Coma," Near-Death Experiences and the Afterlife, 2007, accessed April 07, 2013, http://www.near-death.com/experiences/triggers13.html.
31. Bruce Grayson, "FAQs," Near Death Experience Frequently Asked Questions, June 14, 2012, accessed April 07, 2013, http://www.nderf.org/FAQs.htm. Bruce Grayson is the director of the Division of Personality Studies, University of Virginia Health System.
32. Bruce Grayson, qtd. in Bresee, "The Trigger of Coma."
33. "'Dead' Man Revived Four Months Later," Thestar.com, March 24, 2008, accessed April 07, 2013, http://www.thestar.com/News/World/article/350150.
34. Jennifer Lacey, "Music in the Womb," BabyZone, The Right Music Choices for Baby, accessed April 07, 2013, http://www.babyzone.com/pregnancy/bonding-with-baby-to-be/prenatal-learning-with-music_71701.
35. V. Lemaire et al., "Prenatal Stress Produces Learning Deficits Associated with an Inhibition of Neurogenesis in the Hippocampus," *PNAS* 97, no. 20 (September 26, 2000): 11032-11037.
36. David Derbyshire, "Why Pregnant Film Fans Should Stick to Happy Movies," Mail Online, March 11, 2010, accessed April 07, 2013, http://www.dailymail.co.uk/sciencetech/article-1256990/Unborn-babies-respond-mothers-mood-watches-movie-scientists-say.html.
37. Dr. Oz and Dr. Michael Roizen, "Should You Read to Your Unborn Baby?," Oprah.com, February 6, 2010, accessed April 07, 2013, http://www.oprah.com/health/Should-You-Read-to-Your-Unborn-Baby-RealAge.

38.   Karen M. Moritz et al., "Developmental Programming of a Reduced Nephron Endowment: More than Just a Baby's Birth-weight," *American Journal of Physiology: Renal Physiology*, July 23, 2008, accessed April 7, 2013, doi:10.1152/ajprenal.00049.2008.

39.   Vivette Glover, Professor of Perinatal Psychobiology, Imperial College, London, qtd. in "The Many Benefits of Prenatal Music Stimulation," Prenatal Music Stimulation for Fetal Development and Prenatal Learning, Reduce Stress Levels During Pregnancy, accessed April 07, 2013, http://www.lullabelly.com/benefits.html.

40.   Ann P. Streissguth, Helen M. Barr, and Paul D. Sampson, "Moderate Prenatal Alcohol Exposure: Effects on Child IQ and Learning Problems at Age 7 1/2 Years," *Alcoholism: Clinical and Experimental Research* 14, no. 5 (October 1990): Abstract, accessed April 7, 2013, doi:10.1111/j.1530-0277.1990.tb01224.x.

41.   Don C. Van Dyke and Allison A. Fox, "Fetal Drug Exposure and Its Possible Implications for Learning in the Preschool and School-Age Population," *Journal of Learning Disabilities* 23, no. 3 (March 1990): 160-163, doi:10.1177/002221949002300305.

42.   Julia A. Mennella, Coren P. Jagnow, and Gary K. Beauchamp, "Prenatal and Postnatal Flavor Learning by Human Infants," Pediatrics, June 1, 2001, Background, accessed April 07, 2013, doi:10.1542/peds.107.6.e88.

43.   Caroline Leaf, Brenda Louw, and Isabel Uys, "The Development of a Model for Geodesic Learning: The Geodesic Information Processing Model," *The South African Journal of Communication Disorders* 44 (1997).

44.   Kathy K. Oliver, "Your Child's Brain: The Crucial Early Years," *The Ohio State University Extension*, August 2007, accessed April 7, 2013, http://ohioline.osu.edu/hyg-fact/5000/pdf/Child_Brain.pdf.

CHAPTER 2

1.   Nikhil Swaminathan, "Glia: The Other Brain Cells," *Discover Magazine*, December 16, 2010, accessed April 07, 2013, http://discovermagazine.com/2011/jan-feb/62.

2.   Glenn Elert, "Number of Neurons in a Human Brain," The Physics Factbook, 2002, Chart, accessed April 07, 2013, http://hypertextbook.com/facts/2002/AniciaNdabahaliye2.shtml.

3.   "Human Memory," Intelegen, Inc., 2010, Storage, accessed April 07, 2013, http://web-us.com/memory/human_memory.htm.

4.   Ibid., Forgetting.

5.   David A. Drachman, "Do We Have Brain to Spare?" *Neurology* 64, no. 12 (2005), doi:10.1212/01.WNL.0000166914.38327.BB.

6.   Marian C. Diamond and Janet L. Hopson, *Magic Trees of the Mind: How to Nurture Your Child's Intelligence, Creativity, and Healthy Emotions from Birth through Adolescence* (New York, NY: Plume, 1999).

7.   Caroline Leaf, Marty Copeland, and Janet Maccaro, *Your Body, His Temple: God's Plan for Achieving Emotional Wholeness* (Euless, TX: Life Outreach International, 2007), Audiobook.

8.   Craig Freudenrich and Robynne Boyd, "How Your Brain Works," HowStuffWorks, June 6, 2001, accessed April 07, 2013, http://science .howstuffworks.com/life/inside-the-mind/human-brain/brain1.htm.

9.   Leaf, *Who Switched off My Brain?*, 17.

10. Panayiota Poirazi and Bartlett W. Mel, "Impact of Active Dendrites and Structural Plasticity on the Storage Capacity of Neural Tissue," Department of Biomedical Engineering, University of Southern California: Introduction, accessed April 7, 2013, doi:10.1016/S0896-6273(01)00252-5.

11. Xundong Wu, "Dendrite Morphology and Memory Capacity," DJ Strouse, September 2010, accessed April 07, 2013, http://djstrouse.com/ dendrite-morphology-memory-capacity.

12. *Webster's*, s.v. "Muse."

13. Washington State University, "Sleep Creeps Up: No Top-Down Control for Sleep and Wakefulness," Newswise, November 7, 2008, accessed April 07, 2013, http://www.newswise.com/articles/ sleep-creeps-up-no-top-down-control-for-sleep-and-wakefulness.

14. Simon Moss, "Entorhinal Cortex," Psychlopedia, April 11, 2008, Overview, accessed April 07, 2013, http://www.psych-it.com.au/Psychlopedia/article .asp?id=203.

15. Dick F. Swaab, "Hypothalamus," Brain Maps, accessed April 07, 2013, http:// www.brain-maps.com/index.html.

16. Robert Cooper, "Pituitary Gland," University of Maryland Medical Center, September 19, 2008, Animation, accessed April 07, 2013, http://www.umm.edu/ ency/animations/Pituitary-gland.htm.

17. Candace B. Pert, *Molecules of Emotion: The Science Behind Mind-Body Medicine* (Riverside, NJ: Simon & Schuster, 1999).

18. Leaf, *Who Switched off My Brain?*, 28.

19. Ben Best, "Neurophysiology and Mental Function," III. Memory, accessed April 07, 2013, http://www.benbest.com/science/anatmind/anatmd8.html.

20. Abhijit Naik, "Corpus Callosum Function," Buzzle.com, September 21, 2011, accessed April 07, 2013, http://www.buzzle.com/articles/corpus-callosum -function.html.

21. Swaab, "Basal ganglia."

22. Dr. M. Oz and Dr. M. Roizen, *You Staying Young: The Owner's Manual for Extending Your Warranty* (New York, NY: Free Press, 2007), 106-108.

23. Leaf, *Who Switched off My Brain?*, 38-39.

24. Mohamed Ghilan, "Intelligence: Is It in the Brain or the Heart?" Science, Religion and Philosophy, February 10, 2012, accessed April 07, 2013, http:// mohamedghilan.com/2012/02/10/intelligence-is-it-in-the-brain-or-the-heart/.

25. Ibid.

26. Paul Pearsall, Gary E.R. Schwartz, and Linda G.S. Russek, "Changes in Heart Transplant Recipients That Parallel the Personalities of Their Donors," *Journal of Near-Death Studies* 20 (2002): 192, accessed April 7, 2013, http://www .newdualism.org/nde-papers/Pearsall/Pearsall-Journal%20of%20Near-Death%20 Studies_2002-20-191-206.pdf.

27. Ghilan, "Intelligence."

28. Leaf, *Who Switched off My Brain?*, 71.

29. Rollin McCraty and Mike Atkinson, "Science of The Heart: Exploring the Role of the Heart in Human Performance," Institute of HeartMath, 1999, Cardiac Coherence Improves Cognitive Performance, accessed April 07, 2013, http://www.heartmath.org/research/science-of-the-heart/head-heart-interactions.html.

30. Paul Rosch, qtd. in "Science of The Heart," Emotional Balance and Health, http://www.heartmath.org/research/science-of-the-heart/emotional-balance-health.html.

CHAPTER 3

1. Leaf, *Who Switched off My Brain?*, 72.

2. Pearsall, "Changes in Heart Transplant Recipients," 202.

3. Ibid., 199.

4. Paul Thompson, "Man given Heart of Suicide Victim Marries Donor's Widow and Then Kills Himself in Exactly the Same Way," Mail Online, April 7, 2008, accessed April 07, 2013, http://www.dailymail.co.uk/news/article-557864/Man-given-heart-suicide-victim-marries-donors-widow-kills-exactly-way.html.

5. David Bohm and B. J. Hiley, *The Undivided Universe* (London: Routledge, 1993); Ervin Laszlo, *The Interconnected Universe* (Singapore: World Scientific, 1995); Robert Nadeau and Minas C. Kafatos, *The Non-local Universe* (New York, NY: Oxford University Press, 1999).

6. Amir D. Aczel, *Entanglement: The Greatest Mystery in Physics* (New York, NY: Four Walls Eight Windows, 2002); Roger Penrose, *The Emperor's New Mind: Concerning Computers, Minds, and the Laws of Physics* (Oxford: Oxford University Press, 1989).

7. Stuart R. Hameroff, *Ultimate Computing: Biomolecular Consciousness and Nanotechnology* (Amsterdam: North-Holland, 1987), 17,145, accessed April 07, 2013, http://www.quantumconsciousness.org/pdfs/UltComp_v51.pdf.

8. G.M. Shepherd, "Signal Enhancement in Distal Cortical Dendrites by Means of Interactions between Active Dendritic Spines," *Proceedings of the National Academy of Sciences* 82, no. 7 (1985): 2192-2195, doi:10.1073/pnas.82.7.2192.

9. Eshel Ben-Jacob, Inon Cohen, and Herbert Levine, "Cooperative Self-organization of Microorganisms," *Advances in Physics* 49, no. 4 (2000): 395-554, doi:10.1080/000187300405228.

10. C.R. Wildey, *Biological Response to Stimulus*, Master's thesis, University of Texas at Arlington, 2001.

11. Rupert Sheldrake, Terence K. McKenna, and Ralph Abraham, *The Evolutionary Mind: Trialogues at the Edge of the Unthinkable* (Santa Cruz, CA: Trialogue Press, 1998).

12. Rupert Sheldrake, *Dogs That Know When Their Owners Are Coming Home: And Other Unexplained Powers of Animals* (New York, NY: Crown, 1999).

13. Rollin McCraty, Mike Atkinson, and Raymond Trevor Bradley, "Electrophysiological Evidence of Intuition: Part 2: A System-Wide Process?" *The Journal of Alternative and Complementary Medicine* 10, no. 2 (2004): 325-336, doi:10.1089/107555304323062310.

14.   J.A. Armour and Jeffrey L. Ardell, *Neurocardiology* (New York, NY: Oxford University Press, 1994).

15.   R.C. Frysinger and R.M. Harper, "Cardiac and Respiratory Correlations with Unit Discharge in Epileptic Human Temporal Lobe," *Epilepsia* 31 (1990); R. McCraty and D. Childre, *The Grateful Heart: The Psychophysiology of Appreciation* qtd. in Robert A. Emmons and Michael E. McCullough, *The Psychology of Gratitude* (Oxford: Oxford University Press, 2004), 230-255; C.A. Sandman, B.B. Walker, and C. Berka, *Influence of Afferent Cardiovascular Feedback on Behavior and the Cortical Evoked Potential* qtd. in John T. Cacioppo and Richard E. Petty, *Perspectives in Cardiovascular Psychophysiology* (New York, NY: Guilford Press, 1982), 189-222.

16.   Barbara B. Walker and Curt A. Sandman, "Visual Evoked Potentials Change as Heart Rate and Carotid Pressure Change," *International Journal of Psychophysiology* 19, no. 5 (1982): 520-527, doi:10.1111/j.1469-8986.1982.tb02579.x.

17.   B.C. Lacey and G.I. Lacey, *Studies of Heart Rate and Other Bodily Processes in Sensorimotor Behavior* qtd. in Paul A. Obrist, *Cardiovascular Psychophysiology: Current Issues in Response Mechanisms, Biofeedback, and Methodology* (Chicago, IL: Aldine Pub., 1974), 538-564.

18.   A. Randich, "Vagal Afferent Modulation of Nociception," *Brain Research Reviews* 17, no. 2 (1992): 77-99, doi:10.1016/0165-0173(92)90009-B.

19.   Sandman, *Influence of Afferent Cardiovascular Feedback,* 189-222; Michael G.H Coles, J. R. Jennings, and Patrick K. Ackles, *Advances in Psychophysiology* (Greenwich, CT: JAI Press, 1985), 1-88; Harald Rau et al., "Baroreceptor Stimulation Alters Cortical Activity," *Psychophysiology* 30, no. 3 (1993): 322-325, doi:10.1111/j.1469-8986.1993.tb03359.x.

20.   McCraty, "Electrophysiological Evidence of Intuition."

CHAPTER 4

1.   "What Are Cytokines?" News Medical, accessed April 09, 2013, http://www.news-medical.net/health/What-are-Cytokines.aspx.

2.   Yekta Dowlati et al., "A Meta-Analysis of Cytokines in Major Depression," *Biological Psychiatry* 67, no. 5 (2010): 446-457, doi:10.1016/j.biopsych.2009.09.033; Walter Swardfager et al., "A Meta-Analysis of Cytokines in Alzheimer's Disease," *Biological Psychiatry* 68, no. 10 (2010): 930-941; R. Locksley, "The TNF and TNF Receptor Superfamilies: Integrating Mammalian Biology," *Cell* 104, no. 4 (2001): 487-501, doi:10.1016/S0092-8674(01)00237-9.

3.   Michael T. Osterholm, "Preparing for the Next Pandemic," *New England Journal of Medicine* 352, no. 18 (2005): 1839-1842, doi:10.1056/NEJMp058068.

4.   Kao-Jean Huang et al., "An Interferon-y-related Cytokine Storm in SARS Patients," *Journal of Medical Virology* 75, no. 2 (2005): 185-194.

5.   Locksley, "The TNF and TNF Receptor Superfamilies."

6.   Carol Eustice, "What Are Cytokines?" About.com Arthritis and Joint Conditions, December 1, 2012, Overproduction of Cytokines, accessed April 09, 2013, http://arthritis.about.com/od/inflammation/f/cytokines.htm.

7.   Dowlati, "A Meta-Analysis of Cytokines in Major Depression."

8. A. Hashiramoto and T. Katafuchi, "Mental State and Tuberculosis: Tohru Ishigami, 1918," Brain Immune Media Ltd., April 17, 2009, accessed April 09, 2013, http://www.brainimmune.com/index.php?option=com_content.

9. Thomas R. Blakeslee and Ronald Grossarth-Maticek, "Feelings of Pleasure and Well-being as Predictors of Health Status 21 Years Later," Attitudefactor.com, Results, accessed April 09, 2013, http://www.attitudefactor.com/PWItecharticle .htm.

10. Robert Davis, "Laugh to Your Health," Everwell, April 20, 2009, accessed April 09, 2013, http://www.everwell.com/insights/laugh_to_your_health.php.

11. Healthy Humorist, "The Medical Definition of Laughter," Everwell, accessed April 09, 2013, http://www.everwell.com/fun/healthy_humorist/laughter.php.

12. D. Spiegel, "Effect of Psychosocial Treatment on Survival of Patients with Metastatic Breast Cancer," *The Lancet* 334, no. 8668 (1989): 888-891, doi:10.1016/S0140-6736(89)91551-1.

13. F.I. Fawzy et al., "Effects of an Early Structured Psychiatric Intervention, Coping, and Affective State on Recurrence and Survival Six Year Later," *Archives of General Psychiatry* 50 (1993): 681.

14. H. Yamasaki, "Non-genotoxic Mechanisms of Carcinogenesis: Studies of Cell Transformation and Gap Junctional Intercellular Communication," *Toxicology Letters* 77, no. 1-3 (1995): 55-61, doi:10.1016/0378-4274(95)03272-X.

15. "Why Learning to Forgive Is Important to Your Health," UW Health, October 27, 2010, accessed April 09, 2013, http://www.uwhealth.org/news/ why-learning-to-forgive-is-important-to-your-health/29525.

16. Richard E. Brown, *An Introduction to Neuroendocrinology* (Cambridge: Cambridge University Press, 1994), 297.

17. Dr. Oz, *You Staying Young*, 79-83.

18. Mark D. Rekhter, "Collagen Synthesis in Atherosclerosis: Too Much and Not Enough," *Cardiovascular Research* 41 (1999): 376-384, accessed April 10, 2013, http://cardiovascres.oxfordjournals.org/content/41/2/376.full.pdf.

19. Roy F. Baumeister et al., "Bad Is Stronger than Good," *Review of General Psychology* 5, no. 4 (2001): 323-370, accessed April 10, 2013, doi:10.1037//1089-2680.5.4.323.

20. Ibid., 323.

21. John M. Gottman and Nan Silver, *Why Marriages Succeed or Fail and How You Can Make Yours Last* (New York, NY: Simon & Schuster, 1995), 57.

CHAPTER 5

1. "Stress Related Facts," Stress Less, accessed April 10, 2013, http://www.stressless .com/stressinfo.cfm?CFID=19999547.

2. Ibid.

3. P.J. Rosch, ed., "The Quandary of Job Stress Compensation," *Health and Stress* 3 (March 2001): 1-4.

4. Daniel M. Wegner et al., "Paradoxical Effects of Thought Suppression," *Journal of Personality and Social Psychology* 53, no. 1 (1987): 5-13, doi:10.1037//0022-3514.53.1.5.

5. Louise Smart, "Emotional Detox," Greenwichmeantime.com, Emotional Suppression and Illness, accessed April 10, 2013, http://wwp.greenwichmeantime .com/websites/emotional-detox.htm.

6. Aaron T. Beck, "Cognitive Approaches to Schizophrenia: A Paradigm Shift?" Psy Broadcasting Corporation, Lessons from Clinical Experience, accessed April 10, 2013, http://psybc.com/pdfs/library/Beck_ParadigmShift.pdf.

7. Congreve, William (1670-1729), http://www.brainyquote.com/quotes/authors/w/ william_congreve.html.

8. Alfred Jones and James Strong, *Jones' Dictionary of Old Testament Proper Names* (Grand Rapids, MI: Kregel Publications, 1990), s.v. "Zaphnath-paaneah."

9. Spiros Zodhiates, *The Complete Word Study Old Testament* (Chattanooga, TN: AMG Publishers, 1994), Achor, #5912.

CHAPTER 6

1. "The Cognitive Model," Beck Institute for Cognitive Behavioral Therapy, accessed April 11, 2013, http://www.beckinstitute.org/beck-cbt/.

2. M. Kathleen Holmes, "Aaron Beck, Albert Ellis and Cognitive Psychology," Psychology.info, 2012, accessed April 11, 2013, http://psychology.info/index .php?option=com_content&task=view&id=145&Itemid=2.

3. Ibid.

4. Spiros Zodhiates and James Strong, *The Complete Word Study New Testament* (Chattanooga, TN: AMG Publishers, 1991), Offense, #4625.

5. Kristi, "Hurt People, Hurt People?" Courageous Homekeeping, August 2, 2011, accessed April 11, 2013, http://www.courageoushomekeeping.com/featured/ hurt-people-hurt-people/.

6. Malcolm Gladwell, *Outliers, The Story of Success*, (USA, Little, Brown and Company, 2008): Chap 2, "The Ten-Thousand-Hour Rule."

7. Rob McLeod and Blair Winsor, "3M Case Study: Entrepreneurship," Venture Navigator, May 2007, Sticky Stuff, accessed April 11, 2013, http://www .venturenavigator.co.uk/content/74.

8. *The Lord of the Rings: The Two Towers*, dir. Peter Jackson, perf. Elijah Wood, Ian McKellen (New Line, 2002), DVD.

CHAPTER 7

1. Lord William T. Kelvin, "On the Dynamical Theory of Heat," *Transactions of the Royal Society of Edinburgh*, March 1851, accessed April 12, 2013, http://zapatopi .net/kelvin/papers/on_the_dynamical_theory_of_heat.html.

2. Zodhiates, *The Complete Word Study New Testament*, Convert, #4762.

3. Ibid., Malice, #2549.

4. Henrik Edberg, "How to Overcome Your Worries: 5 Timeless Thoughts from the Last 2500 Years," The Positivity Blog, accessed April 12, 2013, http://www .positivityblog.com/index.php/2009/10/23/how-to-overcome-your-worries/.

5. Ibid.

6. Ibid.

7. William Shakespeare, *Julius Caesar*, act 1, scene 2.

CHAPTER 8

1. Michael E. McCullough, Giacomo Bono, and Lindsey M. Root, "Rumination, Emotion, and Forgiveness: Three Longitudinal Studies," *Journal of Personality and Social Psychology* 92, no. 3 (2007): 502, accessed April 13, 2013, doi:10.1037/0022-3514.92.3.490.

2. Terrie H. Rizzo, "The Healing Power of Forgiveness," IDEA Health and Fitness Association, September 2006, A Hot Field in Clinical Psychology , accessed April 13, 2013, http://www.ideafit.com/fitness-library/healing-power-forgiveness.

3. Leaf, *Who Switched off My Brain?*, 112.

4. Daniel Kahneman, Jack L. Knetsch, and Richard H. Thaler, "Experimental Tests of the Endowment Effect and the Coase Theorem," *Journal of Political Economy* 98, no. 6 (1990): 1325, doi:10.1086/261737.

5. Dylan Thomas, "Do Not Go Gentle into That Good Night," st. 1, lines 1-3.

6. Chip Ingram and Becca C. Johnson, *Overcoming Emotions That Destroy* (Grand Rapids, MI: Baker Books, 2009), 77.

7. Ibid., 49, 66, 57.

8. Ibid., 61-63.

9. Sandford, *Healing the Wounded Spirit*, 120.

10. "Top 10 Common Phobias of the World," Panic Goodbye, September 14, 2010, accessed April 13, 2013, http://panicgoodbye.com/blog/top-10-common-phobias -of-the-world.html.

11. "Anti-stress (somnipathy)," Deta-Elis, accessed April 13, 2013, http://a-ll.dk/ Bioresonance_therapy/DETA-Ritm/Guidelines/9.Anti-stress.htm.

12. Les Stroud, *Survive* (Canada: Harper Collins Publishers Ltd, 2008).

13. Chilton Tippin, "Why Adults Can Learn Languages More Easily Than Children," AccuConference, August 26, 2011, accessed April 14, 2013, http:// www.accuconference.com/blog/Why-Adults-Can-Learn-Languages-More-Easily -Than-Children.aspx.

14. Paul K. Davis, *Thrones of Our Soul* (Lake Mary, FL: Creation House Press, 2003), 53.

15. I. Cordón, "Memory for Traumatic Experiences in Early Childhood," *Developmental Review* 24, no. 1 (2004): 118-119, doi:10.1016/j.dr.2003.09.003.

16. Ibid., 122.

17. Sandi Dolbee, "The Healing Power of Forgiveness," The San Diego Union-Tribune, August 16, 2008, accessed April 14, 2013, http://www.utsandiego.com/ uniontrib/20080816/news_1c16forgivem.html.

18. Everett L. Worthington et al., "Forgiveness, Health, and Well-Being: A Review of Evidence..." *Journal of Behavioral Medicine* 30, no. 4 (2007): 294, doi:10.1007/ s10865-007-9105-8.

18. Berit Ingersoll-Dayton, Cynthia Torges, and Neal Krause, "Unforgiveness, Rumination, and Depressive Symptoms among Older Adults," *Aging and Mental Health* 14, no. 4 (May 2010): 439-449, doi:10.1080/13607860903483136.

CHAPTER 9

1. Zodhiates, *The Complete Word Study Old Testament*, "Heal," #7495; "Giant," #7497.

2.   Ibid., "Scratch," #8427.

3.   Ibid., "Conversation," #1870.

CHAPTER 10

1.   Zodhiates, *The Complete Word Study Old Testament*, "Bite," #5391.

2.   David Centeno, "Top 10 Reasons Why Marriages Fail," Uncontested Divorce NY, April 5, 2011, Financial Stress, accessed April 16, 2013, https://nyuncontesteddivorceattorney.com/top-10-reasons-why-marriages-fail/.

3.   Zodhiates, *The Complete Word Study New Testament*, "Repent," #3340.

4.   Patrick Weidinger, "10 Famous People Who Avoided Death on 9/11," Listverse, December 12, 2011, Gwyneth Paltrow, accessed April 16, 2013, http://listverse .com/2011/12/12/10-famous-people-who-avoided-death-on-911/.

5.   Wordsworth, W., *Ode: Intimations of Immortality*, http://www.artofeurope.com/wordsworth/wor3.htm.

6.   Cleanzclover, "Cope with Guilt or It Will Destroy You," HubPages, November 30, 2010, accessed April 16, 2013, http://cleanclover.hubpages.com/hub/guiltcope.

7.   "Lincoln Never Quits," Rogerknapp.com, accessed April 17, 2013, http://www .rogerknapp.com/inspire/lincoln.htm.

CHAPTER 11

1.   John E. Sarno, *The Divided Mind: The Epidemic of Mindbody Disorders* (New York, NY: HarperCollins Publishers, 2007), 11.

2.   Ibid.

3.   Ibid., 198.

CHAPTER 12

1.   Zodhiates, *The Complete Word Study Old Testament*, "Thanks, praise, confess," #3034.

2.   Zodhiates, *The Complete Word Study New Testament*, "Save," #4982.

3.   Jones, *Jones' Dictionary of Old Testament Proper Names*, s.v. "Manasseh."

4.   Zodhiates, *The Complete Word Study Old Testament*, "Manna," #4478.

5.   Sarno, *The Divided Mind*, 60-61.

CONCLUSION

1.   Harold Arlen and Johnny Mercer, writers, "Accentuate the Positive," recorded October 4, 1944, The Pied Pipers, Capitol Records.

2.   Zodhiates, *The Complete Word Study Old Testament*, "Reins," #3629, #3510.

APPENDIX A

1.   Don Colbert, *Deadly Emotions: Understanding the Mind-body-spirit Connection That Can Heal or Destroy You* (Nashville, TN: Thomas Nelson, 2003), Appendix A.

APPENDIX B

1.   Adapted from Zung, "A Self-rating Depression Scale," *Archives of General Psychiatry* 12 (1965): 63-70.

ABOUT KEN AND JEANNE HARRINGTON

Ken and Jeanne Harrington minister powerfully out of the treasure that God has deposited in them from years of studying His word and seeking His face.

God called Ken Harrington over 40 years ago as a teacher and started giving him revelation while still in his teens. His wife Jeanne has been a prophetic voice in every church they have attended and has consistently spoken into leadership. These ministry callings and their own family journey (three sons and two adopted daughters) have allowed them insights into Kingdom principles.

Ken and Jeanne are pastoral elders and responsible for counseling, prophetic ministry, and prayer. In this capacity, they have ministered to thousands of people and trained hundreds more to minister to the Body. Jeanne is also a recognized prophet and has sat on provincial and national prophetic roundtables.

God has allowed them to minister overseas in Asia, Europe, Africa, the Caribbean, and Central America as well as Canada and the United States. They have seen hundreds set free and have learned to recognize the roots that underlay the destructive fruit in people's lives. This combination of biblical truth and years of practical ministry has given them a unique insight into the power that God wants to release into His Body.